Praise for
RECLAIMING GODDESS SEXUALITY

"Reclaiming Goddess Sexuality *is an instant classic, along with* Sex for One *and* Our Bodies Ourselves. *This book should be required reading for women of any age for developing their sexual identity and for the men who love them.*"
— Nina Hartley, R.N., Sex Educator/Advocate/Entertainer

"Reclaiming Goddess Sexuality *offers powerful new ways of understanding a woman's sexuality—historically, biologically, and spiritually. For any woman seeking to expand her sexual life and for any man wanting to bring greater pleasure to the woman he loves, Dr. Savage's book will offer invaluable insights.*"
— Stella Resnick, Ph.D., author of *The Pleasure Zone: Why We Resist Good Feelings & How to Let Go and Be Happy*

RECLAIMING
GODDESS
SEXUALITY

Other Hay House Titles of Related Interest

Emerging Women: *The Widening Stream,*
by Julie Keene and Ione Jenson

Empowering Women: *Every Woman's Guide to Successful Living,* by Louise L. Hay

Growing Older, Growing Better: *Daily Meditations for Celebrating Aging,* by Amy E. Dean

The Love and Power Journal: *A Workbook for the Fine Art of Living,* by Lynn V. Andrews

Menopause Made Easy: *How to Make the Right Decisions for the Rest of Your Life,* by Carolle Jean-Murat, M.D.

Passage to Power: *Natural Menopause Revolution,*
by Leslie Kenton

Thoughts of Power and Love, by Susan Jeffers, Ph.D.

(All of the above titles are available at your local bookstore, or may be ordered by calling Hay House at 800-654-5126.)

————————————————

Please visit the Hay House Website at: **www.hayhouse.com**

RECLAIMING GODDESS SEXUALITY

The Power of the Feminine Way

Linda E. Savage, Ph.D.

Hay House, Inc.
Carlsbad, CA

Published and distributed in the United States by:
Hay House, Inc., P.O. Box 5100, Carlsbad, CA 92018-5100 • (800) 654-5126 • (800) 650-5115 (fax)

Editorial: Jill Kramer   *Design:* Christy Salinas

Library of Congress Cataloging-in-Publication Data

Savage, Linda E.
    Reclaiming goddess sexuality : the power of the feminine way / by Linda E. Savage.
        p.   cm.
    Includes bibliographical references.
    ISBN 1-56170-607-8 (trade paper)
    1. Sex—Religious aspects—Goddess religion.   2. Sex instruction for women.   3. Women—Sexual behavior.   4. Sex—Mythology.
    I. Title.
BL460.S34   1999
155.3'33—dc21   98-46490
                                                              CIP

ISBN 1-56170-607-8

02 01 00 99   5 4 3 2
First Printing, May 1999
Second Printing, June 1999

Printed in the United States of America

In Loving Memory of Helen M. Savage:
June 16, 1910–March 29, 1998

And to My Beautiful Daughters,
Sarah and Jamie

Contents

Chapter 10: Contemporary Relationships:

Skills from couples therapy give you a blueprint for building your unique model of intimacy. Specific exercises show how to achieve the four basic "walls" of a healthy relationship. A workbook gives you steps to practice with your partner. The skills are also a pathway to finding fulfilling partnerships.

Chapter 11: Awakening Desire and Enhancing

Step-by-step processes expand the erotic senses. Exercises include specific suggestions for awakening feminine desire and heightening enjoyment of partner sex.

The story of the Great Marriage ritual is Inanna's initiation into spiritual sex. It offers an example of the power of the feminine way. Sexual ecstasy brings wholeness through union with the Divine Life Force.

APPENDIX

Preface

The Burning House

Men and women have been in conflict for thousands of years. It is time for us to end the gender wars and pull together to solve the problems that threaten our existence on Earth. We must not continue to blame each other and act out our deep hurts in the form of rejection and abuse. We are like two kids fighting while their house burns down, who don't seem to notice that their lives are in danger because they are so caught up in winning and gaining control.

Low self-esteem is the root of such dysfunctional behavior. Men and women in conflict increase the cycle of low self-esteem as they wound each other. The human psyche has its own way of fighting for survival and growth. If a loved one has gravely hurt us, especially when we were young children or teens, we act to correct that hurt and gain some feeling of mastery over the source of pain. That is our nature. No one accepts hurtful experiences without some internal shift that leads to consequent behavior as well as altered perceptions. In writing about female sexuality, I am addressing one very deep source of hurtful experiences for both men and women. I will explore how sex has become disowned in women. Our sexuality, which should be a source of self-esteem, is distorted by internal pain. This leads to repressed desire and many other sexual difficulties.

I suspect that men and women have been angry at each other for a very long time because what should be healing and life-affirming is not. What should be connecting us to our Life Force and renewing our energy often does not do so. Yet, we can reclaim the promise of our sexuality. While the feminine experience is largely missing in modern adult sexual imagery, it *was* abundantly portrayed as long as 30,000 years ago. These ancient woman-positive cultures have a message about sexuality that we can learn from today.

I am focusing on sexuality because it has been my field of study for more than 25 years. I hope to avoid playing "mine is better than yours" like the kids in the burning house. Yet, it is time to stop viewing women's sexuality as defective. It is time to stop using a male yardstick to judge the adequacy of the female sexual response. A solid base of sexual self-esteem can only come from a truly female model of sexuality. When we can validate female sexual responses, fluctuating desires, and unique rhythms—from a feminine point of view—sexual healing will come from within.

When women are healed of their sexual scars, the sexes can meet as true partners, each with unique power and wisdom. Sexual synchronicity creates unimaginable healing—healing for the souls of the individuals involved, their families, and the earth. I believe that this is what we are all searching for.

— Linda Savage, Vista, CA

Acknowledgments

There are many to whom I owe a debt of gratitude. First is my husband and partner, Gary Reinhardt, who has been the most enthusiastic cheer person for this project from its start. He has nurtured my sometimes irascible spirit throughout, and he deserves a medal for his patience and loving presence behind the scenes. Thank you for being my friend, my support, and my healer.

Another special cheer person and indomitable presence throughout this project is my friend and editing expert, Richard Martin. His tireless attention to detail and his command of the English language made this work far more readable. His impeccable King's College, Cambridge education was put to excellent use. In the final cutting down and editing process, I am grateful for the assistance of Karla Huebner and Jill Kramer.

Neal Tomblin, Wizard of the Internet, and Wendy Walkoe were involved in teaching me the rudiments of word processing that made my life easier as I moved into the age of computer literacy. Dave Harkins was very kind to allow me to utilize his considerable collection of books published 70 to100 years ago about sexuality.

There are many who offered substantive suggestions that contributed to my ideas. Vena Blanchard was especially helpful for the section on surrogate partners, Ina Laughing Winds for the Quodoushka information, and Morgana Taylor for the chapter on spiritual sex. Dwight Dixon, J.D., Ph.D., offered helpful feedback on male/female sociocultural issues.

I would like to thank my wonderful, supportive friends who have been a source of inspiration for a new model of relationships: Danny and Sherry Cooper, Dan Gardner and Vicki Means, Gene Geary and Linda Gray, Rick and Diana Hassan, and my photographer friend John Russo and his wife, Cindy.

◥◤ ◥◤ ◥◤

Introduction

The Great Marriage

AN ANCIENT MODEL FOR MODERN TIMES

The Dream

In 1979, I was living in a spiritual community in San Diego County. As far as I knew, I was going to spend the rest of my life there, building a new and more authentic way to honor the spiritual insights that were emerging in this idealistic period. I had chosen celibacy as a way of honoring my spiritual path. As part of my leadership role in this group, I went to the Findhorn Community in Scotland to study its organizational structure. Findhorn is located on Moray Firth, close to the Arctic Circle. At the Summer Solstice, the land lies bathed in constant light. Only between the hours of two and four A.M. is there a subtle twilight, and on the night of the solstice when the power of the sun was at its zenith, I had a dream as I slept in the heart of this community.

I felt overwhelmed with the most exquisite
loving feeling I had ever known. I was loved and
I WAS LOVE at the same time. I felt incredibly
beautiful inside and out. I was glowing with
an internal light I had never experienced before.
I was Magic; I was a Goddess.

I had been anointed and adorned by handmaidens who seemed to be preparing me for a momentous ceremony. I was aware of a feeling of awesome responsibility, one I was thrilled to be taking on. The thrill I felt encompassed a tumult of emotions. They were also the most sexually intense feelings of my life. The sense of the divine purpose of this meeting was evident. I waited for my groom, my beloved partner to whom I was bound in a spiritual bond that went back lifetimes.

As I moved into a ring of stones on a grassy knoll, I saw him. He was like no one I had ever seen in my life, and yet I knew that I loved him more deeply than anything. I felt overwhelmingly beautiful and had no doubt that his love encompassed me to the core of my being. He trembled with awe at my presence, my body. I was aware of the shimmering day, of the intoxicating smell of the bower of flowers that had been prepared for our joining.

He looked at me with such total understanding that I was sure that he knew me and accepted me totally. He recognized my intense shyness, arousal, and yearning combined as one. I was floating inside, melting in a sexual intensity that he knew would explode as soon as he touched me. And yet, he was in no rush. He banked his sexual passion with the discipline of a great Master. He was a young king to be crowned, a groom at his wedding, and a powerful priest joining my initiation into the great mystery of life.

I awoke from this dream unconsummated. Yet I did not feel the typical frustration of an unfulfilled sex dream. I could still feel the great current of energy that had passed through and around us. It vibrated in my body, even in my awakened state. I knew that this was no ordinary dream and that its meaning might take a lifetime to unravel completely. The feelings stayed with me for days, and occupied my mind and body even in the midst of all the lessons at Findhorn. I knew I was bound to act on the sacred commitment in this dream.

My path led me out of celibacy and out of the isolation of the community into the city of San Diego, where I eventually returned to graduate school and reentered professional life. In the years to come, being trained as a psychologist and specializing in sex therapy, I sometimes pushed the memory of this dream deep into the background of a busy life and practice. Now, 20 years later, I am beginning to act on the commitment I made in my dream state. I am now starting to understand its meaning on a conscious level.

As I researched the mysteries of the Great Mother Goddess, I realized that I had participated in the sacred *Great Marriage* in my dream. I had experienced all of the elements of this rite as powerfully as if I had physically gone through the ceremony. I realized that that dream had led me to the path I was to follow in my life. I am now writing about the meaning of that dream.

Ancient Ways, Modern Times

The enactment of the Great Marriage was performed in all cultures that worshiped the Divine in the feminine form. Celebration of this sacred ritual continued to be performed into the common era until all remnants were violently crushed by the

Inquisition. Understanding the elements that were part of this ritual can help us reclaim the feminine way of Goddess sexuality.

Through the years of work with women and men on relationship and sexual issues, I have formed some ideas of what is missing from the current treatment of female sexuality. We need to look at feminine sexuality from an entirely female point of view, and the Mother Goddess mysteries encompass an untapped source of knowledge about feminine sexuality. We can blend the ancient feminine perspective with a new approach to female sexuality.

The Modern Views

In the summer of 1997, I went to a well-stocked bookstore to review the books currently available on female sexuality. The section on sexuality was a revealing commentary on the quality of information available on sex and women today. Aside from a very few medical "fact" books written by M.D.'s, most of whom were men, there was a plethora of "how to" manuals, including such titles as:

Light His Fire
How to Make Love Six Nights a Week
How to Make His Wildest Dreams Come True
How to Drive Your Man Wild
Wild in Bed Together
The One-Hour Orgasm
365 Ways to Make Love
Sex for Dummies
Seven Weeks to Better Sex
Fantasex

Sizzling Monogamy
365 Ways to Improve Your Sex Life
How to Romance the Man You Love the Way
    He Wants You To

The titles read like a monologue in a stand-up comedy routine, don't they? Most were written by men, and one-quarter were written by a man/woman team. Only 10 percent were by women.

The sad truth is that these titles reflect the level of consciousness about sexuality today, especially regarding the woman's role: to please men and to play the sex kitten 365 days a year. Each month, almost every woman's magazine features articles on how to be better in bed, or attract or keep a man through sexual performance. If all these "how to" articles and books are really making a difference, why do so many couples feel discouraged about sexuality? Boredom in the bedroom appears to be a disease as pervasive as the common cold, for which we all want a cure. The consequence of poor performance seems to be, "If you don't get it right, you'll lose your man." This perspective of woman-as-pleaser-or-else is one of the great tragedies of modern sexual attitudes.

Problems of Desire

I can't count how many women have said, "Sure, I enjoy sex once I get into it. My partner is a wonderful lover, but I just don't seem to find a way to get into it very often." If it were purely a matter of sex feeling good, sex therapy would be simple. In fact, in the 1970s, we all innocently assumed that if we could just teach men how to pleasure a woman and teach women how to achieve orgasm, all would be well. We now know that more is needed.

We used to believe that if we could only get men and women functioning properly, sexual desire would just flow naturally. That is certainly a reasonable assumption. Sexual functioning is a matter of education and specific suggestions applied together with practice. However, all the treatment for sexual functioning disorders, including pills and penile prostheses for erection problems, does not seem to be solving the female desire juggernaut. Sexual desire, especially trouble with low desire on the female side, continues to be the most common problem for committed couples.

A Modern History of Female Desire

For roughly five to eight thousand years, female sexuality has been defined, discussed, dismissed, maligned, and misrepresented in patriarchal societies. The term *patriarchy* refers to the prevailing male-dominated social and political structure that has been reinforced by legal systems and militant power. It does not in any way refer to all men. In fact, only the dominant males in high-status positions truly benefited from the unequal distribution of wealth and access to resources. In these cultures, masculine traits were distorted by the idealized male image of violent and emotionally disconnected warrior heroes.

Under patriarchal law, the rare women who pursued and enjoyed sexual activities in their own way (neither concubine nor wife) were castigated, ostracized, and even killed. The word *sex* meant "intercourse," and it was something men "got" and women "gave," with the purpose of the whole business being simply to bear heirs (preferably male) for the legal passing-on of inheritances. And God help the woman who "gave" it under the wrong circumstances! When medical texts began to say anything about sexuality, the knowledge imparted about women was ludicrous at best. Early marriage manuals exhorted women to submit to what had been reduced to a wifely duty. Female physiology was grossly misunderstood. According to Elaine Morgan, author of *The Descent of Woman*, "Men with the highest medical qualifications pontificated that the very concept of female orgasm was a fantasy of depraved minds and beyond belief."[1] This was less than 100 years ago!

Until the 1970s, psychiatrists considered the clitoral orgasm to be "immature," and assumed that intercourse was the only right way to experience sexual pleasure. Not more than 50 years ago, Kinsey had the groundbreaking notion of actually asking women what they experienced. Since the 1970s, some serious attempts have been made to define women's sexual responses from more objective data. Masters and Johnson studied women responding sexually in a laboratory and proved that women were capable of orgasms, all originating in the clitoris. This ushered in the age of sexual pleasure for women. However, it did not suddenly free women of all the internal bonds. In fact, it merely added the previously male issue of performance anxiety to women's sexual problems.

Knowledge of the physiology of female sexual functioning does not address the deeper mystery of female sexual desire. Most writings describe how to make "it" happen, with detailed descriptions of oral and manual touching. These books and articles remind me of cookbooks ignoring the big picture of thousands of years of cultural conditioning. Women's desire all too often remains elusive, to the frustration of women as well as their partners.

All the effort to "give" women orgasms (as if we did not own them for ourselves), is missing the point. The genital orgasm as the ultimate goal in sexual functioning is still defining sex by a model limited to an essentially male viewpoint. Unless a woman is engaged of her own free will and feeling the desire—unless she is in touch with the power of her feminine way—all the efforts of her partner are for naught.

Men are often the ones to bring their partners to sex therapy. They buy the books and try to persuade women to try this position or learn that technique. These techniques are all empty exercises without the full and active participation of the woman: her body, mind, and soul. Many men will settle for a sexual encounter that engages a woman's body even if it is through manipulation, illusory promises, mental coercion, or even force. But once they have experienced even one encounter when a woman's whole being is engaged, they seek this transcendent experience like the search for the holy grail.

The Power of Sex

There is an irrefutable power in sexual energy. Although it can be misused, the energy itself is transforming. When it is experienced by fully conscious, consenting adults, it is empowering and healing. Sexual union is the best way to experience wholeness that humans can know.

I believe that the power of a woman's sexual desire and responsiveness emanates from her internal alignment with her core feminine energy. When a woman clearly understands and creates the conditions that enhance, *for her*, the experience of her ecstasy, she has the ideal setting for her sexuality to blossom. When a woman can validate her core self and unique approach to her sexuality, magnetic power emerges from within. She feels energized, uplifted, affirmed, and transformed. Her partner will feel it as well. When a woman finds her I AM GODDESS self, she transmutes universal energy and aligns with Life Force. Her powerful sexuality flows through her to her partner. This is the magic. This magnetic force transmutes through her body—connecting her with herself, her partner, and life. The resulting alchemical transformation of the polarities of male and female raises energy beyond the physical. The body-mind-spirit is joined with the powerful source of all energy.

The Wisdom of the Goddess

In order to heal feminine desire, women must reclaim the core of the universal feminine variously called The Great Goddess, The Great Mother, Earth Mother, and Mother of All. The Goddess represents the feminine polarity of the Life Force. She is not outside our experience, but an eternal awareness inside us all. Ultimately, there is no gender for the Divine Goddess. However, by using the image of the feminine, we can break up the judging, sex-negative image of the ultimate authority that has dominated for the last 5- to 8,000 years.

Political and religious domination by patriarchy has led us down a false path—away from sexual pleasure as a freely chosen, mutually beneficial partnership. In order for women and men to experience the divine healing power of sexual union, both must be aligned with their essential core. Long before it was determined that men owned the reproductive and sexual rights to their mates, women conceived and gave birth and engaged in sexual encounters based on their choice. Sexual desire was perceived as the will of the Great Mother Goddess. Children were considered a gift of the Mother, and their legitimacy was never in question. They were accepted and loved in their own right. Any pregnancy was a miracle, and no societal judgment was placed on the woman as a result of her sexual choices.

The worship of the feminine Divine Force gave women an important role in all aspects of life. During the Golden Age of the Goddess, the High Priestess was the Earthly representative of the Great Mother. She always had a consort with whom she enjoyed her sexuality, which was considered sacred. Any child of that union was especially honored. These Goddess cultures were matrilineal (inheritance traced through the mother) and woman-centered, but they were not ruled by women—they were essentially egalitarian. According to author Riane Eisler, they favored a partnership model of male and female relationships.[2] How they viewed sexual relations between men and women is most important for our understanding of the feminine way.

In the female-positive cultures, all paths were open to women and were honored equally: mother, priestess, healer, craftswoman, farmer, surveyor, scribe, and hunter. The choices depended on their abilities and inclinations. Most women chose several roles, as they do now. They were valued in all three stages of their lives: Maiden, Mother, and Crone. They were not ignored once their reproductive capabilities were over. One can only conclude that female sexual desire was not the problem that it has become in patriarchal cultures. I believe that in the old wisdom lie truths that will lead women out of the terrible sexual self-perception they have endured for millennia.

A New Model of Female Sexuality

Women's low level of sexual desire is largely a reflection of the limits that were imposed by patriarchy. Extremely sex-negative messages have been indoctrinated into male and especially female children for the last few thousand years. Women need to internalize the sex-positive, permission-giving, life-enhancing messages of the Goddess cultures and then create the safe, seductive, and honoring settings that work best. With knowledge of ancient mysteries, they can choose to pursue sexual mastery, which in turn leads into the realm of spiritual sexuality.

When a woman is in her I AM GODDESS self, the capacity to feel the Life Force increases. Men, too, can work toward their own alignment with their masculine core, but they cannot make it happen for women. It is not in their power to do so. The power of female sexual response resides purely within the feminine realm. Much of what is still being written perpetuates the myth that it is the man's job to make "it" happen for a woman. This book is a view of female sexuality that is uniquely feminine, without reference to the male model. I want to join with the handful of women who are writing about female sexuality in this new way. In the exploration of ancient wisdom, I will strive to recapture the essence of the feminine sexual perspective that existed before the patriarchal myth that woman was fashioned from Adam's rib merely to be his mate. Instead of emphasizing "how-to" techniques, I'll explore the nature of female desire, and then we will look at how women can really find their ecstasy.

When the feminine way is added into the equation, then healing, life-giving, transforming, sacred sexual pleasuring can be experienced between men and women, which is what sustains long-term relationships. As communities finally become truly egalitarian between the genders, the ensuing partnerships can expand into enriching life on this planet. It is time for men and women—together— to negotiate the solution to the serious problems facing us today.

PART 1:

THE WISDOM OF THE GODDESS

Chapter One

Why Women Seek Sex Therapy:
A Seasoned Sex Therapist's Observations

"Something Is Really Wrong With Me!"

W omen seek sex therapy because they fear that there is something terribly wrong with their sexuality. They have lived so long under the shadow of the male model of woman as pleaser that very few of them have an independent view of their sexual selves. Ironically, women may think that they have too little or too much desire based on what their partners have told them, or what they have learned in their childhood and adolescence. Many women feel that they have "lost" their desire for sex because they do not respond in ways that satisfy their partners. Some women feel that there is something wrong with them because they desire more sex than their partners and have been summarily rejected by men for this. Rarely does any woman think that her sexuality is exactly right.

When a woman seeks sex therapy, she may be at a high level of distress. She has probably struggled alone with her problems for a long time. Even when women come to individual therapy for depression, anxiety, marital dysfunction, or divorce, they report low sexual desire. Many women with low desire never come for treatment at all. Traditionally the focus in sex therapy beyond behavioral education has always been on what is seen as pathological adaptations to earlier trauma or current painful experiences with partners. However, low desire is too common to be attributable to individual pathology alone. Something is obviously wrong with the big picture for so many women to have the same complaint.

Most women go through episodes of lack of desire several times in their lives. I am speaking about normal-range women who do not have a highly disturbed history of rape, abuse, or extremely low self-esteem resulting from toxic families. These women often feel that something is wrong with them because they don't feel sexual desire for their husbands. They will say, "I don't know what's wrong with me. He's such a nice guy." Yet when women hit these "pockets," it is customary to look for the sexual molestation hidden in their background. In some cases, this may be helpful, but in many cases it is misleading or unproductive. Rarely do sex therapists address the life-stage or sociocultural underpinnings that affect the sexuality of all women in similar ways, so we continue to treat women within a patriarchal model that belies the basic conditions in their lives.

There are some important patterns in the issues of desire that need to be understood from a different view of female sexuality. Many of them are based on the realities of feminine life in patriarchal society. While some women even today lack basic information about their sexual functioning, most can achieve orgasm under the right conditions. Even with the ability to "function," which means to become aroused and achieve orgasm, female sexual desire remains all too often elusive. Desire problems are far more difficult to treat.

Sexual desire is a strong erotic pull that is not the same as sexual arousal, which is the purely physical response of lubrication, swelling tissues, and strong sensations in the genital area. Desire is a mental and emotional state, complicated by everything that contributes to our individuality. Sometimes women report shame-provoking feelings because their greatest sexual desire has been in the worst relationships. Many women are confused because the available **partners, their mates,** are the least sexually interesting. They may **feel no desire for their mate,** but once they feel **safe to** disclose their **secret enjoyment of** masturbation, will talk about the desire for self-stimulation accompanied with fantasies. These women often feel greater sexual desire for unattainable partners such as fantasy lovers, famous people, and fictional characters. Some women report no desire for any sexual activity at all.

In order to begin to understand how to heal women beyond their individual differences, we must first understand the underlying conditions, unique to females, that create resistance to *wanting* to function in relationships. There are patterns that have identifiable cultural roots. The special conditions affecting every woman are based on life-stage circumstances, cultural and religious limits on female sexuality, and sexual trauma based on the inherent dangers of being born female in a patriarchal world.

Life-Stage Influences on Desire

I use the ancient tripartite division of women's age stages—Maiden, Mother, and Crone—because it still makes sense. The Maiden Stage does not refer to women who have never had intercourse, but to women who have not entered the Mother Stage. The Mother Stage is defined by childbirth, and the Crone Stage refers to women entering the period surrounding the change of life, and beyond.

It is crucial to recognize that different desire issues relate to different stages of a woman's life. Sexual advice books tend to group all women in the same category when talking about low desire. Young, single women are much more concerned with respect, commitment, and being labeled sluts for appearing sexy.

Their desire problems are a result of lack of security or mistreatment when they freely express their sexuality. Women in the midst of having families are much more concerned about exhaustion, lack of optimal conditions for passion, or wanting sex too much. Women who are approaching the change of life have issues of losing husbands—especially to younger women—subsequently finding sexual partners. These women are struggling with drastic hormonal changes, as well as the loss of traditional role identities. Many manuals virtually omit mention of older women because it is still widely assumed that they aren't concerned with sex.

Despite 30-plus years of sex therapy and sex education, not much has truly changed for women. Maidens are still concerned with maintaining their "virtue" in the face of male pressure. My 23-year-old daughter points out that in spite of the "sexual revolution" (which is a false term) the concerns of her generation are similar to those of earlier times, except that now, AIDS can take lives. Maiden women are more involved in sexual behavior than before, but still feel enormous ambivalence about their desires. Being seduced and abandoned, especially in a society that clings to puritanical beliefs, continues to be demeaning to women. They are overwhelmed with tremendous estrogen- and testosterone-charged sexual feelings—with more opportunities to act on them—but the consequence is still the loss of self-esteem.

Mother Stage women devour millions of romance novels a year. Clearly, their fantasy lives are alive and well, but their real lives do not begin to live up to these romantic scenarios. When they begin sex therapy—sometimes because their husbands are threatening to leave or have already had an affair—they often know what they would like but have given up trying to obtain it. They will listlessly go through the motions of sex therapy "homework" in order to please or keep their man, rather than feeling genuine desire. Some Mother Stage women return to the work-force and meet men who appear willing to give them romantic attention. For the first time in patriarchy, married women are having affairs in fairly high numbers. They are now beginning to abandon their marriages in search of erotic fulfillment.

Crone Stage women are just beginning to emerge as serious players after thousands of years on the sexual dust heap. Women in their 70s are beginning to speak out about their lusty enjoyment of sex. Actress Joan Hotchkiss, a sexy woman in her 70s, stages a monologue drama called "Elements of Flesh," relating stories about her and her friends' sexual experiences. Many who go to listen to her are shocked. "But she's too old," they say. Such is the dilemma of the Crone woman, who also faces abandonment by a husband of 30 or more years, who discards her for a "trophy" wife. After the divorce, she may choose a much younger lover who appreciates her experience, but she faces great moral outrage from friends, family, and society. With menopause wreaking havoc on her body, self-esteem lowered by loss of the traditional wife-and-mother role, and lack of preparation for a career, she too struggles with low desire often worsened by depression.

Cultural Limits on Female Desire

In traditional patriarchal cultures, women's sexuality was ideally confined to the married woman. In order to ensure legitimate male heirs, the Maiden woman was forbidden any sexual experience. Until marriage, any knowledge of her own sexual pleasure was forbidden. Her husband was supposed to be the source of all her experience. Until the last 60 years, marriage came early, and she was often initiated into the stage of the Mother within the first year. Child-rearing, rather than sexual pleasure, became her focus.

Patriarchal wives were supposed to experience only one partner, the husband, who was typically chosen by their fathers. The wife was to submit to her husband's desires, regardless of her own wishes. After she reached the Crone Stage, she welcomed the ending of her "wifely duty," having never experienced much, if any, pleasure from it. In such cultures, older women were not considered sexually attractive, and were not particularly useful because their childbearing function was over. In these cultures, men took on younger second wives, mistresses, or concubines; and older women were largely perceived as castaways. They were tolerated, but certainly not considered sexual beings.

Imagine if our culture told men: "You can have one, and only one, sex partner in your entire life, and then only after you have promised your life and your body to that person. You must submit to what the woman wants, when she wants it and how. If you find enjoyment in the encounter, fine, but it is certainly not necessary. If your erections don't happen reliably or don't last long enough for your mate's pleasure, you will be put out to pasture, while you watch your mate find a younger, more virile partner. You will have a place of honor as father of the children and the first husband, but no more sexual relationships, lest you shame your wife." No one could be expected to sustain any lasting desire under these conditions, but such were the conditions for women's sexuality for more than 5,000 years. If things have loosened up in the last 30 years, and women are now supposed to have orgasms (mostly to validate their husband's sexual ego), the foundation of the culture continues to demean or diminish the female's unique sexual needs.

If you think conditions for women in traditional patriarchal cultures are exaggerated, read the books listed in the suggested reading section to understand the attitudes, advice, and admonitions given to American women just 100 years ago. Or, read the compelling story of one woman's account of sexual life as a Mormon. *Secret Ceremonies,* by Deborah Laake,[1] would be a fine caricature of a patriarchal structure if only it weren't true and happening to millions of women. And if you really want to feel the full impact of patriarchal systems upon women's sexuality, read the books on the history of sexuality, especially during the Middle Ages.

Religious texts and teachings reinforced patriarchal attitudes toward women's sexual activity. This severe structuring and limiting of female sexuality has obviously impacted women's desire. The female sex-negative milieu remains a part of most women's early life conditioning. Although we might like to think current times have changed this situation, it truly hasn't. There have not been more than a few decades when women did not live in terror of the consequences of unwanted pregnancy. It has only been three decades since a significant but small percentage of very brave women felt the personal freedom to pursue sexual pleasure as they have chosen. The moral censure of these women by conservative elements in our culture continues. To examine the cultural causes of low desire in women, look no further.

Lack of Desire as a Result of Trauma and Anxiety

Multiple traumas, severe abuse, or a highly stressful environment can create anxiety-based loss of desire. Anxiety is sustained fear that keeps our fight-flight response operating past the initial crisis. The body's defense system is still prepared for a new danger or painful experience. This physiological reaction can be caused by a perceived imaginary threat, but the source of the fear may not be in our conscious awareness. Anxious feelings continue to stress the body and eventually take a toll on the immune system. They can dampen sexual feelings as well. Sometimes fear can heighten momentary sexual arousal, but it generally does not sustain sexual desire. Anxiety-based low desire can also be caused by repeated discomfort and pain during intercourse. Desire can also be affected by continual anxiety about inadequate sexual performance.

One experience common to many women is some form of molestation. Almost every woman I know has some story to tell of inappropriate sexual touching in her formative years. It ranges from mild inappropriate fondling to severe rape by a relative. Stepfathers are the most common offenders, biological fathers next. According to a 1992 study,[2] one woman in four has been raped, and one in three has been sexually abused. Other surveys, such as the 1994 "Sex in America" study conducted by the University of Chicago, confirm that about one-quarter of all women have experienced forced sex.[3] No one can estimate the scars such experiences leave, because individuals have entirely unique responses to these occurrences. Fifteen years of talking to women and treating victims of molestation indicate to me that all-too-many women have issues with sex that involve coercion, dominance, or violent intent by a male, usually someone known to them.

Sex As a Violent Act

To a significant extent, many women hold the experience of sex as a violent act in their collective memories. The majority of men *are* decent, loving partners; however, it is not possible to talk about desire issues in women without mentioning the history of violence pertaining to them. Just about every woman knows someone who has been raped, forced, molested, or used sexually by men in some unethical way.

"To be born female is to be at risk," says a study by the United Nations Children's Fund. "Violence against women and children is so deeply imbedded in cultures throughout the world that it is almost invisible." Sixty million women are missing worldwide because of gender-related violence. Female fetuses are routinely aborted because ultrasound techniques enable the husband to insist on abortion, even against the mother's wishes.

Female infanticide, child abuse, and domestic violence account for more deaths than all other human rights violations. Up to 130 million women alive today have undergone ritual female genital mutilation, a common practice in 20 countries. More than one million young girls—mostly Asian—are forced into prostitution each year. In India alone, 5,000 women a year are murdered because their dowries are inadequate, yet only one-quarter of the nations in the world have laws against domestic violence. Only 27 countries have laws against sexual harassment, just 17 countries consider rape within marriage a criminal act, and in 12 Latin American countries, the charges of nonmarital rape will be dropped if the woman agrees to marry the perpetrator.

These statistics are current. For the thousands of years that men ruled women with ironclad legal possession, such abuses were legion. Sex crimes and domestic violence were the norm worldwide until the 20th century. They were not even considered crimes, since beating wives was considered a good solution for dealing with "quarrelsome women." Within women's DNA are memories of countless rapes, clitorectomies, beatings, deaths by multiple unplanned births, suicides motivated by repressed anger turned against the self, domestic humiliation, and lives of quiet desperation.

There is a concept in behavioral psychology called *learned helplessness*. It originated in reports of experiments with rats, where the rodents' efforts to escape from a confined space were rewarded with an electric shock. Eventually, the rats simply gave up and cringed in a corner. Even if a passage to freedom ultimately opened up, they did not try to escape. This pathetic and cruel experiment proved what common sense already knew. If you are punished for a certain behavior, you give up trying. For women throughout most of the patriarchal era, there was no escape if your master chose to abuse you or your children.

During the 14th century, women were reviled and punished for being wanton, quarrelsome, capricious, spendthrift, contradictory, over-talkative and demanding.[4] Husbands could and often did bring their wives to priests to be beaten for these "crimes." Low self-esteem is a known consequence of such treatment. Over several thousand years, women have learned to be weak, helpless, and sexually uninspired because being otherwise elicited punishment.

These conditions have marked a woman's way of life for generations and have served as the basis for low sexual desire throughout patriarchal history. Sex manuals that ignore the history of women's treatment in patriarchal cultures are missing the entire context. It would be like ignoring the history of Afro-Americans in our country when examining the psychological problems of black individuals.

Sexual Harassment

One more contemporary cultural consideration must be factored into women's desire problems: the issue of sexual harassment. Again, one need not look into the past, oppressive as it has been, to understand women's feelings with regard to unwanted advances. So much offensive sexual banter, lewd propositioning, and inappropriate touching continues in the United States, where there are supposed to be laws against such behavior, that studies continue to report little improvement. For example, the recent findings from the U.S. Army's own investigation into sexual harassment show that the new regulations have failed to effect positive change to any great extent.

Even in apparently caring and supportive relationships, women experience unwanted pressure, guilt, and shame that taint some of their sexual encounters. Often males express frustration with their partners, who have no idea what is creating the block to sexual desire. Sometimes these men believe that their women are merely withholding *on purpose,* or worse still, assume that the woman is having sexual encounters with another man (or woman). Judging the woman to be intentionally withholding merely compounds the problems related to female desire.

Performance Anxiety

Unfortunately, the need to please is pervasive in women, negatively impacting their sexual desire. Performance anxiety is an issue, even though men retort, "Yeah, but they don't have to get it up; they can just lie there!" But women can and often do "fake it." This always seems to surprise men when I mention it. Typically they say, "Not with me," to which I respond, "How do you know?" This question usually stumps them. Almost *every* woman has, on occasion, faked it. Most women tell me they do it often. Sometimes it's just too much of a hassle to concentrate, relax, or take the time required, so they fake orgasm to please the man. Sometimes the faking becomes a habit, until these women cannot achieve orgasm with their partner present. Desire problems can stem from this kind of performance anxiety, which comes from the need to appear responsive.

Women with low desire used to be called "frigid." This label was often used to browbeat spouses into compliance with male sexual demands. Yet any time a woman consents to intercourse out of guilt, obligation, or a desire to keep her partner happy, she is compromising her sexual enjoyment. If she continues this pattern for some time, she will lower her sexual desire.

Case Studies

Women begin sex therapy because they are afraid that they are not sexually "normal." They have been measured by the frequency and performance model of male sexual demands and are found wanting. They say, "I'm afraid I'll lose my man," or "My husband wants more sex." They also say, "I wouldn't care if I ever had sex again," or "I hate sex; I just do it to keep him happy." They may find intercourse painful because they are not sufficiently aroused, or they may truly desire more sexual activity than their male partners and are humiliated because their mates have made them feel ashamed or abnormal. However, sexual energy is like any other type of energy. It can be transformed but never destroyed. Sexual desire can be awakened and *re*awakened.

The following case studies are true composites of a cluster of similar stories. All illustrate the common issues of desire that are endemic to women today. Each is typical of a characteristic set of desire issues: sexual dysfunction based on negative early conditioning, performance pressure in unromantic conditions, and women rejected for their strong sexuality. These cases encompass the complex interweaving of the life stage, individual history, and most particularly, the cultural foundations of female desire disorders.

Veronica: "I Don't Enjoy Sex; I Think I'm Flawed"

Veronica's husband was not threatening to leave her, nor was he demanding more or better sex. He simply focused his interests on fantasy sex, using on-line pictures and pornographic magazines. The discovery of his activities so upset Veronica that she developed symptoms of a panic disorder, precipitating a trip to the emergency room for treatment.

When we talked about her issues at her first session, she told me that she felt as if her husband committed adultery every time he looked at a picture of another woman. At 29, she was a beautiful, articulate woman, but she was convinced that she was no match for the airbrushed beauties in the magazines. She looked like a cute little girl packaged to appear like a sexy woman. Veronica understood that her sexual desire was lacking. She told me, "I do it once a week so he'll leave me alone the rest of the time." As we talked about her life, it was clear that she had never enjoyed any sexual touching, had never had an orgasm, and found intercourse painful. Her Maiden Stage exploration was so limited by demanding parents that she had little sense of self. She married her first boyfriend after college and wanted a family, but she did not know how to cope with the sexual aspects of her marriage.

Veronica had been conditioned to believe that any sexual contact with a man was shameful. As a young woman dating, she found touching beyond holding hands very threatening. She had been raised in a traditional religious home, and her parents believed that they had done the right thing to protect her from sexual advances of boys. They frightened and shamed her into being "a good girl." She had arrived at the altar a virgin, and tolerated sexual intercourse as a "necessary evil" that men required in marriage. She was a Maiden who was never allowed sexual exploration. She didn't have any sense of physical pleasure, nor any initial desire to learn how her body worked. Basically, Veronica was a stranger to her own body.

Veronica's case was classic for most women until a little more than 30 years ago! In therapy, we dealt with her parental and religious prohibitions and the damage done to her body image and sexual self-esteem. It was fairly simple to educate Veronica about sexual functioning once she had internalized permission to learn about her body. She then enthusiastically pursued finding her own pleasure. Fortunately, her husband was open to the new changes in his wife, and they developed a full sexual relationship. Ultimately, she was able to accept her husband's habit of masturbating while looking at pictures of other women without feeling that her marriage was threatened by his behavior. She felt more secure—with a much freer sense of self—as well as feeling that she had a stronger marital bond.

Clarissa: "I'm Afraid I'll
Lose Him"

Clarissa's husband had an affair several years ago, and the couple had worked about a year in marriage therapy to put the relationship back together again. Recently, her husband had told her that he was not happy with the infrequency of sex and had demanded that she do something about her low sexual desire. She had come to me fearing that he would once again seek a sexual relationship with another woman, and that this time he would leave her. She was angry that he had put so much pressure on her.

When they decided to stay married, Clarissa thought that her husband had put the affair behind him, but he still harbored resentment that Clarissa could not be like his lover. No matter that he had poured his energy into the affair, arranging romantic trysts, meeting his lover's sexual needs with great fervor. He expected Clarissa simply to find a way to become aroused without these special conditions. The fact that he met this other woman infrequently, under extremely passionate conditions, seemed to escape his attention.

In therapy, when Clarissa tried to talk to her husband about her sexual needs, he listened halfheartedly or told her, "I'm just not the romantic type." (As a therapist, I've treated many couples where the husband has said something like this.) Clarissa believed that if she confronted her husband, she would appear difficult, or be called "frigid" and "demanding." Her low desire was partly a result of repressed anger, as well as the unromantic conditions of the setting. Both Clarissa and her husband operated from the belief that if he left her, she would not be able to survive without him.

Clarissa was in a classic double bind. She could not bear her husband to leave, yet she also couldn't find the sexual passion she felt before he had betrayed her. The Clarissas of our current times often have good jobs, run the household, and raise the kids with very little help. They have bought into the societal myth that in marriage, it is the woman who needs the man. The myth confirms that they must do everything in their power to hold on, for they will be lost without husbands. They rarely perceive that their emotional dependence has nothing to do with the reality of their situations. Clarissa might have had to struggle for a while, but she *would* have been able to handle life without her husband.

I am not implying that the solution to this marital problem was for Clarissa to leave her husband, but in order for her to negotiate her needs from a strong position, she had to be able to tolerate the possibility of living without him. Then she could find out how to assert her own degree of sexual pleasure, rather than performing according to her husband's standards. She would also have to address imbalances in the household and child-rearing responsibilities in order to feel free to choose her desired quality of life.

Debbie: "My Husband Says There's Something Wrong with Me"

I worked with Debbie and her husband, a handsome couple in their early 40s who had been married eight years, both for the second time. Their kids from their first marriages were all adults and living on their own. Both partners had good jobs and were healthy. Everything seemed to indicate that sex should have been good, too. They had plenty of time for each other and shared common recreational interests. At the beginning of their relationship, they'd had passionate sex almost on a daily basis, and Debbie was very responsive. They had initiated fun things to do, talked seductively to each other on the phone, and loved to turn each other on in a variety of ways.

When Debbie first came to see me, her desire had gone completely dormant. Her husband blamed her because he could always get an erection. She wanted to feel sexual, as she still found her husband attractive and did not understand what had gone wrong. It was as if her body had turned on her. She felt that, overall, she was a highly sexual woman who'd had a very satisfying sex life in her previous marriage.

As we began to unravel the story, a very interesting dynamic emerged. Whereas Debbie had been sexually spontaneous, wanting to wake up and make love or fall into bed any time of day, her husband had one task he always required of her before any kissing, touching, or sexual pleasuring was to begin. Debbie had to brush her teeth and scrub her genital area thoroughly before he would touch her. As the couple talked, Debbie's husband admitted that he could not stand her female odors. She visited several doctors to try to find the cause. When all the tests yielded nothing and she had to stop using scented douches because they gave her yeast infections, she became discouraged.

This is the progression that led to Debbie's low level of desire. Every time she and her husband made love, she worried that he was silently enduring her odors. Because of that thought, she could not enjoy oral sex. When she used a vibrator, which helped her reach orgasm after she gave up oral stimulation, her husband constantly criticized her "dependence" on an electrical device. He stated that he didn't feel needed and didn't see why she had to use "that thing." Of course he "had no problems," so she had to be really "screwed up." Until we discussed this situation, Debbie had been willing the take the blame for the whole problem. She never even questioned that her husband's obsessive need for hygiene could be a sign of his underlying aversion to her powerful sexuality.

Desire Discrepancy: The Couples' Disease

The most common sexual complaint for couples is desire discrepancy. This means that someone in the relationship wants more sex than the other partner, a situation that often results in conflict and pain. Couples grapple over this desire discrepancy for a long time and often divorce over this issue. Usually it is the male who wants more sex, although the dynamics may be complex, as in Debbie's case above.

Diane and Rob: "Your Way or My Way"

At the heart of almost every desire discrepancy in a relationship is the issue of whose "way" is to prevail. Consider the case of Diane and Rob. They had been married for ten years and had two kids, and had been working diligently in couples therapy for several months. Rob wanted more sexual frequency with less "hoops" to jump through; Diane wanted more sensuality and romance. Over the years, they had come to a "Mexican standoff." Neither one was going to make a change unless the other would. Thus, they had drawn their lines in the sand and waited to be given what they wanted by the other. On special occasions, one gave the other some semblance of what he or she needed, but there was always a price to pay.

No too long ago, Diane (encouraged by the therapy) asked for a "date" with Rob, where they could dress up, have a good conversation face-to-face over a relaxed dinner, and spend the time necessary for her to feel close. Rob agreed, but his body language at dinner showed her that he was bored and simply going through the motions, wondering when they could go home and get to the real thing. Throughout dinner, she soldiered on valiantly, trying to be witty and positive, but feeling awkward and foolish all the while.

Back at home, with the kids over at Grandma's house, Diane set up a wonderful bath, complete with scented candles. She massaged Rob with a soft skin lotion accompanied by lovely music. He began to enjoy the bath-and-lotion segment of the evening, the touching and personal attention. Since Diane was orchestrating the event, she put a greater amount of energy into attending to her husband's needs, really trying to create a mood. Rob's passivity with respect to his own efforts in bathing and rubbing her with lotion annoyed Diane, but she moved on to what he clearly perceived as the "main event." She completed the experience but some-how felt an emptiness that her orgasm did not dispel. Rob could not understand in the next therapy session why his wife stated that she was not thrilled with the experiment.

I have learned over the years of treating couples with desire discrepancy that what most men were willing to do on dates when they were single—that is, what they knew worked very well to seduce women—they now found enormously taxing with their mates. I have heard them say, over and over again, that they did-n't expect to have to work hard "to get laid" once they got married. Some will even admit that they expected marriage to provide them with a willing and available partner for sex *whenever they wanted it*. The meaning of marriage for many men, consciously or unconsciously, is intercourse on a regular basis without the fear of rejection, and without the need to romance a woman as they did when they were single.

When women such as Diane reach a certain point of frustration with their partners, they say, "I don't feel desire anymore." The tendency is for the partner and therapist alike to ask, "What's wrong with you?" when the question really needs to be, "What's wrong with the whole situation?"

Many couples reach a "compromise" that I call "The Concubine Solution." Rather than continuing to struggle (as Diane did) to make something happen "her way," the woman simply makes sure she attends to her husband's needs on some regular basis. The frequency of this servicing is finely calculated, depending on the dynamics of each couple. Women routinely state: "I do him once a week or he gets cranky," or "If I don't let him have at least one blow job every three days, I know we'll have a fight." In order for a woman in a committed relationship to attract the conditions she needs to experience her own authentic sexual response, she will have to fully empower her own desires.

What Women Really Want

After all the years I've been treating couples and women in marital and sex therapy, I have come to a few very simple conclusions about what women really want. First: **Women want to be known *rather than* used.**

Women want the whole process to be about pleasure and not performance (either theirs or their partners'). They want to relinquish the notion of sex as a tool to get or keep a mate, and they want to be honored for their unique feminine ways of pleasuring. They want the beauty of the context of sexual encounters to be more important than the act. They want to be touched in slow, sensual ways. They want to be ravished with intense passion that demonstrates how much their partners need *them*—rather than just needing an orgasm to relax. All in all . . .

Women want to be adored as precious feminine beings!

❧❧ ❧❧ ❧❧ ❧❧ ❧❧ ❧❧

Chapter Two

Ancient Wisdom and Female Sexuality

We are at the dawn of a new millennium. In the 20th century, women acquired some measure of influence in the world beyond the home, yet women's sexuality is far from being the powerful force it once was. The relevance of the ancient women's wisdom is important to contemporary sexual issues because the Goddess cultures honored a woman's sexuality *in its own right*. Revelations of the Mother/Goddess sexual mysteries can lead to the reclaiming of female sexual desire in the 21st century.

There is indeed a feminine way of sexual being that has a unique developmental path. In the new millennium, this information can lead to healing the wounded female sexual psyche. So in this chapter, we will follow the lives of two females, each raised with a prescribed set of mores, beliefs, and child-rearing practices, each of whom supports different views of sex. In this way, we will be able to understand how these radically different social organizations and perceptions of the world affect the sexuality of the two women.

Ancient Wisdom

The earliest known form of religious expression was the worship of the feminine principle of creative power. Divine Woman, Earth Mother, Great Mother of All, or Great Goddess were names given to venerate the feminine as the origin of material form. She was the primal creator of all life, and presided over death and regeneration. As early as Neanderthal times, we find evidence of the worship of Divine Woman. Later, the Cro-Magnons left stone sculptures and cave paintings as symbols of their religious beliefs. In Paleolithic burial sites, the majority of the images depicted the Mother Goddess. In the beginning, as author Merlin Stone says, "God was a woman."[1]

The High Priestess of these ancient societies was viewed as the Earthly representative of the Goddess. She usually had a male consort, or partner, who sometimes reigned as the temporal king. In some cultures, the "Year God" reigned for only one year, perhaps to prevent abuses of power. Royal lineage was always through the priestess, as kinship and inheritance were always traced through the mother. From what we know about the Goddess cultures, women were not exclusive rulers over men. Thus, "matriarchy" is not an accurate description of these cultures. Men and women played complementary roles in what Riane Eisler calls a *gylanic* (partnership) model of social organization.[2]

Some Native American traditions preserve remnants of these ancient gylanic cultures. In these cultures, children belonged to the woman and her clan, and women owned and bequeathed their property. Paternity was not a critical issue, and marriage did not mean the end to sex with others. Both married men and women were likely to have paramours from time to time. Leslie Marmon Silko[3] writes of the old Laguna Pueblo beliefs that are remembered in traditions and stories even today. They tell of the Mother Creator and her sisters who "thought up the world." Since the Creator was female, women were not considered lesser beings, and gender differences were appreciated as signs of Her Grace.

Harmony with the Rhythms of Nature

Rites celebrating the seasons were some of the oldest known rituals demonstrating the people's reverence and respect for the Mother/Goddess. These rites encouraged hope in the continuation of life and gave people a measure of participation in the rhythms of the seasons. They aligned the participants with the natural life-cycle changes and acknowledged the Great Mother for her omnipresence in all phases of life.

An example of the seasonal rituals can be seen in the Celtic tradition of honoring the two solstices (high and low points of the sun) and the two solar equinoxes (night and day are equal). The year began with the Spring Equinox, when day and night are in balance, followed by the "quarter day" of May 1. The Beltane celebrations welcomed the first green shoots, representing the promise of new life. The Sacred Marriage of the Great Goddess took place during the May Day celebrations, to ensure prosperity for all the land. Sexual union was particularly encouraged at this time as a way to honor the life-giving fertility of the Mother.

The next celebration was the Summer Solstice, when the sun is in its ascendancy, followed by Lammas, or the celebration of the Pregnant Goddess giving birth in the August harvest of abundance. Following harvest was the Fall Equinox, when again, day and night are in balance. We still celebrate the next quarter day as All Soul's Day, and the night before as All Hallow's Eve (Hallowe'en). This was called "Samhain" in Celtic, or Summer's End, and was when the Goddess went underground. Solemn rites took place at ancient burial grounds, and the people honored their ancestors. The Sacred Marriage was also enacted at this time. It represented the union of the Goddess with the "Horned One" or the Deer King (horns cross-culturally symbolize male energy).

Finally, at the Winter Solstice, night holds sway over the land. The early February ritual of Candlemas followed, with a procession of torches or lighted candles that represented the beginning of light and the time to sow the seed, which would be reborn again in the spring.

Mother/Goddess Sexuality

The Mother/Goddess was believed to be the source of all form, through the act of giving birth. The Goddess was understood to be *immanent*—that is, she pervaded every part of life. In fact, Earth *was* the Mother/Goddess, so any involvement with the natural world was seen as an act toward the Source of All. It is important to understand that this is the origin of the reverence for nature, the foundation of these cultures. The human body, sexuality, and fertility were highly valued as manifestations of the love of the Mother. Male and female were seen as polar opposites of the same energy of throbbing rhythms that infused all life. Sexual desire was the force that continued pulsating from one to the other in an ever-moving spiral dance.[4]

To the ancients, the female genitals had great magical power as the gate to all life. Death was seen as a return to the Mother's womb. Thus, the sacred caves represented the womb, and entrances were often carved to appear like the vulva.[5] Burial mounds also had *yoni*-shaped (that is, shaped like the female genitalia) entrances, and the walls were rounded. Archaeological evidence of the Neolithic rock paintings, sculptures, figurines, and later mural paintings provide much evidence of the veneration of Divine Woman and Her Yoni.[6]

The Women's Mysteries

The word *mystery* comes from the Greek *mysterion*, meaning "secret rite or ritual." Rituals become secret when the dominant culture suppresses the older cultural wisdom. We know that women's sacred rites were derived from the earlier worship of the Mother Goddess, when the whole community celebrated the power of women's sexuality, fertility, and prophetic visions. In earlier times, death rituals were also presided over by priestesses, who aided the individual's return to the Mother.

The women's mysteries held great importance even during the waning of the Goddess cultures, and after the patriarchal subordination of women. For example, some festivals and secret ceremonies held in classical Greece and Rome were strictly for women.[7] Since only women could give birth, this most miraculous human event was a central theme of women's mysteries. Women were also exclusively the midwives, so the sacred rituals ensuring safe pregnancy and childbirth continued. Female puberty rites, initiating girls into womanhood, and rituals honoring the Mother as giver of grain and civilized laws were also universal themes celebrated in the secret ceremonies.

Sexuality and Self-Esteem

The worship of a Female Divine Force gave women an important role in all aspects of life. In the female-positive, egalitarian societies, women were priestesses, craftswomen, surveyors, scribes, teachers, and warriors protecting their cities. With the development of patriarchal systems, women's roles were diminished, and their value became purely a matter of breeding and domestic functions. What would the two worldviews mean for women's sexuality?

To illustrate the very core of women's issues of sexual self-esteem, here are the stories of two women. One girl, Inanna, is growing up in a culture that follows the ways of the Mother/Goddess. The other, Eileen, grows up in a 20th-century patriarchal culture in the United States. Inanna's story is a reconstruction, based on archaeological and anthropological resources. Eileen's is a true story, altered to protect her identity. The stories of the two women's sexual coming-of-age illustrate the differences between a Maiden growing up in a time of female-positive sexuality, and a Maiden of our times.

A Tale of Two Daughters

Inanna

Inanna lived on the Isle of Crete around 4000 B.C.E. (before the common era). She was the daughter of a priestess and lived with her mother, father, and her mother's extended family. In her grandmother's home, there were murals, tapestries, and sculptures depicting the beauty of nature, and wonderful artistic renditions of human life. One of her most prized possessions was a small, plain clay figure of the Goddess as Nu, the full-breasted, voluptuous Mother of All. It was very old and had been given to her by her grandmother when she was born. When she was very little, Inanna wondered why Nu had no face. Now she knew that no one could visualize the face of the Divine Mother, so she was represented by a woman's body alone.

When Inanna was small, she was taught that her body was an expression of the Divine. She felt no shame about her beautiful form, so she gave little thought to covering her body except for the purposes of comfort or adornment. Her curiosity about the differences between male and female bodies was satisfied by the beautiful nude sculptures in her home. In addition, her culture favored clothing that revealed a frank appreciation for the physical differences between males and females. Her mother had explained to her that in the beginning of time there was only unity, but when the Goddess gave birth to physical reality, she created two opposites that together represented the whole: male and female. The union of male and female in the physical body was a demonstration of the divine unity of all life. Sexual pleasure was a gift to be treasured, and, like all gifts, it had to be experienced under the right conditions in order to honor the Goddess.

Inanna's mother also explained that all relationships were but a reflection of our relationship with the Divine Source. As a result, Inanna knew that she had to respect herself and her body, and honor all others as the same expression of the Divine. Sexual relationships were no mystery to her since she had seen the sacred art of the temple, as well as animals breeding in farms around her village. She knew her mother and father loved each other, as they were openly very affectionate in her home. Her mother was quite willing to answer questions, and as Inanna grew, she would talk to her mother, sharing her concerns about life in general and about her sexuality.

Inanna had shown great aptitude with healing early in life. At the age of nine, she began to accompany her mother when she visited the sick in their homes, and had witnessed birth several times as handmaiden to her mother's skilled hands. She knew she wanted to be a healer more than anything else, and she could feel the strength of the Great Mother inside her as she worked with herbs.

Inanna eagerly awaited the day when she would join the women of her village in the Great Lodge, where all women retired during their moon-flow. She experienced her first blood at the age of 12 without fear or shame. Her mother had prepared her well. All of her female relatives came with her to the Lodge, and she received small gifts from each of them. More important, her beloved Grandmother Nona, as well as her aunts, cousins, and mother, all stayed with her. They spoke of the wisdom and powers of the Goddess that were now part of her new life as a Novice Maiden. Each one told her a story that reflected the wisdom from their life experience. Inanna's grandmother was the last to speak. She told this story of the Divine Woman:

> *In the beginning, the People lived in harmony with the Creator of All Life. Men hunted animals for meat but did not share as much with women. So Mother Goddess spoke to women and told them to gather fruit and to sow the seeds of grasses to make good things to eat. The men wanted some of this good food, because when hunting was scarce, they had nothing to eat. So*

the Mother of All told women to make a trade. Men would provide protection and meat. Women would provide children and the knowledge of plants.

To this day, the Mother speaks to her daughters, and every woman can hear her in her heart. She teaches them how to find the healing plants and tells them about future events and what they must do to be prepared. When you, my granddaughter, are in your moon-flow, you will fast on herbs and roots and hear the Mother as she speaks to you in visions and dreams. Heed her well, and share your visions with the People.

Eileen

Eileen was born in 1950 to a good home with loving parents. Her father was a respected president of a corporation. Her mother had been a gifted teacher who had given up her vocation because her husband did not want her to work, and she now contented herself with charitable activities in her church and town. Eileen's earliest memories included clinging to her mother's winter coat, waiting for her to finish talking to her friends after Sunday choir service. Eileen loved hearing her mother's voice as she laughed and conversed.

Eileen went to Sunday School to learn about God and Jesus, who loved little children. She became well versed in Bible stories about Abraham, Joseph, Jonah, and the other Biblical figures. She never heard any sacred stories about women in the Bible, except for Abraham's wife, Sarah, whose honor was to bear Abraham a son. One unbidden and disturbing thought often intruded into Eileen's consciousness: that God had a penis. It disturbed her that she wondered what He looked like in the nude, for surely everyone knew that the Supreme Being was a male. She had glimpsed her older brothers naked, but it was a source of great shame and confusion. She sensed that there was something wrong with seeing naked bodies, especially those that were male.

Her brothers constantly teased her and demeaned her for being a "girl," which meant something odious and ugly to them. Eileen's mother seemed to believe that her sons must have been provoked by Eileen's naturally assertive behavior and were justified in their teasing. She believed it was for Eileen's own good to learn not to "toot her own horn," which seemed to mean anything she might say about herself that she was proud of. When the teasing turned sexual in nature, it frightened her, but she felt she could not tell anyone how awful it made her feel. Her brothers went to great lengths to get into her room, read her diaries, and embarrass her with sexual innuendo about her female parts.

Although Eileen's father loved her dearly, especially since she was the smartest and most athletic of his children, he was not around to protect her from the teasing and physical assaults. As an adult, she still bore scars from her brothers' bullying. When she had private moments with her father, he would read to her or talk to her about school, and she felt important. At other times, he'd chuckle and pat her behind, which embarrassed her. She knew he thought she was a "cute little girl."

In junior high school, Eileen had seen the film *Growing Up and Liking It*, but it left her with more questions than answers. It seemed to be more about planting seeds than about humans making love. In fact, she understood more about her internal plumbing than about how the sexual act itself would make her feel. Most of the information about sexual activity came from jokes that horrified and disgusted her. She was frightened by the prospect of intercourse, which seemed like it could only hurt.

When Eileen's period came at the age of 12, she was scarcely ready. She was embarrassed to say anything to her mother for two days because they were on a family vacation and she did not want to cause a commotion. As it was, her brothers found out and did tease her mercilessly, brandishing Kotex pads all over the house and making disgusting references. Boys at school snapped her bras whenever they got the opportunity and told embarrassing jokes. Both situations made her wish she had never been born a girl.

The First Blood Mysteries

Special sacred rites surrounded the time of a woman's first menstruation in all Goddess cultures. The first blood rituals helped the Maiden come to understand the mysteries of birth, death, and healing by providing a setting for wisdom to be passed on from the wise women of their families and tribes. Far from "the curse" of modern times, it was a magical and powerful time for a woman. Menstrual blood was believed to have special powers. Only in patriarchal cultures are women seen as repulsive and unfit during their cycles. To those who worshiped the Great Mother, it was the women's *power* during this time that caused them to separate from the daily life of the family and tribe—not uncleanliness.

Women's rites encouraged the newly fertile Maiden to focus within. This development of internal awareness was nurtured in women's lodges, where Maidens often cleansed themselves with purifying diets and baths. Meditation, singing, and learning the wisdom of the ancients also took place on such occasions. The time away from the daily activities of the social group gave the Maiden time to reflect, go within, and develop her feminine gift of intuition. Often, even in later Native American cultures, visions received by women in these "moon lodges" were considered important guidance for the whole tribe. The Goddess cultures emphasized women's power—the power to give life.

Menarche (the onset of menstruation) is a uniquely feminine experience and a fundamental part of women's sexuality. The events surrounding first menstruation are etched in each woman's memory and leave a powerful message about how she is to view herself and her body. In ancient times, a Maiden might learn the secret herbs so she could choose whether or not to allow conception. With these freedoms, there was a very different psychological perception to the significance of her first blood. It was meaningful for the power it proclaimed, not dreaded for the loss of freedom it represented in patriarchal structures.

Let us now return to the stories of Inanna and Eileen.

Inanna

As a Novice Maiden, Inanna was told about the joining of a man and a woman in sexual union. She was told that she would feel powerful emotions and a strong pull from her sexual center when she chose to touch a man in sensual ways. Her sexual desire was the will of the Mother to seek reunion with the other half of humanity. When she was ready, she would feel an incredible pleasure such as she had never known before. This was the gift of the Goddess.

She was also told that this pleasure required her to be in harmony with her own being and that her partner had to understand his own heart in order to blend in harmony with her. Inanna had seen many depictions of men and women in sexual union while gazing at the beautiful art in her home and at her mother's temple. She already understood the mechanics of how male and female joined. Now she began to grasp the great significance of the blending of energy and emotion that accompanied the act. She was taught that she had to work toward her own inner harmony before choosing a sexual partner.

Finally, Inanna was taught about the awesome responsibilities involved in becoming a mother. It was a stage she was not to be ready to enter for many years. She was told of the wondrous powers of the Goddess, which would help and guide her in the process of giving birth. She knew that she could count on her beloved female relatives to support and nurture her through the experience. She was also told of the meaning of surrender to the forces of life within her. She knew she might be asked to give up her own life in the process of childbirth if such was the will of the Great Mother. In time, she would be prepared by her practice of spiritual discipline, her healing studies, and her life experience to be ready for this mystery.

❦❦❦

Eileen

Eileen began to feel strong feelings of sexual excitement at about the age of 13 as she acted out the social rituals of attracting boys and having dates. She was asked to "go steady" at that age without any clue about her own sense of self. She agreed because it made her feel popular and wanted. She loved her boyfriend's kisses, but his sexual touching and attempts to grope her made her feel sick. She made sure they were always around her circle of friends.

When Eileen was 14, she fell in love for the first time. She knew about love from rock 'n' roll songs, but was not prepared for the powerful sexual feelings that "making out" stirred in her. She and her boyfriend necked passionately for what seemed like hours at a time. Fortunately, there was no real opportunity for nude sexual contact. Years later, she realized that she might have been persuaded to have sexual intercourse if it had been feasible. This boy ended up "having to get married" at 18.

From her friends and her church, Eileen knew that it was "bad" to let a boy touch her anywhere below the neck. She spent her first few dating years fending off pleasurable feelings in cars and dark places where furtive kissing took place. Finally, by her junior year in high school, it became okay to pet with a steady boyfriend, but only "above the waist." However, Eileen's boyfriends always encouraged her to go further. All this time, her mother had been a constant source of support for her social problems, but Eileen could not bring herself to talk about the complex feelings that sexual touching and exploration provoked in her. She couldn't admit, even to her mother, that she was doing these things. Even though her friends were all doing them as well, they were too embarrassed to talk about their experiences with each other.

In her senior year, Eileen experienced her first orgasm as a result of her boyfriend's manual stimulation. She was so horrified that she had wet her panties that she couldn't fully enjoy the experience. It was only a year later that a girlfriend explained why that had happened. After that episode, Eileen's steady boyfriend broke up with her. She was very hurt, but she figured it was because she'd allowed him to go too far. She knew it was her responsibility to stop sexual touching. It would be years before she would ever achieve orgasm again.

The Sexual Mysteries

The *Hieros Gamos,* or Sacred Marriage ceremony, was performed in all Goddess-worshiping cultures. The sacred ritual was performed until worship of the Goddess was violently crushed by the Inquisition. In ancient times, the High Priestess might perform the rite with her consort. In later times, the High King or his son was chosen for the male role. The people believed that magic was generated by this Sacred Marriage, ensuring a fruitful harvest, and balancing the male and female forces of the cosmos. Before

the great persecutions, the young king elect was required to perform The Great Marriage as both a symbol of fertility for the land
and a pledge to sacrifice himself for his people, should the need
to defend their land arise.[8]

Let us now return to our two daughters and follow their experience of first intercourse.

Inanna

For five years after her first blood initiation, Inanna
continued her studies as a novice healer. In addition, she
began to train with the male initiates of the Goddess in
the sacred art of bull-dancing, which took place at the
annual spring festival of the Renewal of Life. This dance
depicted male sexual power, represented by the bull,
joining with the Goddess as represented by the dancers.

Men and women trained together for months and
learned to rely on each other for survival as they alternately danced with and leaped over the bull's horns.
Inanna and Tor, one of the young men, became special
friends, and they began to explore their attraction to
each other. They experimented with kissing and sexual
touching, but Inanna had never felt ready to experience
the union of intercourse. The time of the Great Marriage
celebration was approaching, and they shyly acknowledged a mutual desire to meet that night at the celebration fires after their performance.

The day was an eventful one, with the rites of the
bull-dancing following the Sacred Marriage procession at
dawn into the labyrinth at the Palace of the Goddess at
Knossos. The procession went down to the center of

the Sacred Womb of the Goddess, deep within the palace. The torches illuminated the movement of the people who wound around into the womb, and out again as they reenacted the spiral of life, death, and rebirth.

During the bull-dance, Inanna and her friend executed their part with consummate timing, confirming their trust for each other. They were exhilarated by the crowd's appreciation of their skill and beauty. As day became evening, the people returned to their homes to gather food and blankets in order to return to the great bonfires that would be lit at dark with the torches from the procession. The mood was festive and full of expectation.

Inanna was excited. This would be her first experience of sexual intercourse with a man. Many young women she knew had already become sexual, and some had even chosen to be mothers at her age, but she had been drawn to learning the arts of healing and developing her gymnastic skills. She now felt ready for this next step of her growth. She knew that if a child came from this union, he or she would be considered a sacred child of the Goddess. She felt ready for her Mother Stage if that was what the Goddess willed.

That evening, Inanna arrived with her family and joined the community in the games and dancing. As the night deepened, she looked for Tor, who appeared at her side as if drawn by a magnetic force. As the dancing grew more frenzied, their bodies glistened with exertion, and their eyes often met. This was to be their night. Inanna's mother had packed her daughter some food and blankets, and she smiled and nodded as the pair stole away from the fires. As Inanna and Tor found their quiet glen, deep in the woods, they sank down on the blankets. It seemed that time had stopped. Their bodies began to touch, and they moved in the slow dance of primordial pleasure. The hours of ecstasy were a product of their years of spiritual preparation, and a validation of the energy of physically disciplined, youthful ardor. The night was more than they had ever expected and all that had been promised.

Eileen

As teens, the all-important questions Eileen and her friends asked fortune-tellers were: Whom will I marry, how many children will I have, and what kind of house will I live in? School work was vaguely encouraged, but career goals were never emphasized. Throughout her teen years, Eileen continued to experiment with petting, always keeping in mind that she had to remain a virgin so her reputation would not be ruined. Eileen's best friend had suffered socially from rumors that she was a "slut" after having had intercourse with her boyfriend. Eileen's mother encouraged her to remain loyal to her friend and not participate in the other girls' ostracism after the ugly rumors spread. Her mother had taught her that love for a friend mattered more than people's harsh judgment of a girl's sexual choices. But watching what her friend had gone through made a strong impression on Eileen. She had to keep her virginity intact even with all the strong sexual feelings she was experiencing with her boyfriend.

She managed to graduate from high school a "technical virgin" like most of her friends.

In spite of all the pressure of her social life, and the higher value placed on her looks and popularity, Eileen had managed to focus enough of her considerable intelligence on her grades so that in the fall she entered college. She wanted to help people in some way, so she majored in sociology. Her parents said that it was important to have a way to earn a living in case she needed "something to fall back on." Once she entered college, however, the countdown began for that important someone to marry. By senior year, she was expected to be engaged.

In her sophomore year, Eileen met someone her own age, and as they moved from dating to being "pinned" to that highly prized senior year engagement, their experimentation with sex became more intense. After they were pinned, she felt sure enough of his commitment to allow genital touching. However, her desire for sexual union led to a serious discussion of whether they should "go all the way." All the bases had been loaded for quite some time anyway. When they spent hours in sexual touching, her boyfriend would ejaculate outside her, and she had wonderful orgasms through manual stimulation.

Eileen's boyfriend was a "good guy" and a virgin as well. The sum total of his parental sex education consisted of his father telling him, "Don't you be coming home with some girl under your arm telling us you have to get married!" Most of Eileen's college friends had to make the same sexual decisions. Many late-night talk sessions in her dorm led to a search for a liberal-minded doctor who would supply them with "the pill." The birth-control pill was the first truly reliable method to avoid pregnancy. Until then, everyone knew girls who'd had to get illegal abortions, and the horror stories frightened all of them. Although the pill was still unavailable in their state, girls could travel to New York City where it was legal. There they could buy the peace of mind needed to fulfill desires that had been frustrated by years of struggling with their own bodies.

Eileen's first experience with intercourse, although awkward, was a very meaningful event. However, her body had been accustomed to orgasm by manual stimulation, and she could not climax with intercourse. Both she and her boyfriend felt that something was wrong with her continued need for manual stimulation. Throughout the last two college years, they looked forward to the weekends and spent much of their time exploring sexual pleasure. The relationship offered a secure dating life and a safe, available sex partner. The fact that they had very few interests in common escaped both of them, but they were expected to be married as soon as they graduated. Eileen and her groom would go through the charade of a white wedding, symbolizing the bride's virginity, to placate their relatives. Their families were never to know about their sexual exploration.

The Mystery of Sexual Energy

One of the most startling aspects of women's sacred knowledge was the belief that sexuality was both a healing energy and a pathway to raising consciousness. Those who were initiated into this mystery of sexual energy were able to use it for sacred purposes. We know something of these practices from references to the "temple prostitutes," and the descriptions of Tantric rituals. From Rufus Camphausen we learn of passages in the *Tao-te-Ching,* Baul teachings, and Hindu Shakta religious tenets that depict the ability of feminine sexual power to promote healing and ecstatic states.[9] Sexual ecstasy was a way to obtain direct experience of the Divine Life Force.

During sex, powerful endorphins with demonstrated healing properties are released into the system. These same endorphins can also promote ecstatic states of consciousness. Ancient knowledge taught this truth thousands of years ago. The temple priestesses were called *Hierodules*, or the sacred virgins. These women were practicing sexual healing and initiating men into the sexual pathway to expanded consciousness. During the early development of Tantra, women called *Tantrikas* were instrumental in formulating the Tantric practices because they were trained in the tradition of the sacred sexual healing in the Goddess temples.

Ancient Preparation Rituals

An essential part of women's knowledge about sexual energy has to do with the quality of sexual *readiness,* meaning that the female is prepared for this type of sexual experience mentally as well as physically. Rituals using herbs, fasting, bathing, anointing, adorning, and instruction in disciplined spiritual practices were the key methods of preparation in ancient times.

Today, most women perform the ancient feminine rites of enhancing their natural beauty, whether this takes the form of simple cleansing or more elaborate rituals. In the past, women almost always performed acts of purification and adornment with other women. Preparation for any important event in ancient cultures always included bathing, anointing with oils, dressing in beautiful garments, arranging the hair, and many other types of physical enhancement. In the feminine way, it is not a sin to enhance the beauty of the body, but a means to empower feminine magnetic attraction. The ancient origins of adornment are steeped in a special magic called "glamour."

Female Sexual Power

Feminine sexual power has attributes different from the version of passive female sexuality portrayed in patriarchy. The power to attract is the basis of feminine sexual energy. It is a magnetic force, transmuting Life Force energy within the body. The definition of *magnetic* is "powerfully attractive."

Female power to attract has been the source of fascination and fear in men since the onset of patriarchy. The underlying religious message of the last several thousand years is that women must be blamed for arousing men with their "carnal lust." They have been denigrated for distracting men from "more exalted" spiritual pursuits that have been perceived as being in conflict with the pleasures of the body. For this reason, Buddhist monks and Catholic priests may not marry, and Orthodox Jewish and Islamic temples rigorously separate women from men's sight. Orthodox religions continue to require women to cut their hair and/or cover their heads. In contrast, many of the rituals in the Goddess cultures were performed *in the nude* because it is the natural state. This enhanced the female magnetic force.

Fear of women's magnetic power of attraction explains why male-dominant cultures have tried to eradicate the sexual allure of women by attempting to force them into dull and unattractive attire. The apostle Paul exhorted women to be modest. They were to cover their hair and bodies to appear chaste, and they were to avoid looking men in the eye. All this was intended to diminish their power of sexual attraction.

The ancient, feminine magic is called *glamour*. The origin of the word dates back to a derivative of the Scottish *grammar*, meaning "magic." Today the term has become diluted to refer to glittery clothes and make-up. We call movie stars "glamorous" without really understanding the true meaning of the term. In Webster's Dictionary, there is an interesting definition of glamour: "Seemingly mysterious allure; bewitching charm." The word *bewitch* is a reference to feminine power as seen through the lens of patriarchal values. Women are still made to feel guilty for looking glamorous. Young girls are castigated by their families, schools, and religious authorities for even trying.

Today, our culture still resists the seductive pull toward pleasure, but it would be meaningless for society to condemn the power of feminine attraction if there were no cultural prejudices about free, female sexual expression. The magic of "glamour" is the enhancement of feminine magnetic attractiveness. Yet, generating your own magnetic energy extends beyond adorning the external body. It comes from discovering the secret of your inner radiance. Ultimately, glamour is the power to radiate inner light.

Redefining Female Sexuality

From Inanna's story, you can imagine what it would be like to be raised in a culture where sexual desire was a gift and not a sin! As you can see, the worldviews and values of Inanna's and Eileen's cultures are at polar opposites, especially with regard to female sexuality.

One of the most pervasive differences between the Goddess cultures and patriarchal societies concerns the opposing values of sexuality as a natural gift of pleasure versus sex purely for pro-creation. The separation of the pleasurable aspects of sex from its procreative function was an outgrowth of the obsession with Maiden virginity as a way to control male-kinship lines. The only way to ensure that the male's children would be of his own gene pool was to marry a female with an intact hymen. Over the course of several millennia, beginning around 4500 B.C.E., patriarchy crushed the Goddess cultures, recreating legends and myths that served the new values. These new beliefs reinforced the effort to pass on property and positions of power to male heirs. It must have been very difficult indeed to convince people that female sexuality, once sacred and magical, was now evil and harmful. It took much cruel suppression and institutionalized punishment to crush the natural desire of Maidens. The emphasis on sex for pro-creation correlated with the mistrust of female sexual energy *because it was powerful and unpredictable.*

In our two developmental histories, Inanna was taught respect for all relationships and the beauty of the human body. During her first blood rites, she was told about the emotional as well as phys-ical nature of male-female sexual union. The emphasis was on knowing the positive conditions that would lead to fulfillment and pleasure. The Goddess cultures recognized the value of the Maiden choosing her time of first intercourse wisely. However, she alone made the choice and knew that her sexual energy was hers to give of her *own desire.*

Eileen's upbringing left a lot of unanswered questions. Even though she had a strong female role model in her mother, she was not told anything other than the basic facts of procreation. She, like many women today, inherited cultural taboos against sexual touching and the need to protect her virginity. In the face of her strong sexual feelings and the efforts of her boyfriends to override her conditioning, she struggled against her own body. This inner conflict led to subsequent problems with desire and responsiveness due to an *internal chastity belt*. This term refers to a mind-body connection that physically arrests female arousal before the woman becomes carried away and surrenders to her sensations, allowing intercourse to occur as the natural conclusion of her sexual feelings. The internal block can be so severe that some women cannot reach orgasm at all, but feel only the first phase of excitement, if anything. Eileen responded to manual stimulation, which allowed her to reach orgasm yet kept her "intact." Orgasm through intercourse did not become part of her sexual "map" of climax-producing stimulants. It will take a long time for women to overcome generations of such conditioning, which teaches them to fight their own bodies.

The Union of Male and Female:
Two Views of Sexual Intercourse

What was clearly a giving and receiving of pleasure became an act of dominance and submission in patriarchal societies. This stark contrast can be illustrated by pointing to votive plaques that were found in ruins dating from 2000–1600 B.C.E., and artistic representations of rape myths, seen in wall paintings of the classic Greek times.

Recent evidence substantiates that the Mesopotamian terracotta plaque, found at a site of a temple, portrays The Sacred Marriage of the Goddess and the temporal king. This clay image served as an amulet to provide good fortune to the petitioners who made a votive offering.[11] The simple clay depiction manages to exude a sense of intimacy and eroticism that can still enchant us. The lovers are equal in size, and each is holding the other. The Goddess is offering her breast to her consort as he cups her head gently. The image clearly depicts two consenting adults engaging in mutual pleasuring. The gazing eyes are particularly meaningful. This clay carving conveys a sense of respect and compassion for the partner. One can almost imagine that they are looking into each other's souls. As we shall see in chapter 12, The Great Marriage is an excellent symbol for the feminine model of sexuality.

In contrast are the countless Greek myths of the Olympian gods raping goddesses and mortal women.[12] The stories explain the lineage of gods born from these rapes, which were not viewed as crimes. In addition, Grecian wall paintings, vases, and other types of household art depict scenes of satyrs molesting maenads, men beating and sodomizing *hetaerae* (the Greek word for female entertainer), and phalluses committing sexual violence in every imaginable way.

Another contrasting view of sexuality between the Goddess cultures and patriarchy is the so-called *missionary* position of sexual intercourse. Lilith, the first wife of Adam, committed the crime of refusing to allow Adam to mount her in the prescribed, man-on-top position.[13] Man-on-top is still the most frequently performed sexual position of young adult and even married intercourse. Eileen's first experience of intercourse was with her boyfriend on top. Both of them assumed that that was the way it was supposed to be done. When I talk to women, most of them report that their first experiences were the same. Intercourse in this position with the man's full body weight is used to achieve maximum penetration and thrusting. Even if he makes every effort to hold his body weight off his partner, the penetration and thrusting typically become quite forceful in the throes of his orgasm. In the initial experience of intercourse, this position maximizes the painful aspects of penetration for the woman.

From the amulet of the Goddess and her consort in the act of The Great Marriage, it appears that humans did not always see man-on-top as the "normal way." In the side-by-side position, the chance of slow movement enables the female to control the amount of penetration. Both male and female are able to move in pleasurable ways. This is vastly preferable for first experiences. The image of The Sacred Marriage promises mutual, consensual erotic pleasure and the potential joining of heart, mind, and soul.

Chapter Three

The Three Faces of the Goddess

The ancient cultures that worshiped the Great Mother Goddess recognized three distinct phases of a woman's life: the Maiden, the Mother, and the Crone (which means "Wise One"). Women were closely associated with the moon because their menstrual flow aligned with the new, the full, and the dark phases. Their lives bore a similar pattern of division into triads, and so the tides of the moon, the tides of a woman's monthly courses, and the stages of a woman's life are three. Women's life phases are not only chronological stages, but useful divisions of feminine functions and tasks that offer more than rich symbolic meaning. The stages continue to reflect many aspects of female life experience, as each stage represents a profound psychological transformation

The Archetypes of the Triple Goddess

The Goddess figures of the Greek Pantheon and their Roman counterparts, familiar to us today, are extremely limiting in their ability to inspire women because their portrayals of female qualities are stripped of their earlier awe-inspiring powers. For example, Demeter, originally the powerful Grain Goddess, became a grieving woman left to mourn her daughter's abduction with no help. Her only power was to withhold her fertility, precipitating a barren season of winter. Artemis, the Huntress, possessed attributes reminiscent of ancient warrior women, yet had no loving or sexual qualities. The origin of Hestia, or Vesta, was the Guardian of the Sacred Flame. As women were closely confined to the home, her image was demoted from a more powerful central role in the community. She became the Goddess of the Hearth and governed women's domestic activities. Although the following goddess archetypes were chosen from names familiar to us, their significance for each feminine stage is explained with their earlier, more powerful attributes.

Aphrodite: The Free Maiden

The first face of the ancient Mother Goddess is the Maiden. She is exemplified by Aphrodite, goddess of creative energy and sexual love. Aphrodite is called a "virgin" because she is a woman without ties to any male. Aphrodite is often portrayed as athletic, intelligent, and forcefully clever, a worthy adversary of the gods—even to the male-dominant Greek and Roman societies. Her myths tell of a courageous female who maintains her freedom and is capable of using her impressive wit to prevail over more powerful gods. She is, in fact, the most sexually adventurous of the Greek goddesses. Our word *aphrodisiac* is enduring testimony to her image of instinctive sexuality. The recognition of her sexual power is reminiscent of the beliefs of the Goddess cultures. It is her quality of freedom, to choose her partners as well as her creative expression, that makes her a worthy choice as an archetype for the Maiden. It gives us an ideal for the possibilities of this stage, to discover creativity and explore sexuality.

Gaia: The Earth Mother

Inasmuch as Aphrodite symbolizes the creativity and freely expressed sexual energy of the archetypal Maiden, Gaia's image best symbolizes the responsibility of the Mother. *Gaia* is the Greek word for "Earth." The origins of this name for the Goddess reflect the belief of the early cultures that Earth was literally the body of the Goddess. The perception of the Great Mother as being the same as nature is fundamental to the principle of the unity of all life. The image of Gaia as Earth Mother also represents the view that *authority* means the acceptance of responsibility for the well-being of the people and their commonwealth. She protects, nurtures, and cares for her own. The land and its resources were gifts of the Mother to all her people and could not be "owned" by anyone. They were to be shared.

Creation myths in the Goddess-worshiping cultures established the ultimate authority of the Mother. Logically, the creator of life would not seek to destroy it without reason. The early myths of the male sky-gods established their nature as capricious, territorial, and jealous. Legends about these gods demonstrated their ability to destroy out of petty and impulsive anger. In patriarchy, *authority* became synonymous with fearsome and arbitrary judgmental power.

The image of the Mother as a nurturing and responsible authority emerged from observing the natural, instinctive behavior of mothers with their children. In the transformation from Maiden into Mother, new feminine characteristics emerge. Giving birth, as the ultimate creative act, is the profound change that compels women to shift into the Mother Stage's central life task of accepting responsibility for the human life in their charge. The Mother Stage qualities are exemplified by the Goddess as Gaia.

Isis: The Return of the Queen

The Goddess archetype for this stage is Isis, Queen of Heaven. There were many names for her: Astarte, Inanna, Nut, Asherah, Ishtar, and Hathor. *Isis* is actually the Greek translation for *Au Set,* the Egyptian name for their most revered Goddess. Her symbols were the serpent, which represents feminine powers of divination; and wings, associated with the mysteries of death and rebirth. She guided the early Egyptian rulers, who were high priestesses of royal lineage.[1] Their authority was not based on military power, but on their direct connection with the unseen realms of spirit. Spiritual authority was passed on through daughters who received lifelong training in esoteric mysteries.[14] Laws establishing justice were considered to be under the governance of Isis, and subsequent male Pharaohs established their authority by "sitting on the lap of Isis," which was literally the throne.

Isis best symbolizes the Crone woman because she exemplifies qualities of Crone wisdom combined with high spiritual authority. In ancient times, the knowledge of healing and divine prophecy were the province of her priestesses. Prophetic vision, dream interpretation, and divinely inspired guidance are resurgent expressions of Crone wisdom in our times. As we will see, such women are often the wise teachers and healers of body, mind, and spirit. The ancient association of the Goddess with snakes also represents Kundalini, the Vedic term for *sexual energy,* used for sexual healing in the sacred practices of the temple priestesses.

The Psychology of the Three Stages of a Woman's Life

Advancements in health have extended human life expectancy to twice what it was 100 years ago. Yet the tripartite divisions of Maiden, Mother, and Crone continue to be meaningful in women's lives, particularly when we examine female sexuality. Each stage is organized around the *blood mysteries*: menarche (the first monthly flow of blood); childbirth, which is accompanied by blood from birthing; and menopause, when a woman's "wise blood" remains inside her to give her wisdom. These are still powerful landmarks that profoundly influence women's lives. They function as psychological gateways to the change in consciousness required by each new stage.

Even with all our technology, we really cannot change the course of nature and the powerful hormonal shifts that accompany each blood mystery. Most women will experience the powerful changes caused by female hormonal shifts. The emotions women feel, the psychological meaning they attach to the events, and transformational experiences of each stage are outgrowths of the physical timing inherent in the female body.

Intuition

Menstruation, ovulation, pregnancy, childbirth, and perimenopause are such intense internal physical and psychological experiences that they compel women to focus on the internal awareness of the body. This cannot be experienced by males. As author Lynn V. Andrews was told by her Cree Indian teacher, "Go teach ten men how to give birth."[2] It is literally impossible. Women's natural awareness of what is happening inside their bodies, even subtle shifts, is honed by constant internal reminders of the blood mysteries. This direct experience with powerful internal states develops intuition that is grounded in *body wisdom* (see chapter 4). The connection through the body to the rhythms of the cosmos is the foundation for powerful shifts in consciousness in each stage of a woman's life.

The Maiden

The developmental task of the Maiden Stage is *discovering individual creative potential.* In spiritual terms, it can be likened to the Novice preparing to become the Initiate. This can be a wonderful time to learn at all levels: building career skills, experiencing the complexities of relationships of all kinds, preparing for adult responsibilities, and developing a conscious relationship with intuitive body wisdom, which will continue for the remainder of life.

The Maiden Stage primarily signifies a psychological state of learning. The pupil and the apprentice are additional images for this stage. However, today there is an implication of innocence with respect to the term *Maiden* that has been distorted out of proportion to imply a sexuality untouched and literally unknowing young woman, unschooled in any way. This evaluation of Maiden innocence is insulting to the many strong, competent, vastly underestimated Maidens in their 20s. These young women are perhaps the first generation—since the Goddess cultures were eliminated—to explore their potential (including their sexuality) and to enjoy the freedom to learn and gain knowledge in a relatively unrestrained atmosphere.

Sexually, this should be a period of *exploring pleasure,* without the burden of motherhood. This does not mean that the Maiden period should be a time of unlimited sexual activity. There are many lessons to be learned about readiness, self-respect, and appropriate conditions for sexual encounters. However, without the patriarchal concept of the Maiden as personal property, she is free to discover for herself, with wise guidance, her path to sexual pleasure and her unique appropriate limits.

Today, although there is no formal celebration, there is a

transformation of awareness for any Maiden at the time of her first blood. She is now able to bear children, there will be profound consequences if she does become pregnant, and because of her developed body, she is physically attracting attention from males—whether she is ready for the sexual implications of this or not. Every month she will feel emotions she cannot articulate, she will be dealing with hygiene issues unique to women, and she will need to work with her body much more intimately than ever before. She is confronted by feminine differences that mark the end of childhood each time she menstruates. Most women report feeling some aspect of shame and embarrassment, even if only at the level of having to cover up the fact that they are bleeding from a very private part of their bodies. Ultimately, there is the shadow of the awesome power of conception.

The Maiden Stage does not end with first intercourse, but with pregnancy and the birth of the first child. The Maiden Stage may include sexually active and inactive women before they've had children. We shall explore the special case of women who do not physically give birth in chapter 6.

The Mother

The developmental task of the Mother Stage is *accepting responsibility*. The immense psychological changes that accompany the Mother transition are driven by hormones not available to the biological father. The fierce emotions that the Mother feels about ensuring the well-being of her baby are intensely personal, as no one else is as important to the baby's survival. Among the powerful hormones released into the body with birth is prolactin, the nursing hormone, which has impressive properties for fostering the patience and nurturing abilities needed with constant mothering. The shift in consciousness that takes place with first motherhood is the most sudden and powerful of all in life, save the experience of death.

Spiritually, the Mother Stage is a time of the Journey Woman. Giving birth teaches the deeper meaning of surrender through the experience of overpowering body processes. The responsibility of motherhood is constantly being put to the test, as the Mother learns the lessons of compassion. One woman of 30 put it this way: "I can remember the moment when I shifted from being myself to being someone's mother. It was a moment of profound shock. I was home on the day I had given joyful birth to my daughter who was sleeping beside me. I realized, with a flash of awakening, that for 24 hours each day for the foreseeable future, I would be the sole person responsible for my child's life! No one's needs, least of all my own, would take precedence over her well-being. And for right now, her very life depended upon me." Whether the consciousness of the Mother dawns suddenly, as it did with this new mother, or slowly, it is a most profound shift in consciousness from self—to selfless compassion—for another human being.

Once a woman has gone through this passage, she must accept responsibility for another so completely that her sleep, her body, her attention, and her entire existence must be given over to her child. She discovers that what is best for her child may not be in her own best interests at the moment. This changes her in ways that she could not imagine in all the months of reading, taking classes, and talking to other mothers. Many first-time mothers find that they enter into the psychological state of pure mother-hood for many months. Some find it difficult to shift their atten-tion into other areas of their lives, even past the critical first year or so. Women may take on an intensity of focus that excludes everything else. As one woman put it, "Never have I had a role I have taken more seriously in my life!"

Mother Stage sexuality accesses new strengths learned from the experience of childbirth and child nurturing. Surrender and compassion are deep spiritual lessons that carry over to her sexuality. The hormones accompanying gestation and lactation strongly influence her sexual self. Her sexuality continues to develop, but with radical changes engendered by the responsibilities of nurturing children.

The Crone

The developmental task of the Crone Stage is *sharing wisdom*. In Neolithic times, Crone women were the tribal matriarchs. They were the source of wise counsel for important decisions. Crone wise women are still called *Grandmothers* in some Native American traditions. Their heightened awareness of human nature yielded great insight. Spiritually, this is the Mastery phase. The Wise Woman teaches knowledge gained from her education and life experience. It is a time of reaching into her spiritual depths, utilizing her powers of intuition, and finding meaning in her visions from the dream world. Some Crone women are masters of healing at the highest level.

The change from Mother to Crone is a more gradual psychological shift than the one from Maiden to Mother, so dramatically marked by the birth of the first child. It is impossible to use the cessation of the menses as the delineation for this stage because it may take months to several years for a woman to realize that she has had her last one. However, major hormonal changes are happening in her body, long before actual menopause.

The transition begins when a woman notes changes in her cycle. The duration of the perimenopausal period is as much as ten years. The symptoms vary so drastically from one woman to the next that no one, including doctors, can predict the last blood flow. As mentioned, women cannot wait for total cessation of the menses to begin the shift into Crone consciousness. They are given many physical warnings to which they must pay attention. Women are coming to the end of intensive mothering duties, and the physical symptoms are a message that they must consider their own needs above those of others. The symptoms of what is now called perimenopause are the initiation into Cronehood.

The Crone Stage of life, more than any other, is a time of giving back to society the cumulative wisdom of the years. Many women have an urge to speak out, to organize others, and/or to take action. This is only partly because their time is freed from overwhelming demands of mothering young children. In recent times, many women enter Crone years still raising children born later in life, but they seem to have the energy to get more involved in the world at large. It is often Crone energy that leads to changes being made in society. As the Crone woman moves further onto her life path, she feels the urge to teach others and to cultivate her passions. It can be the most productive time in women's lives.

Sexually, the Crone Stage is a potentially powerful one. It is the stage of *sexual mastery*. The ancient Tantric traditions were founded by female masters who understood the sacred power of sexuality and its relationship to the Divine. The Goddess cultures knew it well. Crone women's continued sexuality in ancient times is one of the unknown mysteries. Some older women chose to stay sexually active with their aging mates. If widowed or unattached, they were known to take younger male lovers for pleasure.

Today, many Crone women are seeking sexual pleasure more assertively than ever before. Far from eschewing sexuality, vital Crone women embrace it for the first time in their lives as purely for themselves. Crone sexual response is no longer estrogen-dependent as in the Maiden and Mother Stages, nor limited by the cycles of progesterone as with Mother pregnancy and birth. It has all the potential power that comes from the will of the fully conscious, self-reliant, experienced, sexual self-knowing, wise woman. If she chooses, she can use her sexuality to serve a higher purpose by receiving Divine inspiration and connecting to the Source.

Psychological Domains of the Maiden, Mother, and Crone

Contemporary women can reintegrate their sexuality and reclaim desire by acknowledging all aspects of the feminine way. First, women must consciously view themselves as an expression of the Goddess. Part of this re-imaging is internalizing the archetypes of the Triple Goddess, delineating the three aspects of feminine nature. These aspects are psychological functions within all women. Thus, each of the stages of our lives—Maiden, Mother, and Crone—is also a domain (field of influence) within the feminine psyche. When we become fully conscious of the three sexual expressions of the Goddess within us, we may choose to express any one or all three simultaneously.

The Maiden within us is the playful child, delighting in the wonder of pleasure and sexual exploration. She is longing to be loved. She is the source of our natural curiosity and sensuality. The psychological readiness to awaken sexual energy, and feeling permission "to do what feels good for me" in a safe setting are necessary for the Maiden to come out to play.

The Mother is the loving nurturer, bestowing unconditional acceptance on the beloved, and generating compassionate loving beyond self-gratification. She is the source within us of our capacity to build communion with another in the act of giving and receiving sexual pleasure. The Mother in us takes responsibility for seductive conditions and knows how to surrender to sexual desire.

The Crone is the wise woman within, who can consciously generate healing power. She is the part of us that feels empowered to act on intentional desire, in an honoring setting. The Crone is the teacher, encouraging us to listen to intuition and recognize divine guidance.

The I AM GODDESS self-awareness integrates the domains of the Maiden, Mother, and Crone. The value of integrating the three expressions of the Goddess within your being is to create the ability and the wisdom to express your sexuality more fully.

❦❦ ❦❦ ❦❦ ❦❦ ❦❦ ❦❦

Chapter Four

Reclaiming Your Goddess Sexuality

Where Do I Begin?

Many women feel an immediate compulsion to deal with the issues they have with their spouses when they seek help for sexual problems. Although their mates *do* need to change, I recommend that women concentrate on themselves first. Women should also begin by strengthening their Guardian (the part of us that is aware of our needs, protective of our individual boundaries, and that encourages us to act in our best interests), as change must begin with the self. Beginning with personal work anchors women in their authentic loving selves and helps them develop an appreciation for the complexities of change. Women *can* make new choices, although they may not be able to change their partners.

However, women need not work exclusively on themselves before they seek healthy relationships. Both men and women can remain intimately connected and strengthen their sense of self. For all of you women *and* men reading this book, chapters 8 and 9 will help you examine your personal healing and enhancement needs; chapters 10 and 11 cover the basic skills of couples' therapy that will help you work on your relationships.

How Do I Heal the Wounds?

Keeping the need for connection in mind, we can begin the healing process by looking at problem areas common to many women, including you. Once you have identified the problem areas in your own thoughts and feelings about sexuality, you can move to healing and enhancement. You can heal these wounds by practicing effective mind-body techniques. You may already know much about your strengths, as well as about issues from the past that need closure. You may have done some previous work in therapy, or you may have read self-help books. Another source of insight about your sexuality may come from having thought deeply about your life.

The questions at the end of the following three chapters will help you compile an accurate picture of your challenges and strengths as far as sexual attitudes are concerned. Some of the questions may appear to be unrelated to sex, such as those relating to loss, or your hopes and dreams. Chapter 8, "Making Sense of Your Personal Story," will show why they are relevant. Whether you choose to use the organizational scheme suggested or your own way of looking at your life, you will need some structured data about your experiences in order to find ways to heal old wounds and strengthen your ability to access your sexual desire.

It is very important to understand the mind-body connection and how this operates with all types of healing. Our thoughts, emotions, and body processes are directly connected. Physical feelings can stimulate thoughts and emotions, just as thoughts and emotions can precipitate physical feelings. Researchers in psychoneuroimmunology have amassed compelling evidence that our bodies and minds communicate at a cellular level. Those of us who have suffered from, or worked with, autoimmune diseases have personally experienced ways in which the mind can make us ill or help us heal. The ancient healers knew this, and modern technology is now finding ways to prove it. Remember that whereas *sexual arousal* is a purely physiological response, *sexual desire* is a complex interaction between the body-mind-spirit, with the will acting as a link between all three.

Your healing path will be a personal journey, but you should follow some consciously developed plan using the suggestions in this book, or information you elicit from classes or therapy.

The Psychobiology of Sexual Response

Hormones, pheromones, peptides, and neurotransmitters play a significant role in desire. They influence the sexual "pull" toward an attractive partner or sexy situation. Thoughts and emotions can affect us at the deepest physical level, causing modifications in cells, endocrine function, and immune responses.

In order to work effectively with the mind-body connection, it is helpful to have a clear understanding of the physiological processes of sexual response. To begin with, there are several phases in your response cycle:

1. The **excitement** phase, accompanied by lubrication and vasocongestion (swelling of the tissue with blood)

2. The **plateau** phase, accompanied by maximum vasocongestion and a tightening of the muscles at the outer part of the vagina in readiness for orgasm

3. The **orgasm** phase, which is the rapid contraction of the vaginal muscles and the uterus, producing a pulsing sensation and a feeling of release or discharge of energy

4. **Resolution,** where vasocongestion reverses and muscular tension relaxes

Males have a "refractory period," which is the time needed in order to return to the excitement phase after resolution. Females are unique in that their bodies do not automatically enter the resolution phase after each orgasm. They can return to the plateau phase and move back to orgasm repeatedly without loss of vasocongestion or the "orgasmic platform" formed by the tightening of muscles in the outer third of the vagina.

Several important differences in male and female sexual response cycles cause such frustration and misunderstanding that it is a wonder we ever get it right! First, there is a vast **timing problem** with the excitement phase. Males can move through the excitement phase to plateau and orgasm in two minutes or less, where females generally take much longer, even as long as 45 minutes. The difference in timing probably accounts for 90 percent of all misunderstandings in early sexual experiences. Either the male simply moves at his own rapid pace, having no idea how to satisfy his partner, or he tries for a while to bring his partner to orgasm, then loses interest or his erection after several frustrating efforts. Both partners begin to get discouraged about the length of time the woman may take to reach orgasm. Some couples eventually develop satisfactory solutions after some exploration with each other. However, the difference in timing forms the basis of a complex set of additional misunderstandings that may worsen over time. Most of the erroneous assumptions about "frigidity" are based on the difference in timing, and men's misinformation about pleasuring women. (Chapter 11 delineates some specific suggestions for awakening feminine desire. They provide useful processes for female pleasuring.)

The second male-female difference in the sexual response

cycle occurs in the **plateau phase**. Females may reach this phase and never climax, resulting in enormous frustration and discouragement. A special physiological phenomenon causes a lot of the trouble. The **clitoris elevates or retracts** into the fully swollen clitoral hood, accounting for the apparent disappearance of the clitoris and a complete shift in sensation. Some women describe this as "going numb," but it can also mean that stimulation that was pleasurable a short while ago is now irritating. Many couples give up the effort at this point because they assume that the woman has lost her arousal. However, her sexual sensations are not lost; they have merely *changed.*

The other problem in the plateau phase is that men who **ejaculate rapidly** do not recognize the so-called point of inevitability and move through the plateau phase to ejaculation with no apparent control. "Apparent," because with practice, they can learn to recognize this point, slow down or stop stimulation, and gain control. However, many couples cease any further sexual interaction after the male's orgasm largely due to his disappointment in himself and the couple's belief that sexual encounters must end with the man's ejaculation. This myth is so ingrained that it never seems to occur to some people to ask, "Who invented this rule?"

Sex can mean any sexually pleasurable experience that causes both partners to feel good about themselves and each other. When we're able to reframe the goal as sensual/sexual pleasure resulting in positive feelings about each other—rather than intercourse or orgasm—we can learn ways to focus on the *process* of pleasurable sensations.

All of our accumulated sexual experiences influence our current sexual responses, both positive and negative. When a problem occurs such as lack of desire, sexual aversion, or difficulty with orgasm, we need to search for stored-memory associations as well as current circumstances.

Questions Pertaining to Early Sexual Experiences

On a pad of paper or in a spiralbound notebook, write down your answers to the following questions:

1. How old were you when you first experienced sexual feelings?

2. How did you feel about acting on them?

3. Who told you the most truth about sex?

4. What were your experiences surrounding your first menstruation?

5. What was your experience with first intercourse?

As you read the various case stories in the following chapters, you may find yourself connecting with some of them. Keep your notebook handy to record your thoughts.

Connecting with Your Body Wisdom

As with all of the suggestions offered in this book, the most important source of information about what is useful for you is your own body wisdom. Listening to your body wisdom is a powerful source of what is called "women's intuition," which is anchored in internal physical, embodied experience. The initiations of first blood, childbirth, and menopause focus women on their body sensations. These are uniquely feminine encounters, as is the monthly ebb and flow of the powerful mix of female hormones. When women pay attention to the messages of their bodies, as they must with these natural processes, they develop a connection to their body wisdom. We have been taught to ignore it most of the time, but every woman has physical signs that compel her to pay attention to the process within. This is the source of body wisdom. It is our wise inner guidance, connected to the universal pulse of life. Thus, the physical initiations of the blood mysteries represent gateways leading to new spiritual awareness.

Maidens expand their body wisdom if they are encouraged to listen to their inner voice for guidance. When Maidens are allowed to explore, they develop a keen understanding of personal limits and learn which conditions are right for their sexuality as well as their lives. Mother intuition is added to body wisdom from the Maiden Stage, with the lessons gained from pregnancy and childbirth, augmented by caring for others. In the Crone Stage, menopause fine-tunes body wisdom, which becomes a source of guidance to be shared with others. The fundamental message, "Trust your body wisdom," is the basis for the feminine way of knowing.

It will be necessary for you to develop ways to differentiate between your body wisdom and your automatic fearful or negative thoughts in order to discern wisdom from fear. I once asked Peter Caddy, one of the founders of the Findhorn community, how I could tell the difference between wise inner guidance and my own automatic thinking. He told me, "You can't until you test it." For example, you might ask someone for confirmation about a "hunch" you have had about them. Or you might pursue an idea and take some kind of action. This seems like an arduous method of trial and error, like stumbling over many rocks before you find the right path; however, acting every time on the messages you receive sharpens the distinction between guidance and fear.

For the sake of your sexuality, the goal is to overcome a lifetime of sex-negative conditioning. You will need to separate from your self-defeating beliefs to recognize authentic intuition. Sometimes you will need to go into your dark places, those unexamined repositories of hurts you have experienced in your life, in order to find the distorted beliefs masking communication from your body wisdom. We shall deal with those dark places when we examine your answers to the above questions, and those in the following three chapters. However, you can begin by focusing your awareness on the messages grounded inside your body. With repeated feedback, you will begin to recognize the difference between ordinary thoughts, reactive emotions, and your body wisdom. That "still, small voice within" gets stronger every time you pay attention to your body wisdom. One of the most helpful sources assisting this process is your Guardian Self.

The Guardian Self

In order to express self-accepting sexuality, a woman must listen to her Guardian, which may be thought of as the authentic protective voice that is distinct from the critical, judgmental gatekeeper, which operates on preconditioned thoughts and beliefs. The Guardian is the part of us that acts in our own best interests—knowing our need for connection, but also for solitude. It is the part of us that can foster healthy self-esteem by establishing good *boundaries*. A personal boundary can be considered the border around our individual self. It is the sense of "this is me and that is not me." Think of the sense of self as your garden. The boundaries are the fences around the garden. You may choose to invite someone into your garden, and you may ask them to leave in a moment-by-moment decision. It is *your* garden, and *you* open the gate to let another in. When you have made a commitment to a loved one, that beloved other is not given ownership of your garden, but must respect your wishes for solitude when your Guardian tells you it is time to attend to your individual needs.

Women who believe that they should give ownership of their personal gardens to their mates are vulnerable to co-dependence, and, in more extreme cases, abuse. If this description rings true for you, it is important that you spend time each day using the "My Secret Garden" guided imagery exercise in chapter 9. The concept of boundaries is so important that you should work with the guided imagery long enough to create a clear picture of what your garden and fences look like. You may also need to internalize the sense of permission both to invite your partner into your garden and also to ask him to leave your garden. Such permission also supports the decision to take an action that is in your best interests but not necessarily what your partner wants you to do.

When a woman listens to her own Guardian with regard to her sexuality, she becomes individuated in the sexual relationship. She must be able to say no to sexual encounters that she does not want without the loss of her partner's goodwill. Most women complain that they continue to submit to mercy sex because the consequences when they maintain a contrary stance are painful. They don't want to have to cope with sulking, coldness, withdrawal, and angry behavior, all of which are the result of saying no or insisting on the right conditions before saying yes. When a woman can approach a sexual encounter from an internal locus of control, her sexual power will emerge from within. Her desire will have nothing to do with performing in order to please her partner. Her sexiness will have nothing to do with a perfect body.

In our society, a woman's Guardian needs to reflect a strong belief in the validity of her female gender in order for her to feel sexually empowered. In other words, to take care of our needs, we must love our feminine way. Internalizing the image of the Divine Feminine is precisely the inspiration needed.

Starhawk, author of *The Spiral Dance,* reminds us that the Life Force has no gender, but having thought of God as male for the last few thousand years, we need to reclaim the female-gendered word for the Divine. She says, "*Goddess* breaks our expectations and reminds us that we are talking about something different from the patriarchal Godfather." The name *Goddess* represents the feminine perspective, namely: "Spirituality does not take us out of the world but brings us fully into it."[1] *Goddess* reminds us that our spirit is not separate from our sexuality. To reclaim their sexuality, women need to join their I AM GODDESS awareness with their Guardian Selves. The Goddess is an excellent focal point for acceptance of our female sexuality.

In essence, we must positively choose to receive the Goddess into our consciousness and acknowledge Her presence inside us. The new awareness brings us fully into our sexual nature. The I AM GODDESS awareness stimulates powerful feminine sensuality. It can be experienced every time you feel body sensations: the visual pleasure of sight, taking in the beauty of candlelight or admiring the curve of your throat in the mirror, the olfactory joy of smelling the jasmine in your yard, or the kinesthetic pleasure of feeling the gentle wind on your face or the touch of silk on your skin. When you taste a succulent peach or move to the rhythms of sensational music vibrating in your body, you are experiencing the Goddess who is you and who is all around you. There is nothing new about these sensations. You are simply tuning in to the heightened awareness of touch, sound, taste, smell, and sight as the Goddess's gift of pleasure. You may wish to turn to the "Calling in the Goddess" process in chapter 9 to heighten this awareness. Once you begin to tune in to your senses, you will begin to notice that you are also in contact with your body wisdom.

Sexual Desire and Women's Life Stages

There was a time when women were actually viewed as desiring erotic encounters at least as much as men. In this new millennium, sexuality can become, once again, the life-affirming, healing, joyful connection to the Life Force that it was meant to be. We will be taking an in-depth look at contemporary women in our culture and their problems of low sexual desire. Using the ancient wisdom of the Triple Goddess, the issues will be divided among the Maiden, Mother, and Crone Stages of life. While the issues we look at can be true for women at any stage of life, some are characteristic of a particular one. For men who are interested in helping their partners, the methods suggested in chapters 8 and 9 may provide a useful way to understand experiences unique to women.

Your Personal Story

In order to make the next three chapters meaningful to you on a personal level, please answer the questions at the end of each chapter. You will benefit most from the following pages when you have searched your life for clues to your own mystery. Healing of any kind is a function of finding the right pieces to the puzzle so you can understand your own patterns and what to do about those aspects you'd like to change. The questions are intended to allow you to look at your sexuality in a new way. When we examine your answers to these questions in chapter 8, you can choose methods that specifically pertain to healing and enhancing your unique feminine way.

Just to give you an idea of what we will be discussing, you will be asked to write about seven different areas:

1. Your early messages about touch and sex

2. Your experiences with loss and emotional trauma

3. Life goals and influences on your self-esteem

4. Important lessons of compassion

5. Your ability to speak your truth

6. Automatic thoughts and perceptions

7. Your dreams and visions

When you have completed all three chapters, you will be shown the way to identify key areas that need healing, together with methods leading to assistance and enhancement. Chapters 10 and 11 will give you very practical ways to work with your partner to find balance in your relationship. If you do not have a partner, we will explore ways that can lead to individual sexual fulfillment.

❦❦❦❦❦❦

PART 11:

THE THREE STAGES OF A WOMAN'S LIFE

Maiden

A Broken hymen
*   does not deny me the right to be married in white*
*   if I choose to*

And if it pleases me I will drive five thousand miles
*   only to find what I am looking for*
*   in the place where I started*

And I will take a lover in every place I stop
*   if the Moon tides in my blood*
*   would have it so*

And I do not need to justify the things I do
*   to anyone*

It is enough
*   if I understand why*

Maiden *and* **Helpless** *are not synonymous.*
Virgin *originally meant "complete unto herself"*
*   and didn't have anything to do*
*   with the status of your hymen.*

— Sarah O. Savage

Chapter Five

Awakening: The Path of the Maiden

Discovering Creativity

The Maiden period is a time for *discovery*. The path of the Maiden should encompass exploring and enjoying the pleasures of the body, as well as developing life skills. More than ever before, Maidens should be able to delay entering the Mother stage until their late 20s or 30s. Given our extended life span, there is plenty of time. The Maiden will have opportunities to explore interests and gain skills through education and experience that may lead to the clear and conscious choice of a life path, as long as she is not viewed as merely preparing for life-long mating and motherhood.

Although jobs, college majors, and careers will change in this period of intense identity development, themes derived from the Maiden's exploration will form the threads of a tapestry that she will weave throughout life. Males are clearly given the message that they need to seek out their talents and develop them in their 20s. Yet, young women are often confused by the continuing mixed messages. "Get an education, but be careful 'cause if you're too smart you'll intimidate guys." "Develop your skills, but if you're too much of a jock or too mechanically inclined, you may be seen as a 'dike.'" "Get a job, but don't put too much into it 'cause you'll be raising a family soon."

The premature move toward having a family too often forces

the choice of life partner. Today there is still strong cultural pressure for Maidens to marry as soon as they become sexually active. Our culture continues to view sexually active women in their late 20s as somehow deviant if they have not married. Unfortunately, the myth of "used goods" is still alive and well. Some women admit that they married the first promising male who proposed because they thought that no one else would want them once they had been sexual with a few men.

Maiden Stage sexuality can be a pleasurable and life-enhancing learning process when a woman feels that she has permission to explore. It is an especially critical time of life for female erotic development and for awakening sexual energy, which is akin to a sleeping but powerful cobra. This sacred sexual energy was often represented by the serpent, one of the earliest known symbols associated with statues of the Goddess. *Kundalini*, the Vedic term for *sexual energy,* means "the coiled one."

Exploring sexual pleasure is the foundation for sustained sexual desire throughout life. Sexual arousal and pleasurable self-stimulation are normal and natural for both male and female children. When they are not frightened or traumatized into suppressing these normal impulses, they learn acceptance of sexual pleasure. In the ancient Goddess cultures, sexual pleasure was viewed as a demonstration of the Great Mother's love. In patriarchy, most children are taught to repress sexual feelings using the mechanisms of shame and guilt. Once repressed, sexual energy goes underground until the powerful hormones of adolescence overwhelm these shame mechanisms in most teenagers.

However, since young men and women receive extremely different messages about engaging in sexual behavior as teens, their sexual development is impacted differently. Teen female sexual attraction and exploration raises anxiety for both the Maiden and her family. Often, there is a rush to "legitimize" sexual behavior in the only acceptable outlet available to women in a patriarchal society. The possibility of unplanned pregnancy still carries heavy consequences, and early marriage seems the only way out.

I see so many women in my practice that were required to marry because of their sexual circumstances and are still feeling guilt about it. These women have unnecessarily cut off their self-discovery and individuation by marrying because of pregnancy or because they had become sexually active. They plunge into roles of caretaker for others without ever developing a solid sense of self. Most Maiden women in their late teens and early to mid-20s do not have the wherewithal to make a fully conscious choice of life partner. After some years struggling to make their marriages work, couples who have rushed into marriage come to marital therapy with a host of problems that boil down to the fact that they never understood themselves well enough to be able to choose a mate for life.

The so-called Generation X Maidens sometimes take the opposite position and say they are "never" going to get married because they have such low expectations of anything lasting. They say, "Why should we put any faith in relationships?" because they have seen so many failures and betrayals in their parents' lives, as well as their own. The commitment-phobic men and women of this generation have made it "uncool" to voice the desire for intimate relationships, even though they may experience a deep yearning for them. The fear of rejection has created a type of relationship "nihilism" (the feeling that nothing matters) that requires the verbal disclaimer, "I'm not looking to get involved" upon first meeting someone they find attractive. "Seduced and abandoned" is now played out as "recreational sex with no relationship expectations." However, both men and women suffer the loss of partnership and connection.

Exploring Sexual Pleasure

The ancients understood the powerful sexual forces that emerged in adolescence, and recognized the divine gift of magnetic attraction. Rather than trying to block natural drive, they taught young people how to maintain a balance of body-mind-spirit and to honor the connection to their partners. For example, the Native American Chuluaqui-Quodoushka is a path of spiritual sexuality that emphasizes harmony with every aspect of life. The tradition was handed down orally from generation to generation and was taught to young people of the tribes by specially selected individuals, called Firemen and Firewomen, who initiated them into the deeper mysteries of sexuality. These teachers had been through years of training that included the use of specific breathing techniques, sound, visualization, movement, and awareness of energy centers in the body.

Our present culture recognizes the hormonal drive in adolescence, but continues to try to control natural desire with moral strictures that are ineffective. Society does not seem to understand that young people will explore their sexuality whether we want them to or not. The ancients understood that the young needed to *learn* about the power of sexual energy and to use it wisely.

During adolescence, both males and females get powerful surges of testosterone. In both sexes, testosterone causes a strong urge to masturbate and pursue sexual contact. The testosterone level is less powerful in girls, but still significant. However, additional estrogen causes a desire for cuddling, affection, and approval. Teenage males' greater urge for orgasm and sexual conquest is caused by higher levels of testosterone. Many other hormones, pheromones, and peptides play a part in the complicated dance of courtship and mating, but it is abundantly clear that nature compels young men and young women toward sexual exploration with powerful sexual urges.

Our first sexual experience with a partner is one of the most significant events of our lives. From recent research on the psychological effects of hormones, we now know that the most gender-related hormones, testosterone, and estrogen predispose young men and women to respond differently to the same experience. According to Teresa Crenshaw, M.D., in *The Alchemy of Love and Lust*,[1] men and women are biologically predisposed to respond differently to intense sexual feelings. Testosterone, according to Crenshaw, stimulates the need to be separate. Its effect is to heighten all aggressive urges, not just sexual pursuit. It causes the urge to masturbate even more than to pursue intercourse. Estrogen, on the other hand, apparently causes women to desire closeness and nurturing contact. Females are more likely to seek common ground and accommodate their partners in order to create harmony.

In addition to hormonal differences, motives for sex vary with each individual's early conditioning. Sex for recreation and tension release is quite different from sex intended to deepen the commitment to a relationship. Consider the thoughts of these different people who have just had sexual intercourse:

"Man, I'm great!"
"He must be in love with me!"
"I hope she doesn't cling to me!"
"Now he'll marry me!"
"Oh my God, what have I done?"
"Now she's mine!"
"I hope no one finds out!"
"My parents are going to kill me!"

These are just a few reactions that reflect differing individual perceptions about a sexual encounter. One participant could be thinking, *He must love me*, while the other is thinking, *I hope she doesn't cling to me*. More often than not, this difference in perception leads to hurt feelings and abandonment when expectations of further commitment are voiced.

The "Swept Away" Phenomenon

A woman's perception of a sexual event is influenced by cultural mores, specific upbringing, and history. The experience of a strong sexual response is accompanied by emotions, thoughts, and sensory associations such as smell, taste, and imagery. One of the effects of an intense sexual encounter for women is emotional attachment. Carol Cassell documented the feeling of being "swept away"[2] by an especially strong sexual response to a new partner. Cassell reports that many women are devastated by making the mistake of associating the feeling with romantic love, subsequently not reciprocated by the male. They end up feeling abandoned and humiliated, sometimes repeatedly.

Women of any age may respond to strong sexual feelings with inappropriate attachment because of a first sexual encounter with a partner. However, the swept-away feelings may be most devastating in Maidens who are yearning for a safe setting in which to explore their intense sexual feelings. Often, young women have given the intense hormonal bonding emotions the significance of love attachment, the "riding-off-into-the-sunset-happily-ever-after" kind. They have assumed that their partners have attached the same significance to their sexual feelings. When such women are subsequently abandoned by their partners, powerful feelings of shame often result.

As some pundit once pointed out, all the "sexual revolution" has achieved is to give most men more access to women as sexual partners without responsibility. Although men may be "swept away" by a powerful sexual experience as well, their dominant hormone, testosterone, programs them for conquest and *separateness*. Since estrogen stimulates the desire for attachment, it is no surprise that many more women than men are troubled by feeling abandoned after a powerful sexual experience. The effect of the Maiden's "swept away" feelings can often lead to disappointment and despair. Losing a lover may lead to seriously lowered self-esteem, and in some cases, even life-threatening depression. Take Erin's case, for example.

Erin

I treated a lovely young girl of 14 for severe depression and suicide attempts, the result of having been continually talked into intercourse with promises of love, only to be dumped the following day, gossiped about, and called a slut by the students in her school. The boys had made a game of it. The shame and the loss were so grievous that Erin did not want to continue living. She ended up leaving high school and tried to complete her education at home, but her zest for living had nearly been destroyed.

The Effect of Shame on Sexual Desire

Some of the most damaging influences on a woman's developing sexuality take the form of feelings of shame for exploring pleasure as a Maiden. To this day, the issue of shame for the

Maiden's "promiscuous" sexual behavior has enormous consequences. Even the average girl in her 20s who has postponed family for career is torn with guilt about the number of men with whom she has explored her sexuality. I have treated married couples with children who still argue about how many men the wife had before the husband. Often these women will tell me, in private, about experiences they don't want to tell their husbands. They feel compelled to avoid recounting stories of very pleasurable sexual experiences to their mates in order to protect what they perceive as very fragile male egos. If this information was openly shared, it would be useful in discovering ways of increasing female pleasure. Yet women aren't supposed to refer to something they especially enjoyed with another man. They aren't supposed to know about anything they didn't discover with their husbands.

Shame is one of the principal ways through which society controls women's desire. These feelings may continue to operate subconsciously, even after marriage. In contemporary society, if women have waited until marriage to explore any sexual pleasure, it may be too late for them to be able to access the full range of sexual responsiveness without some therapeutic intervention. In a therapy session, I asked a patient why she cried when we talked about her dressing in her sexiest garb for her new husband. She said, "I'm afraid of what people will think of me."

Shame is an intense emotional charge that interrupts pleasure or taints the sexual experience. Although I have treated men who feel shame about intercourse, Maidens bear the overwhelming cultural impact of shame associated with being seductive, sexy, or promiscuous. The interpretation that society places on their sexual behavior is at the core of female sexual self-worth. It impacts a host of feelings women have about themselves.

One of the great tragedies of sex-negative societies is the denial of female sexual exploration and pleasure during the

Maiden Stage. The nature-defying mandate that young women keep themselves pure, or "tidy," as Princess Diana once put it, cuts women off from the most valuable period for awakening sexual responsiveness. Only 30 years ago, just about every Maiden who had intercourse with a man before marriage felt significant shame. Either their negative self-statements interfered with sexual responsiveness at the time of the encounter, or they began to feel guilt and recrimination afterwards. It is this meaning associated with the sex act that still inhibits female desire and responsiveness after marriage.

Yet time and time again, seemingly well-meaning people inculcate fear and distrust in women for *their own body functions.* Prohibiting women from exploring partner sex is particularly damaging because it may internalize severe blocks to uninhibited sexual response, similar to wearing internal chastity belts. Such body armoring can be the direct result of society's mandate that Maidens fight their own sexual desire. Although the old laws sentencing women to stoning or censure may no longer be enforced, women have internalized deep barriers to expressing their sexuality. Simply teaching married women orgasm techniques does not address the profound disservice already done to them in their Maiden years.

Su Lin

Consider Su Lin, a woman raised in a partially assimilated Chinese household. At the age of 26, she'd already had two unplanned children. She had married the boy who impregnated her, and divorced him because of spousal abuse. She said, "I don't like sex, and I don't think

I'll ever experience an orgasm. It doesn't matter to me." She said this with great conviction. Su Lin is very beautiful and sought after by men, but to her, her body is just an instrument to attract another husband. She believes that it is the man's job to know what to do to arouse her, and since she has never especially enjoyed any male's touch, she assumes that she never will.

Su Lin is the perfect product of a culture that gives its daughters sex-negative messages from birth. "Bad" impulses arouse such profound revulsion in her body that she believes that if she were to explore her own pleasure through self-stimulation, it would be "unnatural." When I told Su Lin that being resigned to never feeling sexual pleasure was a great tragedy in her life, she looked at me in astonishment. "Isn't sex only what men want?"

"No," I explained, "sexual pleasure is as natural to women as to men."

"But I feel dirty whenever I think about it."

"Well," I told her, "you will never know what it is like to be truly alive unless you experience the greatest pleasure your body has to give."

The Banquet

I use the analogy of the banquet when I talk to women like Su Lin who can't quite grasp the profound joy they are missing.

"Picture this." I tell them. "You dress and adorn yourself with the utmost care, preparing for a great feast. With much excitement, you arrive at the feast and are admired by the guests. You stay and watch everyone else enjoying themselves. You go to the banquet often, perhaps every night. You make elaborate preparations, but you are never allowed to taste a morsel of food. How much would you want to continue to go to those banquets? Even if you chose to continue to go or were required to go, you would begin to find the whole experience a source of irritation, and then it would become a source of pain and suffering." This is what it's like to have sexual encounters without orgasm over and over again.

Many young women continue to trade boyfriends, hoping for the Prince Charming who will adore them and give them wonderful orgasms. This is the core of the "he-will make-my-dreams-come-true" fantasy for women. *Not only*, they think, *will he know me so well and love me so much that he will be able to jump through all the hoops of my resistance to overcome my emotional barriers, but he will stay with me and continue to give me such joy for as long as I want.* Such unconditional love is an unrealistic fantasy. Real men cannot make this happen for Maidens. The Maiden must want to discover what it takes *for herself.*

Awakening the Feminine Energy

Our dilemma today is mostly one of *awakening* our sexuality, anesthetized and crushed for so many thousands of years. What each woman needs, for first experiences of partner sex, as well as for all subsequent sexual encounters, is the sense of physical, mental, and emotional *readiness*. Kundalini yoga, Chuluaqui Quodoushka, tantric practices, as well as some of the recent books on pleasuring and sensual touch, all stress gentle awakening of feminine energy and slowing down male sexual response. Breathing, erotic massage, sensual techniques, and many other pleasures can be learned in workshops, from books, and from the exercises presented in chapter 11.

Sexual Readiness

The simple concept of waiting for feminine *readiness* is so fundamental that it is amazing how often it is missing from or glossed over in sex therapy books and advice manuals. There are physical, mental, and emotional aspects to *readiness*; and all three are necessary for female sexual awakening. Men who know how to wait for and tease female desire, delaying more intense sexual touching, know the *physical* key to feminine readiness. In all ancient practices of sexual ecstasy, "ladies first" is a key factor. For example, males who practice tantra with their partners state that the intention is never to progress to a more intense kind of touch until the woman is ready. She decides what she is ready for.

The *mental* aspects of feminine readiness involve perceiving a particular sexual activity as a healthy choice for herself. She must have a reasonably positive image of her body, as well as feel that she has permission to engage in sex. The *emotional* component of readiness is the sense of safety in the sexual encounter.

The Safe Setting

An emotionally safe setting refers to issues of abandonment, as well as those relating to physical harm, pregnancy, or disease. There is an old '60s rock 'n' roll song, "Will You Still Love Me Tomorrow?" The words express the central issue for Maiden women contemplating a sexual encounter, and very little has changed since Carole King composed it. The words speak of the passion and total devotion expressed by the lover as he ardently encourages the woman to have intercourse with him. "Tonight you're mine completely," she says, speaking of the adoring attention women love to receive from men. However, if the sexual experience is followed by rejection, be it the next day, the next week, or the next month, there will be a devastating emotional impact.

Estrogen promotes the desire for closeness, which is the basis of the need for at least temporary commitment. The commitment *need not be for life*, but women need time to repeat sexual behavior, to learn about the marvels of their bodies, and to get to know their sexual partners at some intimate level. They need time to communicate feelings and dreams and to enjoy positive feelings and closeness—not just before and during a sexual encounter—but in the wonderful afterglow. Mutual sexual pleasure should lead to a yearning to repeat the experience with the same person at least for a while. It should lead to a desire to really get to know this wonderful person who has been the source of so much enjoyment.

Emotional commitment in a relationship should not be related to possession. The ideal conditions for feminine sexual awakening have more to do with the intent to develop intimacy, which is the desire to know and be known by the other. Each partner needs to be willing to be vulnerable to the other and to express heartfelt feelings without defensiveness. The Maiden needs to trust that not only will her partner do her no harm, but that he will honor her emotional needs, attend to her physical responses, and *be there for her*—whatever that entails.

The skills needed to attain this intimacy are discussed in chapter 10. The *safe setting* means that the Maiden must have a sense of *emotional* security in order to explore sexual pleasure, along with a sense of permission, and readiness for desire to awaken. However, there is one additional block to female sexual desire. Women must grapple with issues about their bodies. It is essential for reclaiming the feminine way.

Your Body Image

Negative feelings about attractiveness may have led you to problems with sexual desire. The ***Bathing Suit Exercise*** is intended to help you identify negative self-statements you make about your body. You may say things to yourself such as, "I'm so fat and ugly," "I'm so flat-chested," "I really need to lose ten pounds," or even "I can't stand my body." Body-image distortions combine early negative messages about your body and the emotional wounds received from your primary caregivers. These influences undermine your sexual self-esteem. Sometimes they have made you feel unlovable. How you feel about your body and attractiveness has nothing to do with being inherently ugly, but it has everything to do with distorted perception.

Lena

Lena learned to mistrust male touching because her uncle fondled her breasts while pretending to hug her. When she tried to tell her mother about it, she was told to keep silent, yet Lena's mother punished her when she found her exploring pleasurable feelings through masturbation. In Catholic elementary school, nuns angrily mussed Lena's hair and called her sinful when she tried to style it to look like the popular stars of her day. When

Lena did the imaginary bathing suit exercise, she realized that she always avoided looking at herself naked in the mirror. She found herself hating the dull bathing suits she imagined trying on. The young, vivacious girl had turned into a matronly brown hen.

Lena had disowned her feminine body because the message from her mother and teachers was, "Don't be a slut." Her experience of molestation made such an impact on her that she had decided it wasn't worth the trouble to allow herself to shine. One of the negative self-statements Lena found herself saying was, "You're a fat old cow." When she heard herself saying this during the "Bathing Suit" exercise, she began to cry.

The Bathing Suit Exercise

This exercise will give you information about automatic negative thoughts you may have concerning your body. First bring up a picture in your mind, and then please write down your thoughts.

Imagine that you are going to go shopping for a swimsuit. Picture yourself going to the store or mall and entering the store. Be aware of yourself as you approach the rack to choose several styles and colors of suits. Now imagine that you go into a dressing room, remove your street clothes, and try on several bathing suits. See yourself as you look at your body in the full-length mirror. As you continue to imagine what you look like, write down the thoughts that are going through your mind. They should be the familiar and automatic thoughts that come up whenever you try on clothes, especially bathing suits. After you have written down all the thoughts that come to mind, set your notepad aside.

When you're out for the evening, or any time you're in public, pay attention to the critical things you may say to yourself about other women. Maybe you think about their hair, makeup, clothes, or weight. As you reflect on the negative thoughts you may have about these women, go back to your own page of thoughts. Read what you wrote about yourself as you imagined yourself trying on bathing suits. Notice if some of the messages are the same as the critical thoughts you have about others. As you become more aware, resolve to yourself to *stop criticizing other women.*

Also, make a resolution to stop saying critical things about your own body, and realize that as you criticize your fellow women, you also hurt yourself. Try to honor the Goddess in every woman by acknowledging the inner beauty in all of us.

Body-Image Distortions

Along with messages promoting shame, a major influence on the developing Maiden's sexual response relates to distortions in her sense of her attractiveness. The issue of women's negative feelings about their bodies remains a factor throughout life. As one Maiden in her 20s put it, "You cannot be a woman in our culture and not have a body-image problem." It emerges in the Maiden stage, and the effects may be most virulent in this period of a woman's life. In *Reviving Ophelia,* [3] Mary Pipher shows that incidences of bulimia and anorexia are rising between the teen years and the 20s. Although eating disorders are common to women of all ages, these Maiden diseases of severe starvation and malnutrition can be life-threatening.

When a young woman is bombarded with advertising-driven images of perfection, and when she is viewed mostly as a sex object, it becomes her secret obsession to fit these stereotypical images at any cost. What goes in and out of style concerning female body fashion is cruelly arbitrary. Marilyn Monroe and huge-bosomed women like Anita Ekberg were considered perfect when I was growing up. With my small breasts, I felt that I just couldn't compete. The current perfect "10" has very little body fat, exaggerated muscle development, and narrow hips, which is actually contrary to what makes us female. My mother used to say to me, "You're built to have babies" when I used to complain about my pear shape. As a teen, that didn't comfort me much, but now I value her wonderful wisdom. She was trying to tell me I was *feminine* shaped.

When Maidens are perceived primarily as objects of beauty, they lose their way to finding their core sense of self. Beauty may not be all that matters, but the cultural message is that Maidens present themselves as acceptable sex objects first and foremost because their task is to secure a marriage proposal. Those who doubt that contemporary women continue to see this as a goal should read *The Rules.*[4] Emphasis on arbitrary and impossible beauty standards leads to distortions in female self-statements ("I am ugly, fat, unacceptable") and serious emotional disturbances.

Risky and dysfunctional behavior results from a desperate need to prove worthiness as a sex object: unwanted pregnancy and premature motherhood to prove femininity, unprotected or forced sex to keep a man, or painful intercourse just to keep a partner happy. Even without risky behavior, there is deep emotional confusion held inside by many Maidens, leading to serious depression and anxiety disorders. The habit of negative self-statements develops into lifelong patterns of persistent depression.

The billions of dollars spent by women on makeup, hair, plastic surgery, and clothing are the result of their extreme insecurity about their image. Most women rely on judgmental "others" or internalized critical voices to tell them how they look. Here is a case study showing how this perception impacts sexuality.

Nancy

Nancy's mother would criticize her constantly, saying things such as, "Fix your hair, you look awful"; or "Don't eat all that bread, you'll get fat." The boyfriend she attracted into her life was, of course, similar to her mother in his critical messages about her weight. Now she compulsively overeats and hears a voice inside telling her, "You're fat!"

Nancy left her boyfriend because of the never-ending emotional abuse, but her internal critical messages stayed with her. She realized in therapy that she always pictured herself as the "others" saw her. The voice inside of her was commenting on her looks in the way she had been taught to see herself. Nancy's sexual desire was blocked by the same spectator voice that grew louder as soon as she took her clothes off. Even after she had lost weight and started dating, she could not go beyond the feelings of sexual excitement during courting. As soon as the relationship moved into sexual touching, Nancy's arousal sensations shut down, and she felt confused and frightened.

When I taught Nancy to catch the internal critical messages, replacing them with positive affirmations, she began to focus on her internal experience of energy. When she had a choice of what to eat, she now asked herself, "Will this give me the energy I need?" When she examined what happened in a sexual situation, she was able to more appropriately judge her readiness for a particular touch. She learned to stop the critical voices and listen more attentively to her healthy Guardian Self. She could now ask herself, "Do I really want to engage in this activity with this person?" She could decide if the relationship was giving her energy or draining her.

❧❧ ❧❧ ❧❧

At some level, we all recognize that beauty comes from within. Inner strength generates a *luminosity* promoting *true beauty*. As Marianne Williamson points out in *A Woman's Worth,*[5] feminine beauty is not a function of hair, clothes, or makeup, but a reflection of the light within. When women hold sacred their unique and special feminine energy, they feel beautiful from inside. It takes courage and some determination to choose to stop the internalized critical voices, especially when bombarded with societal images with which we cannot possibly compare. However, overcoming those voices is well worth the effort. Chapter 9 offers exercises to end the paralyzing grip of negative self-statements on self-esteem and sexual desire.

Leslie Marmon Silko tells a wonderful story in "Yellow Woman and a Beauty of the Spirit."[6] Half Laguna Pueblo, Silko grew up looking "different" because she was not exactly like her Native American friends but didn't look completely white either. She explains that, "In the Pueblo world, beauty was manifested in the behavior and in one's relationships with other living things." No one would have thought of calling a woman beautiful who was mean-spirited, self-centered, or disconnected from her people. On the other hand, no one would think a woman ugly, no matter what her outward form, if she truly expressed a loving heart.

A beautiful person was healthy, and by that the Pueblo meant she was in harmony with herself.

The Heart of the Matter

As much as women complain about their hips, buttocks, breasts, or waistlines, the yoni is at the heart of most women's body-image distortions; it is their ultimate disowned body part. How women really feel about the seat of their sexuality is a much more serious issue of body image that they rarely, if ever, talk about—even in therapy. Yet these feelings are central to desire disorders in women.

The Sanskrit word *yoni* refers to the entire feminine sexual system. This system is far more extensive than the meaning of any commonly used terms. This term will be used throughout the book because it encompasses the external vulva, internal vagina, the complex organization of nerves of the clitoral system, and the whole pubic area. *Yoni* is more female-positive, being newer to Western terminology and not having the limited connotations of other terms. For instance, the word *vagina* is commonly used to refer to the whole female sexual system as if it were analogous to the penis (as in "boys have a penis, girls have a vagina"). This has perpetuated a gross misunderstanding among young and not-so-young men and women about female sexual functioning.

If sex is defined as intercourse, behavior essential only for procreative sex, the vagina would be considered the primary female organ because it is the passageway to conception. If sex is defined as pleasure, the vagina is no longer the principal source of feminine sexuality. Most adults have heard the word *clitoris*, but young girls are rarely informed that this word describes their principal organ of sexual pleasure. The patriarchal bias toward sex for procreation is perpetuated by the use of *vagina*, which refers only to the internal canal.

The vagina is a source of much pleasure *for the penis*. Most couples are dismayed when the woman finds that friction applied to the vaginal walls does not result in her orgasm. It is still hard for men to understand that what feels so good to them is not enough for their partners. Countless women have told me that their husbands think there is something wrong with them because they cannot achieve orgasm with minimal stimulation apart from intercourse. The general myth persists that women "should" enjoy this as much as men. It is as if we expected men to attain orgasm from nipple stimulation (something that produces much sexual pleasure for women) and considered them defective if they needed any other kind of stimulation.

The woman-centered sexual perspective shifts the focus enormously. If visiting anthropologists from another planet were to interview a few sexually secure women, they might describe male-female sex quite differently. In fact, alien researchers might not immediately see any connection to procreation in what they were told by these women about the things they enjoy. Pleasure would appear to be the purpose of the interaction, and there might not be any emphasis on one particular sexual act, but a long list of pleasurable activities in no particular sequence and with no particular finale.

Our alien researchers might take notes on touching, eye contact, playful or seductive moods, sensual bathing, passionate kissing, and embracing. They might list the clitoris as a primary sexual organ because it gives the women such joy, but they might also recognize that the entire body is an organ of pleasure, with the yoni as the source of sexual heat. If they published their findings, we humans would recognize that their data was biased because it would be obvious that they had interviewed a rare and small percentage of the female population.

Sadly, most women do not accept their yonis as a most precious treasure. Men refer to their scrotum as "the family jewels," name their penises affectionately, and often admire their organs in mirrors. Rarely do women admire their external vulva, or appreciate the wonderful shapes and colors of their labia. When we enter into therapeutic discussions, all women who have low desire admit to feelings ranging from discomfort to disgust about the looks and odors of their yonis. Most have never really looked at their yonis with their legs spread, and they report feelings of aversion or horror at the thought of doing so. Most women tell me that they have always thought of the vaginas as "dark" and perhaps "dirty" or "icky." If they are given an opportunity to view them with a speculum and hand-held mirror, they are surprised that it is a lovely, clean pink. The "Yoni Exercise" in chapter 9 is a way to begin to heal some of these negative feelings.

Women also report that they believe their partners, husbands, or boyfriends must certainly have the same perceptions. Projecting their own repulsion onto men may be justified by experiences with their current partners or reactions from men in the past. Many men have admitted in my office, "It's not my favorite part," yet these same men express dismay that their wives do not want them to have cunnilingus (oral sex) performed on them.

Suzanne

Suzanne, who had previously had a very high desire for sex, told me this story. Her husband loved her to perform oral sex on him, and during their honeymoon, she summoned the courage to ask him to return the favor. He obliged her, and the experience was extremely pleasurable for her until his reaction at the end. Very quietly he got up, went into the bathroom, and vomited. What truly amazed me is that he continued to perform cunnilingus on her on a fairly regular basis, vomiting each time. Needless to say, any enjoyment she would have normally received diminished until she was able to bring herself to participate in nothing but "duty" sex.

I have treated many cases where women have experienced similar, if less extreme, reactions to their yonis. Amazingly enough, many, if not most women, accept this revulsion to their yonis as natural. Oral stimulation is one of the most pleasurable sexual experiences for a woman, yet the most common reason for women refusing to receive it is that they believe that their yonis are viewed by their partners as being somewhat unsavory. Even when partners insist that they enjoy giving pleasure in this way, most women will report disturbing thoughts that intrude on the pleasurable physical sensations, blocking their ability to achieve orgasm.

Influences on Sexual Desire: The Maiden Years

As long as shame is paired with sexual feelings, women will not feel the full force of their desire, even when given apparent permission to be sexual. Together with negative feelings about their bodies and being conditioned to associate sexual desire with shame, many women have repeated experiences of giving in to their desire and being abandoned. They say, "He didn't call," "I saw him with another girl," "He said I was too possessive," or

"He wants to date others." It's no wonder that many Maidens have psychological blocks embedded in their sexual-response systems before they ever find a committed partner.

Sexual interaction arouses the most powerful human emotions, which is why sex has been one of the most proscribed of all activities. The emotional experience can be so transforming that patriarchal society has rules to protect Maidens from any sexual involvement until it is "safe" to allow her to respond in the appropriate setting of marriage. By then, the window of opportunity for maximum sexual enjoyment may be buried.

We have seen in the coming-of-age stories of Inanna and Eileen that the different cultural worldviews influenced their assumptions about their sexual self-worth. These, in turn, shaped their perceptions about their sexual experiences. As little girls, they learned either to love or be ashamed about naked bodies. They learned to value their intelligence, skills, and place in society, or they learned how to feel inferior to the other half of humanity. These lessons were all part of forming opinions about their ability to enjoy sexual pleasure. Naturally, there is a wide variety of individual responses to such influential cultural messages, but such carefully shaped attitudes *directly affect female sexual experience*.

The following questions will help you understand your personal story. You will be writing answers in order to apply this personal information to the suggestions on healing in chapters 8 and 9.

Making Sense of Your Personal Story: Part I

1. Did anyone abuse or abandon you? How did you react to the experience?

2. What losses of loved ones did you suffer in your life? How have you coped, and what resources have you discovered?

The Power of a Mother

Fire and lightning she is you are I am

Mothers of any animal species have been known to
fight off attackers twice their size
in order to protect their children
But sometimes children need to make their own mistakes
You always knew, even when I didn't

Elf child of an elf mother told me once that we were
descended from the faeries
conceived in the desert raised on a
mountain and given an Indian name

Earth child elf child ruled by Mercury master messenger
Was I even in the womb bringing a message to your soul?
Tapping out Morse code onto your belly with my tiny feet

Now we two who once occupied the same body
have come to a place where we can learn from each other

And she would gladly trade her life for mine if it came to that
(it never will but) mothers
are the only ones allowed to love unconditionally

NEVER underestimate the power of a mother

To a little girl the most important thing is simply to be listened to
even if she starts a protest march in the kitchen
because she doesn't want to wash her hair

Mother is the word for God in the heart of a child
true for me even though I never learned to call you "Mother"

— Sarah O. Savage

Chapter Six

Initiation: The Circle of the Mother

The Transformation

Each of the three stages of feminine experience requires a transformation of consciousness. To transform means to remake. With each stage, the woman is remade into a new self. She carries the old self within, but, like a butterfly from a chrysalis, she emerges in a new form. With each transformation, she is building the strength of the Guardian Self. In every life stage, there are different tasks and parallel growth in a woman's sexuality.

Motherhood requires the abandonment of the self-absorption and selfish pleasure that have been enjoyed by the Maiden. Nature provides the woman nine months to prepare for birth. The experience itself is a rite of passage for the new Mother consciousness. The act of giving birth is unique to the female. Because every woman in labor knows that despite all our modern technology, she may face her own death or that of her child's, the experience of birth confronts the Mother Stage woman with a unique understanding of the close connection between life and death.

Mother Stage women must take responsibility for their sexual experience. Because of the enormous responsibility they accept with family, Mothers will need to take a proactive stance with sex. This is the stage in which women will most likely notice an unusually low level of sexual desire. However, after the early child-rearing stage, women may also feel the highest level of sexual desire of their lives.

The Circle of the Mother

The Mother is in the center of many competing roles that lead to many more complications in life than before. Usually she has a relationship with a partner to sustain, children to raise, a household to manage, and these days, she works to create extra income for the family. If she has found a creative skill in her Maiden years or develops one during the Mother Stage, she is drawn to pursue her personal path as well. The term *Supermom* reflects the enormous energy demanded by all of these roles. The developmental task of this stage is accepting responsibility. More than at any other time in her life, the Mother will be required to surrender her personal needs, her desires, and even her body to the needs of her family.

Initiation

The beginning of the Mother's bonding with a child born of her body is a very special initiation experience, the blood mystery of childbirth. Surrender is the most profound element of this initiation into Motherhood. Almost every woman who has experienced even a few hours of natural childbirth knows what it means to have to surrender to body processes that cannot be controlled. We learn important mind-altering techniques simply to survive the agonizing hours of labor. Just about every woman emerges from her first birth experience changed for life, her journey unique to her, yet essentially binding her to every other Mother.

Giving birth sets the stage for a shift in conscio,
compassion, a deeply satisfying and formidable ci.
Mother consciousness gives women a very special powe
power to activate energy from the heart. One woman expres,
this shift as a feeling that some part of her just "clicked in" as she
began to nurse her child. For some Mothers, the click is instanta-
neous, but for many it takes time with their babies before they
truly feel the full force of the nurturing instinct. There is no question that nature *intended* for women to feel so completely
absorbed that they ache when they are separated from their
infants. Le Leche League calls it "falling in love with your baby."

Compassion is fundamental to mothering. It is practiced daily
to cope with the extraordinary demands of nurturing an infant.
The Latin root of the word *compassion* means "to suffer together," but it has come to describe "deep sympathy," or the ability to
truly empathize with another's feelings. It is essential for a
woman's growth in this stage of the feminine way and is an
important developmental milestone that can also be practiced by
women who do not give physical birth.

Women Who Do Not Give Birth

Giving birth is a creative act. It is the ultimate transmutation
of energy into matter, but other creative acts bring inspirational
ideas into being. For example, many women "give birth" by
transforming creative energy into artistic expression, new organizations, problem-solving legislation, and so on. Women have told
me that they felt "pregnant" with their ideas and "bursting" with
the urge to give birth to them. This is a universal expression not
limited to either gender, but the metaphor relates to the direct
experience of women.

Compassion is learned in the act of nurturing others, including nonbiological children. The quality of compassion is critical to our survival at this juncture in our evolution, and needs to be practiced by males and females alike. Yet, it is considered an aspect of the feminine way because it is fundamentally linked to the lessons of caring for an infant.

Unselfish, nurturing love must be perfected in the Mother Stage, along with the central task of accepting responsibility. It can be developed without the necessity of giving birth, but it must be consciously practiced. As Marianne Williamson says in *A Woman's Worth,* we are meant to nurture and care for all children of the planet. It does not matter if what we care for is not our biological child; we must express the feminine power of nurturing love or pay a heavy price.[1] In *A Woman's Book of Life,* Joan Borysenko points out that 20 percent of all women in our culture remain childless.[2] These women find other ways to express Mother Stage nurturing love.

Many women have mothered younger siblings or have become excellent stepmothers. In addition, many women embrace opportunities involving community projects that make a difference for others. These women rescue plants and animals, volunteer for organizations such as Hospice, and so forth. Increasingly, women have become ministers, therapists, and self-help speakers. In these ways, they "give birth to souls."[3] Louise Hay, respected author, lecturer, and the founder of Hay House (this book's publisher), describes the concept in this way: "I know I have had many children in my many lifetimes. This lifetime I do not have them. . . . The Universe has filled my life with rich experiences and has made me a surrogate mother to millions."[4]

How women learn compassionate love is a personal story, but most women relate intuitively to the powerful Mother image. It is part of the feminine collective consciousness that connects us to our mothers, grandmothers, great-grandmothers, and our distant matrilineal past. Feminine compassion is the ability to connect with other living beings, and nurturing is built into our feminine core. It may even be part of our gender-specific DNA. Mother consciousness is one of the most deeply imbedded and powerful sources of wisdom and courage that exists *in our bodies*. Fierce protection for our young and intuition about others' needs are important components of this consciousness.

Mother Stage Sexuality

Even if a woman does not experience childbirth, she still feels the pull of natural rhythms each month when she must surrender to her body's tides. The powerful and rapid shifts from high estrogen/low progesterone, to low estrogen/high progesterone, which trigger premenstrual moods, cannot be ignored. There are powerful physical and emotional effects. Most women have learned to flow with these shifts so gracefully that they do not realize the extent of their emotional adjustments and behavioral adaptations. As a woman, you adjust to your body every month because you know there will be repercussions from ignoring the internal changes.

In order to respond sexually, you must listen to your own body. It is thought that there are four sexual desire phases for women. These phases are:

1. **receptive**, determined by high levels of estrogen when women are most open to penetration and closeness;

2. **seductive**, when estrogen is mixed with oxytocin, prog-

esterone, and other hormones to produce an "on-the-prowl" desire;

3. **active**, when higher testosterone levels cause an aggressive pursuit of sex and orgasm; and

4. **aversive**, when progesterone is at its peak and the woman would be wise to "just say no" to sex.[5]

Learning to *surrender* to the body's natural rhythms means that you must honor all the signals. It means allowing sensual feelings to develop when your timing is right. It also means not overcontrolling a sexual encounter to allow only "acceptable" sexual behavior that limits sexual surrender. It means letting go of thoughts and tuning into the sensations of the body. It also means knowing when conditions are not right and acting in your own best interests. One of the most wonderful methods of experiencing surrender to sensations is one you already know: **dance**. There are bumper stickers that read, "Shut up and dance!" Dancing is a simple way to heal the split between mind and body.

Maiden women have plenty of estrogen to enhance their receptivity to sexual advances *and* relatively high testosterone compelling them to pursue sexual interactions. However, so many conditions operate against sexual desire in Mother Stage women that they need all the romance they can get. Yet, in this stage, husbands are less likely to behave in ways that are seductive to their mates.

Seductive Settings

Men often complain in sex therapy that they want their wives to initiate sex. A husband might say, "I would like her to ask for sex at least a third of the time." Many men keep score as to how often their wives initiate sex and use this information as a form of emotional blackmail. This method is always doomed to failure, as is sulking. However, these desire-dousing behaviors continue for years, causing relationship disturbances. They form the basis of **the concubine solution** mentioned in chapter 1 ("I do him once a week or he gets mad"). Never does this behavior enhance female sexual desire. What is needed are the seductive conditions that worked in the couples' courting days, as well as anything else that can create a sexy mood.

Postpartum Mother Stage women have new circumstances as well as hormones working against sexual desire. Prolactin, the nursing hormone, creates abundant nurturing feelings and the desire for touching, but does not promote the desire for penetration. With postpartum depression and hormonal shifts, it is a wonder that female desire ever returns, but miraculously it does. The new responsibilities of the Mother Stage do not mean that couples should resign all hope of finding sexual pleasure. It does mean that Mother Stage women require the most positive mind-sets and conducive settings in order to sustain sexual desire. They need *seductive* conditions.

The Crisis of the "New Kid on the Block"

The birth of the first child often signifies the time when problems in a couple's sexual relationship are likely to develop. Just as the Mother's hormones and instincts discourage frequent intercourse, her partner may increase his sexual demands and find it hard to understand that her lack of sexual desire does not constitute a personal rejection of him. Often the subject is not broached until years later, but couples tell me that sex started to diminish after the first child's birth. The woman reports that she focused on her tasks of mothering and wanted more help and fewer demands from her mate. The issue of women's total absorption in mothering and the need for help with responsibilities can lead to an impasse that results in the Mother being abandoned.

Ellen

"We had nine years together as lovers before we became parents. I thought I had done everything right." Ellen's husband had just informed her that he was in love with another woman. She had given birth to their second child six months earlier, and their daughter was three years old. Both Ellen and her husband were in their mid-30s and had been married 13 years. The early years of their marriage had seemed like a wonderful partnership. They had numerous interests in common since both were backpacking enthusiasts and loved camping in the wilderness. Ellen's job as a computer specialist had made it possible for her husband to finish his master's degree while she supported them. When he was offered a laboratory research position, Ellen cheerfully relocated so he could pursue his career. They both decided that it was time for a family, so when their daughter was born, their life seemed complete.

The cracks in the perfect scenario began to show at that time, but the couple assumed that the stress would be temporary. Ellen's sexual desire waned as her attention shifted toward the awesome task of nurturing the young life they had created. Although the sexual passion of the earlier years was diminished by the needs of a growing infant and the inevitable time constraints, Ellen thought that she and her husband had reached a mature balance between their roles as parents and their marital relationship. She even set aside time each week to devote to her husband since they both agreed on the need for "dates." When their second child was born, the demands of young mothering intensified. They had planned this child carefully so that their daughter would be toilet-trained and ready for preschool. They had also discussed the husband's need for attention and continued to negotiate solutions for the time-management problems of young family life. Ellen's husband's admission of betrayal was like a bomb detonated in the middle of paradise.

After several half-hearted attempts to reconcile, Ellen's husband stated that he did not want the responsibility of two kids and a full-time family; he liked the sexual intensity of his new relationship. He expressed some regret for hurting Ellen but decided that he preferred being a part-time father. What infuriated Ellen was that they had mutually agreed to have their two children. He had, in effect, signed on for a contract and then said, "I'm sorry, I've changed my mind." He did not seem to grasp the enormity of his decision to leave his kids. Ellen's Mother consciousness would never allow her to abandon the day-to-day nurturing and raising of their kids, but her husband's consciousness allowed him to do just that. His new lover never intended to have children and planned to devote all her attention to him. He seemed to believe that his sexual needs and personal fulfillment were justifiable reasons to break his commitment.

It is common for men to engage in their first affairs after the birth of a child. Even worse, pregnancy is a time when women start being physically abused. This lack of participation in what the ancients considered the "Sacred Trinity" is clearly a distortion of parenting responsibility. In patriarchy, priority given to male sexual needs is often considered natural because "that's just how men are." For many centuries, this has been an acceptable reason for husbands to seek sex with another woman.

The Sacred Trinity

The archetype of the trinity is much older than Christian doctrine. The Divine Female principle was left out of the trinity in patriarchal interpretations (Mary was a mortal woman and not considered part of the Holy Trinity), which created a grossly distorted view. The natural trinity always was, and still is, Mother/Father/Child.

The combined crisis of the conception of a child and subsequent birth of a new life profoundly affects the sexual relationship of almost every couple. All the wonderful nurturing and compassion that a male expects to receive from his mate is suddenly shifted to their baby. Some disgruntled fathers feel overlooked for the first few months of the child's life. Any sympathy paid to the new father's feelings of being excluded seems to overlook the fact that his reaction is simply immature.

The reality is that the father needs to put Mother and child first. To do this at a genuinely deep emotional level requires him to accept his responsibility as father. He must have a greater understanding of the change that has taken place in the Mother's consciousness in order for any sexual contact to be successful. His mate is now gravely responsible for the life of another human being, and she will need him to accept his role as parenting partner and support *for her*. This is the beginning of the compassion flowing the other way.

The father is not overlooked in the concept of the trinity unless he chooses to defect. His protective arms surround Mother and child, creating a safe and harmonious environment for essential, early bonding to take place. This is an extremely important role. He is now expected to take on the role of protector, perhaps for the first time. He must do everything necessary in order to minimize Mother's stress.

All too often, men do not bear this emotional responsibility well. I have been involved in many cases where the father actually functioned less effectively and left more of the practical details of life to his wife than ever before. Sadly, pregnancy as well as childbirth is a common reason for abandonment of the Mother. Men often start having affairs, with the excuse that he needed sex and she was not available.

Princess Diana

Princess Diana became a symbol for many women struggling with issues in the Mother Stage. She actually conformed to the patriarchal, moral imperative and "kept herself tidy." She was the perfect virginal vessel for the seed of the future king. The marriage fit the patriarchal ideal: a very young innocent female and a much older, established male (there was a 12-year age difference). The fact that Prince Charles had had numerous sexual partners was well known, tacitly accepted, and viewed as natural. Diana became a mother 11 months into the marriage, which conformed to another patriarchal ideal. Two years later, she produced "a spare heir," and her job was complete. Although Diana had said many times that she wanted more children, we now know that Charles returned to his lover, Camilla, soon after Prince Harry was born.

The royal family winked at Charles's indiscretion, and when it became obvious that the marriage was failing, the palace allowed information about Diana's bulimia and bouts of depression to be leaked to the press, hoping to pin all blame for the failed marriage on her. They didn't count on this thoroughly modern woman taking the media into her own hands and telling the truth about Charles's infidelity. She openly admitted her own failings and exposed the circumstances of the marriage on TV. She became a symbol for all Mother Stage women who have been rejected, discounted, and betrayed by their husbands.

Through her public suffering, Diana paved the way for other women to recognize and grapple with their own painful circumstances. She had beauty, money, and high position. She was someone who should have "had it all," but she had the same problems as many Mother Stage women. This is why she was so admired and loved—not because she was perfect, but because she was flawed.

Her life struck chords for Maiden Stage women as

well. They could see that "my Prince will come" was not the solution to their adult lives. Diana set an example for survival and transformation because she eventually found a meaningful path for her self-expression through compassion for others who have suffered. She found her sense of self in what she cared about rather than in her marriage. Above all, she never neglected her Mother responsibilities.

The Nurturing Father

Fortunately, there has been a resurgence of paternal responsibility since the 70s. This is a return to the natural Mother/Father/Child trinity. Many men have embraced the role of father, and it is no longer the norm for men to wait for the birth of their children in waiting rooms or on the golf course. Also, men don't customarily remove themselves from child-rearing duties during the first year. Fathers are holding and nurturing their infants, thereby experiencing emotions that had been purposely suppressed by patriarchal conditioning in the past.

Perhaps humanity is returning to a more egalitarian way of life. We are witnessing the resurgence of feminine qualities in many other ways, exemplified by extolling the strength of vulnerable emotions. Daniel Goleman's *Emotional Intelligence*,[6] a study of the importance of emotional aptitude for success, gave us data that reports what women have always known. Those who can monitor body sensations for useful information about their feelings and have empathy for others have more satisfying human interactions, promoting overall success in life. As part of the resurgence of feminine values, Riane Eisler founded an organization, The Center for Partnership Studies, dedicated to balancing masculine and feminine energy in the world. The message is: *It Doesn't Have to Be This Way.*

Dysfunctional Role Imbalances

After the early stages of infant care, the crisis is over and the long process of child rearing begins. There will be 18 years or more of "chopping wood and carrying water" that is emotionally and physically challenging. This is when the bulk of sexual-desire problems surface. When couples come in for treatment, they have already made a positive step by talking about the problems and deciding to seek help.

Anger's Role

Overworked women are angry women. Anger plays a major role in low levels of female desire during the Mother Stage. It is one of the most effective blocks to female sexual desire and functioning. Female sexuality is not programmed to respond well to anger, which most often inhibits women's desire. Conversely, testosterone may be responsible for linking anger and sexual feelings because of its role in aggression. Perhaps this is why rape, which requires male physical arousal, is possible.

Most Mother Stage women desperately want to feel sexual desire and enjoy sexual pleasure, but they don't know how to bypass their anger in order to do so. When a woman does not acknowledge her anger, she becomes depressed, which is also damaging to her sexual desire. Yet it is not a matter of "getting over it," as many books imply. It is a question of addressing the roots of the problem. When women seek help, they are baffled by the fact that their anger could be blocking sexual feelings. They tell me, "I don't think my sexuality even exists anymore." What they really mean is, "I no longer know how to access my sexual feelings." Female sexual energy is indestructible, but in these cases, it lies dormant.

When carrying the majority of responsibilities during the child-rearing years, the Mother will inevitably feel resentment. Even today, most working women still bear the responsibility for 80 percent of the domestic tasks. For a long time, men have been raised to believe that simply "bringing home the bacon" is the sum total of their duties in the domestic equation. Now that most women return to the workforce at some point, we have a major imbalance of role division that has not been sufficiently acknowledged as a cause of low desire.

Cindy

Cindy came to me with extreme anxiety because her husband suddenly announced, "I'm not happy." She was perplexed because she had thought everything was fine. She was struggling so hard to get through her day of endless child care, food preparation, diapers, and cleaning (dogs, kids, carpets) that she hadn't even noticed when he stopped giving her affection. She not only carried the burden of the household and the kids, but she worked on the weekends to bring in extra money. She said: "Honestly, I was relieved that my husband wasn't approaching me for anything. He was one more need to take care of, and I just wanted everyone to leave me alone for a while."

Cindy is typical of women today. She tried to be the perfect mother, homemaker, chief cook, bottle washer, and wage earner. The role of wife had taken a back seat, and her attitude was, "Can't he see that I'm up to my eyeballs? He's an adult; he can wait." Obviously, her husband had reached a crisis point and was screaming for attention.

Cindy felt that she was being asked to give up some of her maternal responsibilities in order to meet her husband's needs, specifically for attention and sex. He had said, "Meet my needs or I'll leave." What had appeared to be a partnership in raising three young children had become her job. Cindy had been functioning quite well under these circumstances, having given up her personal development to meet the constant demands of a young family. She even gave up hope of any substantial help from her husband. But when he voiced his need for attention and demanded that she do something about it, Cindy reached overload.

Certainly, she could not abandon her Mother Stage development. Cindy's nurturing instincts ran too deep. As nature intended, her children's needs came first. She loved her husband and wanted to continue the partnership to which they had committed when they married. As she put it, "I can't shift from Mom to sex kitten at the drop of a hat." The couple needed marital therapy to help them negotiate the best solution possible.

Cindy's need for time alone or for relaxation with women friends had to be addressed as well. With improved communication and negotiating skills, she saw the possibility of working out a third alternative acceptable to both of them. She and her husband developed a sense of teamwork that led to her sexual desire resurfacing due to the communion she felt with her partner. Cindy no longer felt the stress of being responsible for everyone's happiness.

If you are holding too much stress inside of you, your sexuality is going to shut down. Many times when couples seek counseling and the issue of the overwhelming demands of the woman's roles is broached, the male will say things such as, "Well, your standards are too high," or "Why don't you learn to tolerate the mess (or the noise) like I do?" Not all men are so passive about the problem, however. Recently a woman approached me after a presentation and said, "I want you to know that our sex life improved enormously when my husband started doing the dishes."

"I Don't Care If I Have Orgasms"

Women who state that they do not need orgasms may have histories of minimal experience with sexual pleasure. Some may be "good girls" who wait for the right man, or they may have had few sexual experiences prior to getting married. They climax rarely, or only under certain circumstances, often because their response cycles may take up to 45 minutes and they need a lot of time to relax. Since around 70 percent of all women do not climax with intercourse alone, most of these women are uncomfortable

asking for the time or touch required. Some may have been faking orgasm for many years, and their partners are totally unaware.
They have despaired of having the pleasure they want because it
is just too much effort.

Betty

Betty had waited a long time—until it felt right to
her—to experience sexual intercourse. She expected
her husband to know what to do and to perform perfectly without either one of them having any knowledge
of her particular sexual needs. When the initial experimentation did not satisfy her, she began either to fake
orgasms so she would not hurt her partner's feelings, or
she simply encouraged him to climax quickly to "get it
over with." Like many women who say they don't care if
they have orgasms, Betty says she does not worry about
her lack of pleasure. She claims to enjoy the closeness,
yet she rarely engages in sex.

❧❧❧

Some Mother Stage women who report having little or no
interest in orgasms with their partners can climax through self-
stimulation, where it is much easier to achieve just the right touch
without fear that their partner will tire before they climax.
However, such women have been unable to transfer the ability to
attain orgasm into partner sex and find it embarrassing to tell men
what they need. Over the course of a 10- or 15-year relationship,
their mates may have behaved in ways that communicate fatigue
and boredom while stimulating them. Women commonly give up

hoping that their partners will enjoy stimulating them for as long as it takes them to climax.

Some women who have become discouraged about their own sexual pleasure in the Mother Stage may have had patient lovers sometime in the past who took the time necessary for them to achieve orgasm. Yet, these women are not getting the same kind of attention from their current partners. Oral stimulation is one of the most pleasurable ways for women to achieve orgasm, but many men do not have the stamina for it, so both parties give up easily.

I often recommend that women use a wand-type sport massage vibrator that can be very effective in freeing the couple from fatiguing activities that may not guarantee any orgasmic release for her. It can be used in addition to partner stimulation and during intercourse. It is a wonderful way to shorten the time of the response cycle and build a sense of sexual self-confidence. For the first time in their lives, these women can count on having an orgasm when they choose. Women who feel confident about being able to climax become very interested in repeating the experience as often as possible, in safe and seductive conditions.

The banquet analogy used in the previous chapter is appropriate for Mother Stage women who claim to be uninterested in their own pleasure. They have gone to that banquet too many times without feasting on anything. When they can create the optimal conditions for awakening their sexual energy, they have an opportunity to taste all the wonderful and varied pleasures possible.

Women with Greater Desire Than Their Mates

High-desire women in our culture are really closer to the norm of women raised in the Goddess cultures. The ancient wisdom recognized an incredible capacity for sexual energy in women. Those societies expected and encouraged women to express their full desire for sexual pleasure. However, it is women's sexual *power* and their capacity for such intense pleasure that threatens and infuriates certain men who are unsure of their own sexuality. The archetype of the wild woman is as frightening as it is fascinating. Consequently, the patriarchal marriage laws were, in part, a way to control the sexual energy of women. If their sexuality remained unbridled, who knew what would happen?

How, then, have we come to such an impasse with respect to female desire that women would say, "I don't care if I never have sex again"? Ann Landers recently quoted a letter in her column entitled "Glad to Be Sexless." The contributor wrote, "There are many of us who consider sex an unhygienic and degrading experience that must be endured to have children." The writer continues by assuming that if women chose not to have a family, they would seize the opportunity to have platonic marriages. Ann's wonderful humor comes out in her reply, "Never say never," she says. "You might just meet someone down the road who makes you eat your words. You can play with the cat for just so long." With this testimonial to women's current awareness that they can enjoy sex for their own benefit, we shall examine the many women who feel rejected because they want sex *too much.*

Kate ("He Makes Me Feel Dirty")

Kate had grown up as a "wild child" of the 1970s and entered into the Mother Stage prematurely. She had struggled as a single woman to raise her child and com-

plete her education. She finally found a new life and sta-
bility in marriage in her 30s. She knew that her relationship with her new husband was extremely compatible.
They both loved family life and had common values,
recreational pursuits, and friends. Except for his sexual
passivity, she thought she had found the right mate. At
first she didn't mind initiating sex on every occasion
because she had a strong sex drive and loved arousing
him. As time passed, he began rejecting her, complaining
of fatigue, illness, or work. When Kate confronted him
about his lack of interest, he told her that she was too
aggressive and it made him uncomfortable. She decided
to try a more subtle approach.

When she finally came to therapy, Kate was
depressed, anxious, and she lacked confidence. During
the months in which she had tried being more subtle, her
sexual encounters with her husband had diminished in
frequency from weekly to zero. Every time she dressed
in a sexy outfit, her husband criticized her. He took pains
to avoid her when she undressed, buried himself in his
computer when he came home, and refused to discuss
their sexual issues. He said that Kate was too obsessed
with sex, which made her unappealing. He was completely disinterested in her, and she was so deeply
wounded that she sincerely believed that she was disgusting.

The reality was that Kate was actually an attractive
and lively woman who really loved sex.

Mary ("I'm Told I'm Just
Too Much")

Mary had been the star of her class in high school: cheerleader, student leader, and homecoming queen. She became pregnant by the captain of the football team and married at 17. Subsequently, she had three wonderful kids and built a successful construction company with her husband. During their 20 years of marriage, he continually criticized every part of her body. Her breasts were too big, her bottom was too round, her skin wasn't creamy enough, and so on. Even more damaging, he found her enthusiastic orgasms and lusty noises disgusting, and actually covered her mouth when she expressed her sexual pleasure verbally. Mary was multi-orgasmic and very responsive to touch.

It was a miracle that Mary never completely allowed her husband to annihilate her sexuality, but he did create many obstacles to her self-esteem and natural expressiveness that took a lot of courage to undo in the years after their divorce. She had stayed in this sexually repressive marriage because her family told her, "You made your own bed," and she had to prove to everyone that she really hadn't made a mistake. Mary's husband's parents never let her forget that if he hadn't felt obliged to marry her, he would have been considerably more successful. They viewed her as being from "the wrong side of the tracks," and not good enough for their son.

As luck would have it, after Mary had developed the internal strength to leave the marriage and thrive on her own, she dated two other men who were intimidated by her powerful sexuality. Both men had problems with erectile dysfunction. They were unable to get hard enough to penetrate, or lost their erections fairly soon after entering her. These men had been struggling with their sexual problems before they met her, but each, in his own way, tried to blame his erectile failures on Mary. She was too noisy, too demanding, too wet! Rejection of a woman's strong sexual desire is a common ploy among men whose sexual self-confidence is very fragile. Sadly, women tend to feel bad about not being able to seduce such men effectively.

⋘⋙ ⋘⋙ ⋘⋙

When I treat a couple where the woman wants more sex than the man, I know it will be complicated due to the fact that they represent the opposite of the "normal" desire discrepancy in our society. Both the woman and the man feel bad that their situation differs from the familiar scenario: "Guys are always horny, and women have to push them away." When it is the woman who gets pushed away on a regular basis, it disturbs the foundations of her belief in herself compared to what is "right" or "natural." In patriarchy, the woman is not supposed to want more sex than her partner.

Women Who Love Sex

In Gina Ogden's study of easily orgasmic women,[7] the experience of feminine sexual satisfaction is described in much broader terms than physical release. These women's sexual interests went far beyond the range of a typical sex researcher's focus on physiological response. Ogden defined a three-part continuum of pleasure-orgasm-ecstasy that more completely describes women's sexual experience. The theme that surfaced repeatedly in Ogden's interviews with easily orgasmic women was their expanded view of sexuality.

Although women who are highly responsive said they were able to enjoy recreational sex, they universally spoke of the importance of an intimate connection with their partners. Feeling an emotional connection integrating romance, love, and commitment were important factors in sustaining high desire. In addition, the deeper experiences of communion—"heart to heart, soul to soul, mind to mind"—were important for their most ecstatic sexual moments.[8] These women defined their feelings of desire, arousal, and satisfaction in an enormous range of erotic possibilities that extended far beyond the physical. These reports expanded Ogden's research into the phenomenon of spiritual sex (see chapter 12).

Taking Responsibility for Sexual Experiences

Once you know what kind of stimulation pleases you and what factors make the setting seductive for you, you are capable of taking responsibility for your sexual experience. Knowing that women have an expanded capacity for sexual desire and pleasure in conducive settings may help encourage you.

It should be abundantly clear by now that when either partner perceives a sexual interaction as a performance or a duty, both lose. Unfortunately, conventional sex therapy techniques such as touch exercises are often interpreted as a way to teach the mechanics of touching to please the partner. If the woman is only motivated to do these exercises in order to learn how to please her partner (so he won't abandon her or have an affair), she will go through the motions without significant increase in sexual desire.

Jackie

Jackie came to sex therapy with her husband because of their desire discrepancy. He insisted that she learn to enjoy the sex experience and had often threatened to leave her because she did not. The touch exercises and subsequent individual work taught Jackie to have more reliable orgasms, and her husband felt satisfied. Now she was able to climax with the correct stimulation. However, his need to control their sex life continued with his pattern of insisting on contract sex. This is an agreement, usually driven by the male's need to have some reliable interval of time or number of episodes in a week, when he can count on having intercourse with his wife. The contract might be, "We will have sex three times a week unless you're having your period," or "Every Saturday when the kids are in bed (or away or napping) we will have intercourse." In such cases, women tell me privately that they are relieved when their periods arrive. They know that they can relax for a while.

Surprisingly, Jackie's story is not at all unique. Such contractual arrangements surface quite regularly. In fact, some therapists seem to think that this is a good solution to male complaints! In reality, though, insistence on this type of contract leads to female resentment and avoidance. It also leads to irritation of the vaginal membranes as a result of a lack of arousal. Eventually, contract sex can lead to painful intercourse.

If you feel relieved when you have a "good excuse" not to have intercourse, you may have unwittingly submitted to a non-verbal contract with your mate. Taking responsibility for your sexual experience includes not yielding to pressure to relieve the male's anxiety about when he can count on intercourse. It should be obvious that when *contract sex* is carried out without fail, regardless of the psychological conditions, feminine desire is bound to become dormant.

Sex must be reframed as an erotic experience in which both partners take responsibility for their own sexual pleasure. The vital element in defining erotic experiences is *pleasure.* Defined in this context, it has infinite possibilities. Erotic encounters may not necessarily include intercourse or may not always culminate in orgasm. Partners must represent themselves from a Guardian position by asking for what they want. Each should be willing to support the other for mutual pleasuring.

You must be accountable for acting in your own best interests by communicating desires and refusing unwanted touch. When you find yourself silently wishing for a special touch or you lose interest because the form of stimulation is not pleasing, you must actively change the situation to make it more satisfying. If you silently endure uncomfortable or boring sexual behavior without saying anything about it, the result drains the overall energy and health of the relationship. Another word for such silent suffering is *accommodation.* Unfortunately, women have been engaging in it for a long time.

A balanced sexual partnership is essential for sustained sexual desire. Long after the early kinds of mutual pleasuring have lost their luster, both men and women are afraid to discuss the problem with their partner. It is difficult to be really specific about changing the kind of touch, tempo, sights, sounds, and any other details related to sex. However, the communication skills outlined in chapter 10 can help you voice your needs while eliminating defensive reactions.

Among women, there remains an unspoken understanding that the male sexual ego is very fragile. Most women have learned through hard experience that it is not nice to shatter the man's illusion of himself as the *Great Stud Lover*. Women know better than to jump on the bandwagon and suggest changes in a man's style. He may recoil in a huff if she says something like, "Honey, can you touch me gently?" or "I really would like you to wait until I'm ready before you enter me." If you wince at the thought of saying something like this, you need to work on your Guardian and your assertiveness skills in order to develop the courage to speak up. You owe it to yourself and your partner to participate fully.

It is even more important in long-term relationships for women to use their Guardian in assessing their readiness for a particular sexual activity or for a specific type of sexual stimulation. This principle starts with sensual touching and kissing and goes all the way to penetration and beyond. As a woman taking responsibility for your own sexual experience, you must not give in to pressure to be rushed, simply because your partner's tempo is ten times more rapid than yours. *You* are the only source of information about your readiness for intercourse. If you go ahead too soon, you will eventually start resisting the idea of attending the banquet.

The pattern of yielding to your male partner's timing, when it becomes chronic, is perhaps the greatest source of the gradual loss of female sexual desire. You may actually believe that it isn't important to respond fully in a sexual encounter. You're likely to relinquish your own needs in the service of pleasing your mate. The demise of desire can be so subtle that you may not realize you've sabotaged yourself until you've practiced this pattern of ignoring your needs chronically. The following scenario is an example:

The husband asks for sex before rising for another busy day. The wife says to herself, "We don't have much time, and the baby will wake up, so what's the harm in a quickie? He'll be much happier and easier to live with." When she has more time, it is too much bother to try to relax enough to complete her response cycle. Men often collude with their partners in allowing this accommodation to persist. He may say, "Are you sure you're okay with this?" She reads the signals of his yawns, lack of eye contact, and waning interest after his orgasm. She says, "Sure, Honey, I just enjoy the closeness." With that, he gives her a big hug and tells her what a great wife she is.

There are times when a woman truly feels good about a sexual encounter without needing to achieve orgasm, since the goal is both partners feeling good about themselves and each other. Physical pleasuring can mean an infinite variety of mutually satisfying activities without having intercourse or climaxing every time.

As you begin to risk asking for what you want, it will become clearer what you *do* want. During each experience of asking and receiving the right touch, look, or sound that intensifies your sexual feelings, you'll discover more and more about the depth of pleasures that you find you enjoy. If you must ultimately leave a bad relationship because your partner does not want to change, learn, or grow, so be it. Just be sure you've worked hard enough on yourself to be able to verbalize your desires before you give up. By all means, visit a sex therapist if your efforts are not working.

Making Sense of Your Personal Sex History: Part II

Once again, please use a notebook to write down brief answers to the following questions.

1. Right now, if your partner asked you to do something you didn't want to do, could you say no?

2. Who was a Woman of Power in your life? How did she influence you?

3. If you have not had children, how have you expressed nurturing compassion for others?

4. Can you communicate what you want to your partner? Which feelings remain undisclosed?

Chapter Seven

~~~~~~~~~~~~

Mastery: Reclaiming the Wisdom of the Crone

"Never underestimate the power of a woman."
— Tag line for the *Ladies Home Journal*

The Transformation

Maiden creativity continues to live within women as they accept responsibility as Mothers. As women transform into the Crone, they also carry their Mother selves within. The Crone Stage is delineated by the emergence of a new self resulting from another blood mystery. In the ancient cultures, this was the time when women retained their "wise blood." As the First Blood was the gateway to Maiden life, and as Childbirth was the gateway to the Mother, accordingly, Menopause was the gateway to the Crone.

In order to prepare for Cronehood, women must attend to the transformation process that precedes it. Perimenopause is the crucible that brings us to a new phase of adulthood. From the spiritual perspective, perimenopause is an initiation. Women who attend to the messages of their bodies move through a valuable period of growth. On the other side is a level of unparalleled awareness and the task of *sharing wisdom*. Hot flashes are the fire that refines us and directs our consciousness to a new level of body wisdom. Shamanic tradition holds that the symptoms of menopause are purifying the woman, challenging her to relinquish old habits and come to a new understanding of herself and her chosen path.[1] Cronehood is a consciousness that women must learn to embrace rather then fear.

Crone women may find support from women previously viewed as competitors. Friendships forged during Crone years are profoundly empowering. A free and fiercely assertive sexuality can emerge from confrontation with emotional issues of aging and loss. There is also the potential of dramatic new energy motivated by the desire to make changes in society.

The Crone Stage is potentially the most powerful one, because women who have come to terms with themselves are now ready and willing to work on societal issues that are close to their hearts. Often they are effective in mobilizing other women who share their passion to collaborate on projects, increasing their effectiveness. Collectively they have a newfound assertiveness that makes them tireless campaigners for chosen causes. As one female psychotherapist put it, "These are the truly dangerous women." They have the conviction to carry out their purpose, and the wisdom to become message bearers for change.

Contemporary Crone women have the opportunity to give birth to the creative self, which may have been left by the wayside. They are becoming leading speakers, teachers, writers, and policy makers in our culture. As Crone women declare themselves to be the spiritual authorities they were meant to be, their ancient and future power to transform the planet will at long last come to the fore.

Sexual Mastery

There are many possible paths open to Crone women. Sexual mastery is one of the sacred ways that women can embrace.

Contrary to all the common misinformation and prejudice imbedded in patriarchal assumptions about women, the Crone Stage has the potential for continued sexual development. Those who have pursued personal growth with their long-term partners may enjoy a new level of sexual pleasure with their mates. Crone women who do not have mates may also follow the path of sexual mastery, but they will need to take care that they are being honored by their chosen sexual partner.

Women may be considerably motivated to pursue this new developmental path because it can lead to the most powerful sexual experiences of all. Not every sexual encounter will be a direct experience with spiritual energy, but the fact that it is possible is interesting to many Crone women. Sexual mastery utilizes women's intuitive healing abilities in combination with sexual energy. It facilitates the deepening contact with body wisdom with consciously developed *intentional sexual desire*.

Intentional Sexual Desire

With *intentional desire*, Crone women may learn to focus on a new sexual response that is different from earlier times. Sexual desire in the Crone Stage is affected by lower levels of estrogen in relative proportion to the levels of testosterone. Although women do have an assertive mix of hormones, it does not feel like the sexual "horniness" of their youth. Some women are more familiar with feeling the estrogen-dependent, receptive sexual response. When their bodies stop producing abundant estrogen, they report that they do not feel any sexual desire, not having learned to attend to a different source of sexual response. Intentional desire is derived from the focused will.

Crone sexuality extends beyond what society deems appropriate and proper behavior for a woman "of a certain age." Intentional sexual desire comes from an inner resource that accesses a deeper sexuality, transcending instinctual, hormone-driven responses. It can be understood as a purposeful action: to heal, to commune with a partner, to seek mutual pleasure, and to play with universal energy. Intentional sexual desire may be used for the practice of spiritual sexuality, and the potential for deeper experiences with the great mysteries of life. *The Sacred Marriage*, which is the ancient practice of spiritual sexuality, will be described in detail in chapter 12.

Sexual Mastery and Healing

Pursuing mastery can revive an interest in sex. Crone sexual interest often goes beyond simply experiencing pleasure and physical release. The healing potential of sexual mastery may motivate Crone women to reclaim their sexuality because it is rejuvenating. Sexual healing means playing creatively with sexual energy at levels where partners must honor each other as expressions of the Divine.

In order to explore the power of sexual healing, we shall examine the experiences of modern surrogate partners. Surrogate partners are a special kind of sexual healer practicing today. They are a contemporary echo of an ancient, sacred path of the *Hierodules,* or sacred virgins of the Goddess temples. Today's sex surrogates practice a form of healing once performed by specially trained women who offered sexual healing for those who came in need.

The interest in healing that is prevalent in the Crone Stage of life becomes intensified for many women because of the initiation process of menopause. In the Crone years, women have the potential to become sexually self-responsible as never before because of courage gained from facing menopause and finding solutions that challenge conventional notions.

Menopause

More than in any other stage, Crone women cannot take their bodies or their health for granted. Women learn to listen to their bodies and respond to the messages during menstruation, pregnancy, and childbirth. In this stage, they are confronted by new, seemingly mysterious physical and emotional challenges from another major hormonal shift. The symptoms accompanying menopause can include migraine headaches, weight gain, hot flashes, sleep disturbance, low energy, depression, and poor concentration. Most women find these symptoms impossible to ignore. They serve as a warning to women, enabling them to make intelligent decisions about their bodies.

The medical perspective considers menopause a manageable illness that should be treated aggressively with the best of modern chemistry. Yet, we do not know how to reliably account for each woman's unique response to hormone therapy. Premarin, a form of estrogen, is the popular medical choice because it is assumed that estrogen withdrawal is the *cause* of menopause. However, dosing the body with this type of estrogen may not always be in women's best interests because we do not know exactly how much is absorbed nor the outcome of long-term use. There is a more balanced formula called "tri-estrogen" that can be prepared at any pharmacy with a doctor's prescription, but few doctors recommend it because they are insufficiently informed.

Other choices are often overlooked. So-called precursor hormones have been recently identified, such as DHEA and a new "superhormone" called Pregnenolone. These hormones occur naturally in our bodies and are capable of producing other desire-boosting hormones such as estrogen, testosterone, and androgen. They may be especially helpful in counteracting physical symptoms inhibiting pleasurable sex and have shown promising results in contributing to our overall health. With all the alternatives, it makes sense for women to investigate choices, including homeopathic preparations and traditional herbal remedies.

Crone women have started taking their health concerns into their own hands. Because of their body wisdom, they are motivated to pursue alternative methods of treatment and healthy living. They are sharing both their frustration and their triumphs with health regimens that really work. Whatever the choice of medicine, Crone women must add some form of regular exercise and healthy diet for overall robust health leading to abundant sexual desire.

Menopause and Sexuality

Let's examine the role of menopause in the psychology of female desire. Crenshaw[2] cites a London study of women that listed the following problems reportedly starting during perimenopause: loss of interest in sex, aversive reactions to any sexual touching, vaginal dryness, painful intercourse, loss of clitoral sensation, decrease in orgasm, and thinning of the skin leading to irritation. Yet, slightly over one-third of the women in the study reported loss of sexual interest, and even fewer women reported the other symptoms. This leaves us wondering about the experience of the other two-thirds. Since the focus was on the pathological problems of menopause, the positive side was not examined.

It is alarming to contemplate the ongoing symptoms of hot flashes, dizziness, heavy bleeding, mood changes, painful joints, drying body membranes, heart problems, and even suicidal feelings. There is no question that perimenopause impacts sexual desire during episodes of these symptoms. Fortunately, they are intermittent in most cases. More important to continued sexual activity is how women and their mates respond to these episodes. Menopause may be unnecessarily perceived as an illness with the assumption that it is "all downhill from here," so couples may unnecessarily relinquish the hope of pleasurable sex. Supportive skills that build intimacy are especially critical at these times.

The onset of Crone years may be seen as a psychological fork in the road, one path leading to relinquishing feminine sexuality altogether, and the other leading to a rebirth of sexual possibilities. Currently, there is a new recognition of older women's desire for sex. Fortunately, there are increasing numbers of older women defying conventional stereotypes. They may even have younger male sexual partners.

Crone women with strong self-esteem, who have internalized a sense of permission to be sexual, survive the physical and emotional changes of menopause by continuing to access their life-affirming sexual desire. At first, they may be surprised by the fact that they are not sexually responding in familiar ways. Once such women realize that perimenopause is not fleeting, they utilize the sexual body wisdom they have gained, in order to function well under the new circumstances.

As a way of coping with the perimenopausal symptoms that affect sexual functioning, you will need to expand your sexual self-esteem. You can begin by accessing a deeper level of permission to be sexual, so that your image of "sexy" is not synonymous with "young." You need to rework your concepts of physical readiness in order to respond to the changes in your

body sensations. Learning to make adjustments to different physical timing and touch requirements will enable you to retool your
sexuality. The coping skills you need include sharing information with other women and learning from their experiences.
Women's wisdom has always been a matter of collaborative
sharing, and there is certainly a lot to share.

To gain a feeling of sexual empowerment, Crone women need
to view the physical changes as a *necessary process*. Its purpose
is to strengthen and add insight, which facilitates the emergence
of the "wise woman." Perimenopausal symptoms are preparation
for the transformation of the last of the blood mysteries. Women
are *meant* to go through this challenge, as they were destined to
go through the childbirth process. Both initiations are powerful,
natural processes.

Germaine Greer shakes up conventional notions about older
women with a very thoughtful book called *The Change*.[3] Greer's
message is that the *climacteric,* as she calls it, is an opportunity
for a woman to examine her life. It may be that the reduction of
estrogen in the female body allows women to find their sense of
self outside their caretaking roles. She points out that estrogen is
the "biddability hormone,"[4] which mediates women's *submissive-
ness*. Crenshaw confirms that estrogen is the source of the *receptive* sex drive.[5] When women no longer play the role of self-
sacrificing caretaker or "contented cow," as Greer writes, no one
seems to appreciate their newfound assertiveness. As Joan
Borysenko puts it in *A Woman's Book of Life*, "Ballsy behavior is
supported by ballsy hormones."[6]

Shedding the caretaker role may be difficult, and you may
need to work through personal issues about both your assertiveness and your aging process as an ongoing part of your growth
toward positive sexual interaction.

Sexuality and Aging

The current panic over medical solutions to menopause derives from a profound fear of growing old and especially *looking old* that has reached paranoid proportions in our times. Our culture is so aversive to aging that the new wave of chemical solutions to menopause seem like a response to the scare tactics from our childhood: "The bogeyman will get you." The message is: If you don't take this or that pill, you will have serious bone loss, heart disease, and you will look old. In contemporary society, *old* is synonymous with *sexually unattractive*.

What is even more alarming is that women sometimes choose to overdose by taking four times the recommended amount. Perhaps they think that if estrogen will keep them looking young and feeling sexy, *more* is even better. If you have considered all types of estrogen and have discussed the possible alternatives assertively with your physician, you have made an informed choice.

Since initially, the crisis of aging sets off a panic in most women, they must resist the immediate reaction to deal with the fear by blindly taking the latest and greatest chemicals. These may be desperate measures. Such women are going to need to directly confront their psychological issues with aging.

The Aging Crisis

At the Crone Stage of life, we revisit our body-image issues of the Maiden years. Yet even women who were confident in their Maiden body image and managed to survive the Mother years with a continued sense of beauty are vulnerable to an emotional crisis. They become alarmed by the loss of elasticity and the pull of gravity that will eventually defy the most rigorous beauty regimens. If a woman has been a slave to society's concepts of beauty, she may avoid sexual activity, unable to tolerate the painful thought of a lover's rejection. For some beautiful women, the only choice is to become a recluse, as did Greta Garbo.

Since our feelings about our attractiveness influence our sexual desire, the more we dwell on negative feelings about how we look, the worse the effect on sexual desire and responsiveness. Some women never realize that they can feel sexy at any age. There is at least one psychological crisis to be found lurking around the 50th birthday. The moment of realization that: "Oh my God, I don't look young anymore." You become aware that the image in the mirror is older and more wrinkled. Yet many women tell me that they still feel 19 inside their 50-year-old bodies, and it comes as a surprise to see an older woman in the mirror.

A woman's crisis of aging is the loss of her illusions about her once-youthful attractiveness. Even with the miracles of plastic surgery, she cannot ignore her aging. Sadly, some women can never accept the loss or find a way to expand their sense of beauty beyond the norms of our culture. They may remain eternal princesses, always chasing after the next expensive treatment. Their style is a copy of youthful fashion, and at times, these aging princesses look downright silly. Some women go through a period of yearning to return to their youthful look, but grow to accept a new, unique sense of self.

Crone women should never give up their basic pride in their appearance, but beauty at 50 or 60 or 70 is a *mature erotic beauty*. Once women appropriately mourn their previous self-image and come to terms with a new stage, they begin to get a second wind and pursue a new ideal. Only then will they attain beauty that reflects a sense of feeling at ease with themselves.

Mature Erotic Beauty

A valued male friend of mine described what he found sexually attractive about certain older women. He said that there was something undefinable about them, a sense they communicated that they were at ease with themselves. Obviously they cared about their bodies and good grooming, but they had clearly found a style that suited them and were not mindlessly obedient to current fashion. They seemed to exhibit a flair for vibrant and sensual colors, and the cut of their clothing complimented their feminine curves, but did not scream, "Look at my body parts." Most important, these women glowed from within. It was this *luminosity* that he found so enormously attractive.

In the new millennium, the good news is that Crone women have learned to refocus on overall good health as the central issue of aging, rather than beauty. When they target *health* rather than *aging*, they are more likely to appropriately resolve the loss of youthful beauty as their ideal. Many women are discovering the joys of walking, healthy food preparation, and herbal remedies. Revival of the ancient healing arts and the ability to blend them with modern health knowledge makes Crone women ideal leaders in the growing field of alternative health.

Mature beauty stems from a woman's sense of personal authority and the richness of her life. The mature erotic woman will have integrated her Maiden creativity, Mother compassion, and her growing assertiveness. Such women possess the quality of harmony with self, valued by cultures such as the Laguna Pueblo. Beautiful Crone women have continued to grow and are following their sacred path of power. These are truly *luminous* beings of great worth. Such beauty can only increase with age. This is the promise of *mature erotic beauty*.

Sexual Desire and Loss

The issues relevant to the Crone Stage of life, which impact sexual desire, generally concern loss: loss of the illusion of youthfulness, loss of a mate through divorce or death, and the most pernicious loss of all, loss of self-esteem, which is at the core of depression. Although depression can debilitate women at any stage, any of the Crone Stage losses can precipitate depression, making women particularly susceptible.

Even women who have never had symptoms of depression before can suddenly find themselves on a disturbing emotional roller coaster. The profound hormonal changes and inevitable losses of the Crone Stage will increase the likelihood of an episode of depression in the perimenopausal years. Yet, Crone sexual desire does not inevitably decline without good cause. Some women subconsciously rebel against hurtful experiences with partners who have betrayed them. Their bodies may be acting in response to a decision not to allow feelings of sexual attachment ever again to render them vulnerable to such painful loss.

Jane

When I first saw Jane, she was hanging on by a thread. Her dignity was in shreds, and she had no idea how to continue living. Her husband of 29 years had informed her that he wanted to live apart and had no interest in marital counseling or reconciliation of any kind. He just wanted out. She was deeply depressed, with all the classic symptoms of poor sleep, extreme

fatigue, no appetite, and suicidal thoughts that were fortunately too vague for her to act on.

When we talked about the history of her relationship with her husband, a pattern of extreme co-dependence emerged. She had married after college, and her
husband had been her first sex partner, although she'd
had a few boyfriends before him. He had informed her
that he was not the kind of man who enjoyed any cuddling, hand-holding, or any other affectionate touching.
She would have to accept it if she wanted to marry him.
Jane knew she was a warm person who loved to touch,
but she made the classic mistake of assuming that with
enough love, she could change him.

Over the course of their marriage, their sex life consisted of uninspired intercourse, with the goal being her
husband's orgasm. There was little touching and no cuddling afterward. Jane rarely had orgasms and had abandoned the idea of any sensual experience for herself. As
time passed, sex was reduced to a few sessions of per-
functory orgasms for her husband.

Jane had built her work around her husband's business, and her organizational skills had been the backbone
of his success. With his defection, she was losing her
career as well as her mate. But the straw that truly
broke her was information she received just weeks after
she had started therapy. One day, after another session
of questioning from her, Jane's husband admitted that he
had found someone younger. He proceeded to tell her
how fulfilling he had learned a truly sensual relationship
could be, and he was discovering how much he enjoyed
all the deep emotions and physical affection he had
missed in their relationship!

Imagine the betrayal this woman felt. She was so accustomed to making excuses to herself for her husband's behavior that it took time for her to rise out of her deep depression and allow herself to feel justifiable rage. Of course, after the rage over his treatment of her came an analysis of what had made it possible for her to tolerate the lack of affection during all those years. Now she says that she never wants to be involved with another man again.

Losing to "Jennifer"

One of the most painful ways a woman can lose a partner is to a younger woman referred to as a "Jennifer." The book *Jennifer Fever* [7] described the syndrome of older men pursuing much younger women in the desperate hope to feel young again. This theme was dramatized in a very successful film entitled *The First Wives' Club*. It owed its huge appeal at the box office to the large group of women who had lost out to "Jennifers" or who knew friends who had. The movie obviously struck a chord in the hearts of its female viewers.

The sexual consequences are serious for Crone women who have focused their entire adult lives on their husbands' needs. Until recently, a husband taking a younger woman as a bed companion or second wife was the *norm* for patriarchal men. Wives were expected to suffer in silence while their husbands dallied with the maid or the servant girl or had a woman "on the side" who was supported in a separate household. Now women are objecting publicly to these excruciatingly humiliating experiences.

Popular opinion used to hold that once a woman "dried up,"

she had no right to a sex life unless she managed to keep her husband. Even then it was assumed that she would tolerate her husband's infidelities because he had the right to an active sex life for as long as possible. If her desire was low, doctors assumed that it was a result of hormonal changes rather than inadequate stimulation by an inattentive partner. However, among sexual options available to the current Crone pathfinders is the choice of considerably younger men as part-time lovers or even mates.

Older Women, Younger Men

By choosing a younger sexual partner, women are asserting their sexuality in ways they could not have imagined years before. The trend reflects Crone women's internalized sense of permission to have active sex lives with men who appreciate their assertiveness and sexual self-knowledge. Society may still frown on older women with younger men, but the women who have empowered themselves to act on their sexual desires find this avenue highly gratifying. As long as such women are honored, the elevated self-esteem and healing sexual pleasure is deeply rewarding.

We have many examples of women who have chosen to regenerate their sexuality rather than "go quietly into the night." One such woman is Margaret Mead, one of the most famous social anthropologists of the 20th century. According to an account by her daughter, Mead went through a sexual transformation in her Crone years. Mead's daughter reported the story in Gail Sheehy's book on menopause, *The Silent Passage*. She stated that her mother looked prettier and dressed more dramatically in designer clothes after starting a new romantic involvement.[8]

Loss of Sexual Desire and Depression

It is normal to feel depressed about disappointments or to feel occasionally disillusioned. This type of depressed mood is part of everyone's life. Also, it is considered normal to feel depressed over a loss such as the death of a mate or another loved one. The concern about depression and its effect on women's sexuality refers to a more chronic and debilitating variety that can sap our strength and zest for living. One of the hallmarks of this type of depression is long-lasting disinterest in sex.

Andrea

Andrea did not like the image of herself as a depressed woman. She had not desired sex in several years, yet she wanted to be more available to her mate. As we examined the causes of her depression, she discovered that she was deeply angry with her husband. The union had been an affectionate one in the early years but had run aground as a result of her husband's affair ten years before. Although they had decided to stay together after having marital counseling, Andrea still harbored considerable anger over his betrayal. Her depression was a silent reproach for her husband's violation of their intimacy.

Andrea yearned for the lost closeness with her husband, but she was depressed because she could not ask for the intimacy she truly craved. She could not move in the direction of her own growth until she could release her anger over her husband's betrayal and acknowledge that she still desired the connection with him. Once she was able to mourn the loss of the innocent security she had felt before his affair, she could accept and function within the changed circumstances of her life. She also became aware that she needed to communicate her needs to her husband. Andrea was able to set behavioral goals for change, such as suggested in chapters 8 and 9. She developed the assertive skills she needed to speak about her desire for closeness and to face the terror of her husband's rejection. This led to the resurrection of intimacy in the marriage.

The outcome of taking a proactive stance was a growing sense of power on Andrea's part. She began taking responsibility for her sexual experience by insisting on conditions in support of her sexual pleasure. In therapy, the couple learned intimacy skills that produced the sense of communion Andrea desired. Her sexuality blossomed as never before, and her desire manifested itself with a sensuality that led to her sexual empowerment.

Sexual Empowerment

Empowerment means the process of internalizing a sense of personal power. Many things can stimulate a woman to feel more of her own power, but the perception has to come from her own psyche. The difference between *empowerment* and *power* is that the latter can be used to imply the use of force to obtain what is desired. There is a significant difference between having *power over* a person or situation and being *empowered*, which means acting in one's best interests. Feminine empowerment is defined in this context as claiming for the self what is fair and reasonable to fulfill needs and feel satisfied, without harm to another.

Sexual empowerment can be described in the same way, in the context of a sexual situation. It refers to an inner confidence about your feminine sexuality that belies the physical image seen in the mirror, on a day when you may be feeling your age. Due to changes in the female body during the Crone years, there must be a new consciousness of acceptance of these circumstances.

Being e*mpowered* implies a state of awareness of the internal strengths of emotional compassion, focused will, and clarity of intention. An empowered Crone woman manifests her energy in a way that reflects the spiritual strength she has gained from all the feminine initiations. This strength describes a sexual *Woman of Power,* whose desire is an intentional surrender to the will of the Divine. Her purpose is to work with the energy, call it Kundalini, Life Force, or the pulsing spiral of the Source of All.

The Power of Sexual Healing

Sexuality as a force for healing is still rarely discussed in sex therapy, yet was once considered a sacred healing art in the Goddess cultures. Unfortunately, there is no scientific research describing the curative effects of sexual energy on diseases of the mind and body, but I would like to recount an experience that profoundly and directly focused my awareness on the ability of sexual energy to heal at many levels.

My Story

Having had the dream of the Sacred Marriage during my stay with the Findhorn Community, I returned to my own community in California and continued a life of celibacy for a year. However, I came to understand the meaning of my dream as a message urging me to consciously express my sexuality. I knew that when the conditions were right, I would be open to a sexual relationship. I particularly remembered the incredible sensation of surrender in that dream, but I needed a sense of communion—such as I had felt with the lover in my dream—in order to resume a sex life.

I was aware that I had not had that sense of communion in my marriage. My decision to become celibate had been partly motivated by the experience of living with a compulsive womanizer. My husband had been a typical charismatic leader who used his position of power to gain access to sex partners. Most of the women were insignificant to him, but each time he told me of a new episode, the emotional pain I felt cost me dearly. In fact, my immune system had become so stressed that I developed Crohn's disease, which is an autoimmune bowel disorder with excruciatingly painful symptoms.

I have often asked myself why I tolerated such behavior without leaving. But anyone who experienced the turbulent sexual revolution in the 1970s will remember innumerable examples of experiments with group sex, open marriage, and ménage-à-trois relationships. We actually believed that we had liberated ourselves

from possessive jealousy. Everything that spelled "structure" was suspect—not only monogamy, but all other
establishment values were overthrown in the headlong
race to build a truly New Age.

I had discussed my hurt feelings with my husband,
only to be told that jealousy was an outmoded way of
thinking. It was my problem to fix. I spent a lot of time in
group encounters and bizarre growth experiences during that decade. I was trying to fix my inappropriate jealousy, only to be groped by other charismatic leaders
who were, themselves, trying to use their positions of
power to have sexual access to me! Eventually I got the
message when I acknowledged my body wisdom. All the
nonsense about my jealous feelings being invalid was
really a manipulative ploy. It suited some men to talk
about female jealousy being inappropriate, but when I
took my husband's free-love philosophy seriously, he
could not handle his own jealousy!

After a few attempts at meaningless sexual encounters, I found a man who believed in New Age sexual
freedom and actually had an open marriage. His wife and
I bonded and agreed to a trial four-way marriage. We
had all read The Harrad Experiment, and we were eager
to try group marriage. In the context of a mutual interest in spiritual sex, the other man and I developed a
sense of communion from past-life memories. However,
the experiment in honest and openly shared sexuality
ended with my husband going emotionally off the deep
end. The problem was that I truly enjoyed sex with my
new "husband." It transpired that he was only comfortable with the age-old double standard of patriarchy, and

I wasn't supposed to enjoy other men.

After leaving my marriage, deeply scarred by eight years of emotional upheavals, I thought I might never be sexual again—until my dream led me to a renewed awareness of spiritual sexuality. I met a man who shared my spiritual values and had, himself, been celibate for some time. I had just been released from the hospital following a serious flare-up of Crohn's disease, and weighed less than 80 pounds. I resembled a walking skeleton. This man's attraction to me miraculously transcended my emaciated physical state. We decided to have a sexual relationship.

The incredible joy I felt in the new, loving communion with a kindred soul lifted my depression, which had been caused by physical and emotional pain. We shared a level of sexual energy that led to a direct experience with sexual healing. I remember feeling infused with a powerful, luminous force that soared beyond ordinary sexual satisfaction. During several sexual encounters, I became aware of drawing healing from the universe through the energy centers of my body. I experienced cosmic orgasm, a moment of union with the Life Force, which seemed to vibrate the molecular structure of my cells at a faster rate. At times, I would lose contact with my physical boundaries, and I would move into a suspended state of timeless, boundless fusion with a clear light that I knew to be Divine Love.

This sexual healing had little to do with the personal relationship with my partner. It was beyond personality or particular boundaries. I had learned about spiritual sexuality but had never formally practiced it. I don't think my lover truly understood what was happening, but he recognized my ecstatic state and respected the need to suspend interaction. This allowed the experience of "being in the moment" to last as long as possible. It was the honoring setting I needed in order to heal at all levels of body, mind, and spirit.

When my doctors released me from the hospital, just before I started this relationship, I was to gain some weight and raise my red blood count with iron shots. They needed to see enough improvement to be able to proceed with surgery. My doctors told me that the inflammatory process had gone on too long with too much damage, and they planned a colon resection, or possibly a permanent colostomy. I never did have the surgery. When I returned to my gasteroenterologist one month later, he was astounded at the difference in my physical condition. The change in my appearance was so drastic that he could hardly believe it.

My doctor took me around to each of the other doctors' offices and asked them if they remembered seeing me one month before. He proudly showed office staff and nurses how much I had improved. He asked me what I had been doing, but I never did tell him the true origin of my recovery. It wouldn't have made sense to him anyway. I let him feel good about his prescribed medical regimen and continued my remission for many years.

I did tell trusted friends that I'd had an experience that left me utterly convinced that sexual energy was indeed Divine Life Force. I had felt the electrical current passing through me so clearly that no one could invalidate my extraordinary experience. It was a most compelling direct encounter with universal healing energy, yet it was difficult to find words to describe the moment of boundless, timeless existence in "light/energy." Years later, I was to learn that the Goddess cultures utilized the healing power of sexual energy. Spiritual sexuality to these societies was a way to achieve profound ecstatic states.

My miraculous recovery led me to a new phase of accomplishing goals that were long overdue. I enrolled in a clinical psychology doctoral program, and as part of my graduate program, I found ways to make sense of my experience. I was able to put clinical words to my healing in a research paper. I studied the visualization techniques that were new at that time, used with serious immune-system disturbances. I worked with different mind-body techniques such as autonomic training, biofeedback, relaxation, guided imagery, and other alternative techniques available. However, I could not find references to the use of spiritual sexuality for healing. I did not realize then that it would ultimately lead me to become a sex therapist.

My path led me to a little-known center, the only one in San Diego working with sex surrogates. Most sex-therapy techniques used at that time centered on the Masters and Johnson behavioral model of working with couples. Treatment of sexual dysfunction before their Human Sexual Inadequacy book was published in 1970, typically consisted of long-term verbal psychotherapy. The Masters and Johnson model of sex therapy focused on learning the mechanics of sexual functioning and developing communication skills to express sexual needs. Such skills still comprise the basic framework of sex therapy.

I became so fascinated with Surrogate Partner Therapy that I based my doctoral dissertation on the women involved in it. The concept of therapeutic sex was controversial, but Masters and Johnson had published statistics indicating very successful results working with surrogate partners and men who did not have mates. I knew intuitively that they practiced sexual healing, and have since realized that Surrogate Partner Therapy provides clues to the practices of temple priestesses in ancient Goddess cultures.

Hierodules: The Sacred Virgins

The ancient *hierodules,* or sacred virgins, were referred to as "temple prostitutes" in the scholarly writings of those who first read the Sumerian tablets. The Latin word *prostitute* literally means "he who stands before," and meant one who sells something. Their choice of terminology reflected the prejudices of their patriarchal upbringing, as the sacred virgins of the temples did not sell sexual favors. The conservative researchers who read about sex in holy places were horrified by the images this evoked. Sex had been totally separated from spirituality for centuries, and priestesses engaging in sexual healing outside the bonds of marriage was a morally inconceivable concept.

The *hierodules* were really priestesses of the Goddess, having been disciplined in spiritual training for many years. Their sexuality was used as a direct instrument for channeling the Life

Force. Sexual union with partners transformed the regenerative powers of the Great Goddess into healing the body-mind-spirit. What we know about the sexual healing practices of temples can be inferred from references to them in the Sumerian tablets recovered from archaeological sites at cities such as Uruk. These cultures believed that the Goddess was present in the temple, and the priestesses were direct links to Her.

Surrogate Partner Therapy resurrects this aspect of their holy work. The ancients understood that sexual energy was a never-ending cycle of giving and receiving. The following section is based on my experiences with some of the most compassionate healers I have met.

Surrogate Partners

The origins of surrogate partner therapy began with the research of Masters and Johnson. The idea was attractive to sex therapists who had been reading about Masters and Johnson's successful outcomes with this treatment. Surrogates were trained in conventional sex therapy and relaxation techniques and communication skills, as well as the medical aspects of sexual dysfunction.

The stereotype of the gorgeous temptress who teaches the mechanics of sexual performance, or pleasures the client to heights of sexual ecstasy could not be further from the truth, yet many people have watched slick, pornographic films portraying this image of sex surrogates and even female sex therapists. One of the key issues in the initial session, when the client and surrogate partner meet, is the surrogate partner never seeming to fit the "perfect 10" ideal the client had in mind. Surrogate partner therapy challenges the notion that the success of sex is dependent on the woman's physical attributes or techniques. Many men assume that they need the right female packaging to function sexually. The client's experiences with surrogate partners, most of whom are Crone women, refocus his attitudes about sexual functioning away from this notion and onto his own process.

Adele

Adele was a Crone woman when she started surrogate partner training. I interviewed her for my dissertation because she provided an outstanding example of successful surrogate partner therapy. She was one of the most courageous and energetic women I had ever met. She described her work with sexually dysfunctional men with great enthusiasm. Her particular emphasis was sensual touch, and she subsequently published an excellent handbook about touching for pleasure. It was clear that she believed in the power of sex to heal. One of her favorite exercises with her clients was the mirror exercise.

Adele would routinely do the mirror exercise after a couple of private sessions in which she would establish trust and help the client get comfortable with her. Exercises such as hand caress or face caress were practiced to develop a comfort with safe, pleasurable touch. The mirror exercise consisted of standing nude with the client in front of a well-lit, full-length mirror. First, she described her own feelings about her body. Then it was the client's turn. She invited them to discover, as if for the very first time, the shapes and textures of their bodies. They were asked to talk candidly, without self-criticism, about what they saw. When they were aware of negative thoughts, they were reminded to recognize them and set their judgments aside. Adele would say, "Just notice your thoughts, and stay aware of feelings without investing in them." Usually her clients' awkwardness about feeling exposed and talking about their bodies would neutralize the social posturing that occurs in dating situations. The honesty that began to develop paved the way for practicing healthy communication skills, a central part of the treatment.

The unique aspect of Adele's work was the population she specialized in treating. Adele was a miracle worker with disabled men. Contemplating mirror exercises done with male paraplegics, limb amputees, multiple sclerosis sufferers, and so on, gave new meaning to the significance of this exercise. Adele had the capacity to give these people unconditional acceptance, and her compassion combined with a no-nonsense approach to the realities of their situations made her healing extremely effective.

She and her client reached a deeper level of emotional connection. Adele was never patronizing to these men, nor did she treat their limitations as invisible. She focused straight at the core of their issues of self-esteem and was tremendously compassionate and supportive. Her willingness to touch and be touched by them allowed them to develop an acceptance of their sexuality. Most single men in these situations only had a small chance to find mates because they had no confidence in their ability to function sexually.

With the surrogate partner therapy, they were able

to face their limitations and practice alternative methods of sexual expression, adapted to their bodies. Adele's nurturing ways and empowered sexuality gave them confidence in their ability to please women. Her presence and ability to bring their attention to the quality of the relationship taught them more than sexual functioning. They learned to operate in the context of a relationship. Often their lives were turned around.

Adele is an excellent example of a sexually empowered Crone woman practicing sexual mastery. The story illustrates the holy work of sexual healing as it was done in the ancient temples of the Goddess. Most of surrogate partner therapy develops communion with the partner, teaches expressing vulnerable feelings, deals with shame, and establishes appropriate conditions for sexual readiness in order to surrender to sensations of desire. This is essentially a feminine approach to sexuality.

Making Sense of Your Personal Story: Part III

1. As a young girl between the ages of 9 to 12, what was your dream for your future (something you wanted to be, do, or have)? How much of that dream have you fulfilled? What do you still need to do?

2. What does your body wisdom tell you that you must do for your health and sexuality? What rituals, meditations, or other practices help you receive guidance? What could you do to develop them?

PART III:

THE POWER
OF THE
FEMININE WAY

Chapter Eight

Making Sense of Your Personal Story

A s you work on making sense of the patterns in your life, you can build on the strengths of what you have already accomplished and also look at areas that need healing. You may find that you have many positive influences with regard to your sexuality. Your personal story should not reveal anything radically different from what you already sense about yourself. This chapter will organize this information better, focus your understanding of it, and give you some direction about what to do once you are able to see it clearly for yourself.

There are seven basic areas with regard to your sexuality:

1. Issues of mistrust and sex-negative messages

2. Wounds from primary attachments

3. Self-esteem and control

4. Distortions of compassion

5. Fear of self-disclosure

6. Perceptions blocking your vision

7. Inspiration and guidance

These areas correspond to each of the seven domains of the seven chakras, or energy centers, of the body. If you are not familiar with the concept of chakras, using the seven areas is still an excellent way to organize your understanding of the influences on your sexuality.

CROWN: 7th chakra
Illumination
Guidance

THIRD-EYE: 6th chakra
Perception
Visualization

THROAT: 5th chakra
Communication
Self-disclosure

HEART: 4th chakra
Compassion
Divine healing

SOLAR PLEXUS: 3rd chakra
Self-esteem
Personal power
Control

SEXUAL/SACRAL: 2nd chakra
Attachment
Desires

ROOT: 1st chakra
Security
Survival
Trust

Early Sexual Exploration and Sex-Negative Messages: First and Second Chakras

How old were you when you first experienced sexual feelings? How did you feel about acting on them? Who told you the truth about sex?

We all have some degree of guilt or shame associated with our developing sexuality. Shame and guilt are socially motivated emotions, intentionally evoked by caregivers to prevent acting inappropriately. For example, Gina was told *ad nauseam* by her mother, "Boys only want one thing," and "Don't let any boy touch you." This instilled fear of exploring sex as a teen. Her parents used fear as a way to prevent her from devaluing her virginal status. She had not been able to eliminate fear-based sexual prohibitions and enjoy her husband's touch after marriage.

Sherry constantly heard her father say, "Why buy the cow if you can get the milk for free?" She often felt degraded after intercourse, even with her husband. Those of you reading this may have had parents who talked in platitudes about sex, as in: "Save it for the one you marry." Or, you may recall, "They didn't tell me anything." In either of these situations, you have automatic thoughts and uncomfortable feelings to overcome.

Messages about self-stimulation follow the same pattern in households where the parents were uncomfortable with sexuality. You may have been caught masturbating and associate shame with wanting to pleasure yourself. These feelings continue to operate in your subconscious as powerful blocks to sexual desire. Shame and guilt may have dissuaded you from sexual activity, but they may also indicate sources of taboo sexual fantasies. These forbidden images may still arouse your most intense, sexual feelings. In chapter 9, we will explore fantasies and self-stimulation.

Identifying people who told you the truth about sex helps you understand the source of positive attitudes. One woman's source was an older cousin who was about to be married. Her cousin told her, "It's real fun with the right guy." That encouragement allowed her to explore sexual pleasure with her steady boyfriend in high school. Her adjustment to marital sex was enhanced by this exploration. Much traditional sex therapy provides the counterbalancing voice of the therapist as a source of permission to explore sexual pleasure. Whatever the sources of information, they have made a significant difference in your developing sexuality and your attitudes about relationships between men and women.

First Blood Experiences—Self-Esteem and Body Image: Third Chakra

What were your experiences surrounding your first menstruation?

The way your first blood experience was handled strongly influences your sexual self-image, yet many women do not realize it. Recently, I attended a women's full-moon ceremony in my community. We gathered in a circle and recounted our first blood stories. Most of us related some tale of embarrassment or humiliation from which we had learned shame or loathing for our natural body processes. However, some of the stories were truly enlightening because they were so different. The women told of special celebrations honoring their new Maiden status, conducted by a beloved female relative. The women's stories about positive support and festive events gave us great inspiration and a goal for the future. The stories inspired many of the women to seek ways to initiate their own daughters in the spirit of the ancient, feminine way.

First Intercourse—Personal Power and Self-Esteem:
Second and Third Chakras

What was your experience with first intercourse?

First intercourse is a major rite of initiation. In our culture, it is usually not very satisfying for women. When women recall their first intercourse, their answers fall into three categories. One group says that it was painful or disappointing. They report thoughts such as, "Is that all there is?" or they tell me, "It got better after a while," or "It didn't hurt as much over time," but their first intercourse was a negative experience. Some of these women may even say, "I hated it and still find it uncomfortable."

Another group of women respond with, I don't really remember what I felt," or "I guess it was okay." This group has blocked out memories of the first defining moment of male-female genital sex, and they are unaware of any issues stemming from it. The third group says many things about their first intercourse. They say they desired the experience or looked forward to it. Even if it was awkward, they had many opportunities to repeat pleasurable exploration with their lovers, enhancing their sexual responsiveness. They talk about the conditions that made their first experiences positive. Rarely do I hear, "I loved penetration the first time," but women of this group fondly recall their first love relationship, which included intercourse, and are likely to feel the most empowered about their sexuality.

Loss of Basic Trust and Security: First Chakra

Did anyone abuse or abandon you? How did you react to the experience?

If you have been neglected, physically harmed, or sexually abused by a parent, relative, or trusted adult, you have been deeply wounded. You may find intimate relationships threatening. Your early care taught you that caregivers failed to meet your needs, or they actually hurt you. They may have failed to attend to your cries, neglected your needs for nourishment and cleanliness, and damaged your sense of security. Your experiences with negative touch determine your ability to tolerate and express physical affection, the foundation for healthy sex. You may *function* sexually, but block feelings of intimacy. Such barriers to intimacy erode your sexual desire in a long-term relationship.

Many people assume that these early experiences have no bearing on their current sexual relationships. For example, you may think that you were no more disadvantaged than others, that physical abuse was just strict discipline, or that you adapted to the neglect. In my experience, most people downplay their neglect and abuse until they are confronted with circumstances that tap into their buried feelings. Many learn not to trust, which creates the desire to control loved ones, due to such early rifts in primary attachments. A supportive, therapeutic environment is necessary to deal with the issues associated with physical and sexual abuse.

Attachment—Early Wounds in the Affectional Bond: Second Chakra

What losses or rejection from loved ones did you suffer in your life? How have you coped, and what resources have you discovered?

You may have sustained a loss, disappointment, or heartache as a child that raises anxiety when you have attachment feelings. *Attachment* refers to the sense of connection and closeness that we all need from the primary caregivers in our lives. This relationship is called "the affectional bond" because we learn to express and receive affection, which impacts us throughout our lives. The early mother-infant bond is the basis for the ability to form attachments throughout life. Our mothers, or other family members who provided nurturing, are the initial "significant others" to whom we attach. If we are separated, it causes serious issues in our psychological development.

Primary relationships teach us whether our needs for attention will be met or not. Holding, visual attention, and nurturing touch are all part of our attachment needs. If your mother was distant or unavailable, you may have experienced significant anxiety as a child, producing a need to control loved ones as an adult. On the positive side, you may have had a good foundation of loving, nurturing parents. This has probably resulted in a reasonably secure childhood that gave you tremendous insurance for the slings and arrows of later life. Any losses in adult relationships may have been painful, yet the foundation of good experiences with early nurturing may have mitigated the devastation.

There are at least three significant attachment losses in the childhood through teen years that impact sexuality: loss of a parent through death or divorce, and loss of adequate parenting. Some of you may have had alcoholic, drug-addicted, mentally unstable, severely depressed, cold, distant, seductive, or emotionally abusive parents. All of these problem parents have one element in common: They could not or would not provide adequate, emotional nurturing for you as a child.[1] Your parents may have been emotionally cruel, withholding affection, but quick to deliver critical messages. This deprived you of the chance to build healthy self-esteem.

Two additional losses in teen years affect adult sexuality: the betrayal or loss of a cherished friend, and your first "broken heart" in adolescence. These are critical to developing sexuality because they teach either valuable skills for negotiating and ending relationships, or ways to detach from attachment needs in order to numb the pain.

The losses, tragedies, and challenges of your life may have taught you much about how to cope. Take stock of all the lessons that strengthened your ability to face life's adversities with courage, and consolidate your knowledge of resources you have internalized. There are times you challenged yourself to grow by confronting your circumstances, overcoming depression, anxiety, grief, despair, and loss of faith. Please make a list to which you can continue adding. This inventory will inspire you to continue facing adversity.

Co-dependence and Control: Third Chakra

Right now, if your partner asked you to do something you didn't want to do, could you say no?

When there are attachment problems from your early life, you may feel the need to control others, whether directly or through subtle manipulation. *Co-dependence* is centering your attention on *the other*. It is the illusion that you can somehow fix your partner's problems, control unwanted behavior, or get to him to change. Many women, as well as men, hold tenaciously to such illusions, which are permanently doomed to failure. Such behavior inhibits sexual self-expression and blunts sexual desire. Co-dependent women accommodate their partners' desires and bypass lack of sexual feelings to engage in sex, simply to please. Bypassing feelings to accommodate your partner erodes your sexual responsiveness.

This question directly targets your ability to stay individuated in your relationship. Acting in your own best interests is the opposite of co-dependence. Listening to your Guardian includes validating your body wisdom. You can refuse your partner's request when it is not in your best interests, and soothe your anxiety about his reaction. If you were totally honest in your answer to this question and you find it hard to say no, you need to strengthen your boundaries. If you practice the "My Secret Garden" exercise faithfully, you will begin to set limits on unwanted behavior and act in your own best interests more often.

Self-Esteem and Personal Power: Third Chakra

Who represented a Woman of Power in your life? How did she influence you?

We have been looking at what presented problems in your life. Now you can examine inspirational feminine role models who may have contributed to your self-esteem. Each of us has heard of women of power. You know them. They are women who radiate a sense of potent inner life, which manifests in their energy and determination. They may have been leaders where you grew up or lived as a young woman. Your role models may even have been nationally or internationally known.

Such women did not need material wealth to exude feminine power, yet they were a force to be reckoned with, wherever they chose to focus their energy. Some are quiet forces for good in helping those with difficult struggles. These women understood what was required to foster self-esteem, and they were unstinting in their values. They are the ones who used their gifts of intuition or acted on their convictions. Some women of power operate in the public sector. You may have read about them or listened to them speak. In any walk of life, these women were empowered by their inner light and offered guidance to others, perhaps even to *you*. These women, through their courage, intelligence, and achievements, added significantly to your sense of personal power.

Distortions of Compassion: Fourth Chakra

What do you need in your relationship with a partner? Can you imagine being able to have these qualities in your life?

If you get involved, perhaps repeatedly, with men who are abusive, rage at you with explosive anger, or are cold and distant, you may think that your love will save them from their withdrawn or violent behavior. However, you are distorting your compassionate, heartfelt love by enabling such relationships to continue. Compassion sustains satisfying sex with a long-term partner only when it is experienced as reciprocal. Without reciprocal compassion in a committed relationship, you will have a wellspring of resentment.

If you deny your resentment in order to appear to be a loving and giving partner, you will be like an empty vessel, having poured out all your caring with nothing left to give. Such distortion of your natural nurturing and compassion damages female sexual desire because it results in sexual accommodation, without any genuine sexual energy.

The classic statement, "I don't really need to have orgasms; I just want to know that he's enjoying it," or some other variation of that theme, is a distortion of compassion and a loss for both partners. If you have isolated the sexual part of yourself from your "good girl," loving self-image, you may be unable to access genuine desire. You may feel helpless because you cannot respond to your chosen mate. If you are unable to integrate sexy behavior with your wife-and-mother image, you may have internalized a distorted view of compassion and disowned your sexuality.

Developing Compassion: Fourth Chakra

If you have not had children, how have you expressed nurturing compassion for others?

You can assess your current integration of Mother compassion, without having children, by identifying the things you have done to foster your nurturing skills. Early role models of nurturing and compassion may have influenced your own development of these qualities. In your relationships, you may have gone from the feeling of "this one is mine," to loving communion.

Sexually, you may be expressing the Mother domain by generating Divine Love from the heart as a source of sexual healing for you and your partner. You may have experienced the shift from personal attachment desire into selfless love for another, facilitated through your compassionate acceptance of your partner as a gift of the Divine.

Self-Disclosure—Telling the Truth: Fifth Chakra

Can you truthfully communicate what you want to your partner? Which feelings remain undisclosed?

The ultimate goal of communication is telling the truth about yourself. Self-disclosure is difficult because it is hard to be honest with yourself if you feel considerable shame. It is also hard to tell your partner the truth about your most vulnerable feelings. One of my patients expressed fears about being honest with her partner. She wrote, "Why am I afraid to tell you who I am? I'm afraid that if I tell you, you may not like me, and that's all I have." Thus, the desire to tell the truth competes with the very real fear that if you show your true colors, you will be rejected. As you work with the skills in chapters 10 and 11, notice how often fear emerges when you practice self-disclosure.

If you remain aware of what makes you avoid saying what you feel or want, you develop the capacity to relate more of your vulnerable feelings. Your goal should be to communicate deeper truths about yourself outside your comfort zone. You can be truly *known* once you have faced the fear responsible for your discomfort. Your ability to tell the truth about yourself deepens your capacity for intimacy and intensifies sexual desire.

Perceptions Blocking Your Vision: Sixth Chakra

As a young girl between 9 and 12 years old, what was your dream for your future? How much of that dream have you fulfilled? What do you still need to do?

The dreams you had between the ages of 9 and 12 are strongest because your idealism about your creative potential had not yet been overwhelmed by the cultural mandates to "be a girl." You may have negative self-perceptions from feeling disillusioned or inadequate because you have not achieved your ideal goals. When you've lived up to your potential, you have a positive view of yourself. Most of us fall somewhere in the middle. During stressful times, we tend to block achievement by holding damaging self-perceptions. If you think your work is unfulfilling, you can still pick up the threads of dreams you had as a girl.

Women who hold dreams of their own, independent from having families, do not have the "empty nest" syndrome. You may have started on your personal path by returning to school or finding meaningful work outside the home. You may be feeling a new sense of identity from developing your creativity, unrelated to being a caregiver. If you've felt some measure of success, you may have paused in your career path in order to be a mother. You may also have continued your career after having had children. All these choices are excellent if you've felt fulfilled.

In order to start realizing your dream, refer to "Creating Your Vision" in the following chapter. Sexual energy released from the sixth chakra is an ancient source of shaping reality with extraordinary results. You can visualize a desired goal with the powerful release of orgasm.

Inspiration and Vision: Seventh Chakra

What does your body wisdom tell you that you must do for your health and sexuality?

You can ask your body wisdom for guidance about health and sexual needs throughout your life. Once you listen to your body and ask questions of your own inner healer, you can take appropriate action. Sexual desire, like good health, is ultimately a matter of balancing all the body systems, including your psyche. When you pay attention to your sexual needs, you are tuning in to the energy of Life Force.

The current trend of women taking testosterone or even Viagra to shore up their sexual desire is quite disturbing. In the new millennium, we must reverse the trend of endlessly taking pills or seeking surgical solutions and ask ourselves *first,* "What is out of balance?" The Guardian is an excellent source of information. How often have we heard someone say, "I know I should stop smoking, but . . ." or, "I'm not getting enough exercise, but I just don't have the time"? Listen to your inner voice—really *listen.* Then take action. This has great value for enhancing your will.

Much of our behavior overrides the voice that tells us what we need to do for ourselves to experience greater sexual pleasure. If you work on optimizing your own sexual expression, sex with a partner becomes increasingly pleasurable.

Opening to Guidance: Seventh Chakra

What rituals, meditations, or other practices help you receive guidance? What could you do to develop them?

Please consider developing conscious rituals and meditation techniques that allow you to be open to guidance. Create your unique ritual, knowing you are enacting the ageless mystery of the feminine way. In developing your own rituals, you will need to gather items that are important to you. Rituals need to be personalized, infused with your own creativity. You can borrow from ancient rituals, such as honoring the four directions of the Native American Medicine Wheel. The Wicca tradition uses rhythmic poetry and movement. You may want to work with the ancient feminine magic of glamour, or Eastern practices of meditation and chanting. Some additional suggestions are offered in the section on "Creating Your Vision" in the next chapter.

There is another form of ritual, useful for clearing your automatic thoughts and perceptions so that you become open to guidance. It utilizes the cleansing properties of fire. Write down your unwanted habits, feelings, fears, and old wounds. Then burn the paper in a specially prepared fire, in a safe container such as an abalone shell. Put a lot of thought into what you intend to eliminate from your life.

The seventh energy center is the source of transcendental sexual experiences. The sense of merging with cosmic energy without physical boundaries at the moment of orgasm is often described as "being in the moment of boundless bliss." Ancient and modern visionary experiences describe feelings of being "bathed in pure light." It is cosmic orgasm, the direct experience of the self as pure energy.

Chapter Nine

Healing and Enhancing Your Sexuality

You *can* heal the problems from your past experiences and relinquish their influence on your sexuality. Patients tell me, "I really want to feel desire. I don't know why it's not working." Sometimes it is necessary first to eliminate thoughts and beliefs, preventing you from surrendering to sexual desire. Negative thoughts can arouse disgust, aversion, and even fear. These emotions can hinder otherwise pleasurable feelings. Such emotions block the effects of physical arousal even when the conscious mind tells us it *should* be time for sex.

You must also engage your will in the conscious decision to reclaim your genuine desire. Just the fact that you are reading this book probably means that you have come to value yourself and are choosing to enhance your sexuality. To engage your will, you must go beyond examination of thoughts and emotional reactions, and challenge distorted beliefs that block the ability to focus on your goals. Methods such as guided imagery, conscious visualization, lucid dreaming, and affirmations communicate with the subconscious.

The following processes draw on many disciplines and traditions: psychodynamic theory, cognitive-behavioral techniques, Jungian imagery, Shamanic methods of focusing awareness, meditation techniques, body therapy concepts of energy, Ayurvedic principles, and anything else I have found helpful. The guided imagery can be read onto an audiocassette and listened to as often as you like.

To begin with, the following process is intended to strengthen your core sense of self and help define your personal boundaries.

My Secret Garden:
Guided Imagery

Find a place where you will be undisturbed and comfortable for about 20 minutes. Begin by breathing deeply as you move mentally through your body, relaxing your head, neck, torso, arms, and legs. As you gradually begin to relax, close your eyes and take deep breaths of fresh air, feeling the pure air cleansing your system of all stress. You will feel very peaceful and relaxed.

Imagine walking along a lovely outdoor path, leading you into a garden. It is your garden and very special to you. Imagine the path, whether made of stones, gravel, wood chips, or simply tamped earth. Envision all the natural surroundings leading up to your secret garden as vividly as possible. As you approach your garden, notice if there is a fence or wall around it. Visualize the structure, and imagine how it is constructed. It may be made of wood, brick, concrete, or carefully clipped hedges, making a boundary between the surrounding area and your garden. Also imagine the entrance to your garden. Is it a gate that swings wide open and closes automatically, or is it a barrier that needs to be pushed open or removed in order for you to walk inside? As you imagine yourself walking inside your secret garden, notice how you feel. Can you see the surrounding area from inside, or is the wall so high that you feel totally enclosed?

Inside your garden, notice all the wonderful plants and trees. Imagine any swings, benches, or other ornamentation that comes to mind. Imagine yourself tending to your garden. This is your own special place, and you may make changes in your garden in any way you like, anytime you wish. Perhaps there are weeds to be pulled, or there is overgrowth that needs to be cut back. Imagine planting things, or simply enjoying the wonderful sights—the colors of flowers; the bright shades of green; and the cool, brown earth. Notice the wonderful smells of flowers and plants. Enjoy the sounds of the wind, or the calls of animals or birds that may be part of your garden. All your senses are alive in this special place.

As you spend time in your garden, you may decide to build a different fence or any other kind of boundary to partition the outside world from your own space. Take a moment to imagine what you would like to add to or eliminate from your garden. Your images will change over time, and you will always be able to choose what you want to do with this special place. Now, take a moment to say good-bye to this place that is yours alone. Then imagine yourself leaving by the entrance and walking down the same lovely path. As you move away from your garden, notice how you feel right now. Slowly bring your consciousness back into the room, and feel your body supported by the floor, chair, or mattress. When you are ready, open your eyes.

Creating Your Vision

In order to create lasting change, you must direct your will toward your goals. Having a vision of where you would like to be is the best way to provide motivation. The following are some ways to build a vision and manifest steps along the path:

— Treasure mapping is a wonderful way to begin to visualize what you really want. It consists of tearing pictures out of magazines and pasting them onto a large piece of cardboard. The pictures represent aspects of what you would like to manifest in your life. You do not have to think a lot about this because it is best to let your right brain have free rein. You could also use drawings, clay figures, or any other artistic medium. Some pictures can depict feelings you would like to experience, such as joy, success, tenderness, or hope. After you begin to get a sense of what you want from your life, you can set goals to move toward your vision.

— You also might try developing a mission statement for your life. Author Laurie Beth Jones suggests a useful process in The Path.[1] Think of one of the four elements: fire, earth, air, or water. Which one would you identify with? For example, I found that I identified with two elements—fire and water are equally represented in my being. Write down some adjectives applying to the one or two elements you have chosen. Put the words "I am" in front of each of these adjectives and see how they fit. If you have difficulty finding adjectives for an element, you might use ideas from attributes associated with the four directions of the Native American Medicine Wheel. Many traditions describe specific animals and qualities that go with the four elements. Also, refer to the book Woman at the Edge of Two Worlds, by Lynn Andrews, for a wonderful description of these attributes as they apply to women.[2] All this symbology may help you see patterns and a cluster of meaningful characteristics in your personality.

Laurie Beth Jones states that your mission statement ideally consists of one or two succinct sentences that could be understood by a young person of about 12. The statement should be a summary of your purpose in life. As you are writing your mission statement, you may find yourself struggling with a sense that what you are saying may be too grand. For example, I wrote: "My commitment is to contribute to the healing of the planet by promoting healthy relationships and self-love." I had trouble at first seeing myself in such a lofty role, but I encourage you to write what is really in your heart. You have your own unique purpose, and it is your gift to everyone.

Calling in the Goddess

This is a process that allows you to experience and acknowledge the Goddess within. Begin by creating a safe space for yourself where you can be alone without distractions. You may decorate the space with crystals or other objects that are special to you in order to remind you that this space is now your sacred place. You will need to be upright for this exercise, so you may want to put down a special blanket or pillow to sit on.

Practice breathing from your diaphragm by placing your hands at your sides, under the bottom ribs. Feel yourself pushing your hands away from your ribs as you breathe deeply. Now, experiment with making primal sounds. Chanting aligns you with the pure sound of harmony with the Source. The most effective sounds are those that end with vowels. Use open sounds such as They, Aah, Ho, Hey, Oh, or Yah. Find a rhythm that appeals to you and a tonal note that is pleasing to your ears. Spend some time playing with your own chant. If you choose, add a drumming rhythm with your hands or an instrument you enjoy.

Imagine the Mother/Goddess as an image, a presence, or any way you can perceive Her, in harmony with your personal beliefs. You are allowing new awareness to build. As you continue to offer your song to the Divine within and all around you, imagine the Goddess being charmed by your rhythm, dancing on the waves of sound. If you feel moved, begin to dance with Her, moving in the beautiful rhythm of life. Whatever your body chooses to do, let it happen. Notice if there is new energy taking you with it. Enjoy the playful movement, sound, and rhythms you create.

As you feel energy building, imagine that you can project creative, playful, loving energy out and around you. Send out your energy with each deep exhalation and primal sound. Practice sending love to all that brings you such pleasure. Express your own sacredness through movement as you feel the inspiration of Spirit. Allow loving awareness to transform you as you complete your time with the Goddess. When you're ready, return your body to the ground or floor. Allow yourself a moment of relaxation, lying still and inhaling the wonderful magnetic field you have created. Allow it to feed your body and soul as you relax and breathe it in. When you feel complete, go through your daily activities with the rhythm continuing to pulsate inside you.

Thought-Stopping

Critical thoughts and judgments are powerful blocks to new experience. Most of us have strong, internalized judgments that form the critical messages and dire warnings we hear from within. Understanding that some judgments originate from internalized sex-negative conditioning may help you overcome them. Your judgments and core beliefs operate as gatekeepers to change, and you can eliminate them.

Several methods of thought-stopping are used extensively in psychotherapy to eliminate the negative thoughts that are toxic to your system and block your ability to grow. A short version of the technique follows. It may be your most important tool in pulling yourself out of a downward spiral of sinking feelings. Both depression and anxiety increase when automatic, unbidden thoughts go through your mind repeatedly.

First, concentrate on what you're thinking when you're feeling sad or anxious. When you listen to yourself, you may hear the voice of "reality" warning you about some dreaded consequence if you do or neglect to do something. Such thoughts may sound like criticism, calling you stupid, or telling you something awful about yourself. Write down these automatic thoughts, especially the ones that are negative self-statements. Most of the time we are unaware of automatic thoughts. The more you pay attention, the more you begin to see repetitive patterns.

The second step is to choose a destructive visual image. Imagine your visual image destroying your negative self-statements. Don't worry. You will be destroying your automatic thoughts, not people or things. It is never wise to send negative energy to others; you would only be creating harm for yourself. You can gleefully destroy your own thoughts with no ill effects whatsoever. You may want to see your thoughts in a picture, as characters, or words on a screen. Your image must be vivid enough to see the thoughts being destroyed.

Some of the visual images people choose are explosives, crashing waves, blasting shotguns, napalm, lightning, and for the computer-literate, DELETE. Whatever image you choose, keep using the same one, because it will become familiar to you. Do not choose something that alarms you, but keep in mind that this is your destructive force, so there is no harm to you. I have used lightning, which used to scare me as a child. Now, I love the power it represents because it is my lightning.

The third step is to replace the negative thoughts with a positive affirmation. An affirmation is a positive statement about yourself stated in the present tense. For example, "I am completely comfortable with my sexuality," is something you would like to be true, but is yet to become reality. Once you choose an affirmation, use the same one repeatedly until your feel it is automatic, similar to a mantra, which means "sacred sound." Repeat the same short affirmation for about a minute as a way to "jam the radio frequency" and prevent the negative thoughts from returning. Once the negative thoughts stop for a while, they may come back. Just repeat the whole process over again.

A list of affirmations specific to women's sexual issues follows. They are useful in developing your sense of sexual empowerment.

Sexual Affirmations

Affirmations work as vitamins for the soul. When you repeat a consciously chosen phrase over and over, your subconscious begins to believe the truth of that statement. Repeating affirmations can help you make significant progress in releasing negative conditioning and acting in new ways. Sexual self-esteem can never come from your partner. Partner validation must be seen as the icing on the cake

Find a time each morning—in bed before you get up, or while you're preparing for the day—to repeat your chosen affirmation for about five minutes. You may decide to say it in front of a mirror. Pick just one affirmation that really warms your heart. You do not have to believe it to be true in the present, but you are going to affirm its truth. Each day for at least one month, starting at the beginning of a lunar cycle (the new moon), repeat your affirmation over and over to yourself. Add it to any personal ritual that feels good.

Each night before you drift off to sleep, repeat your affirmation for several minutes. Morning and evening affirmation exercises do not take much time, but they stimulate the psyche toward healing. You may find yourself risking new behavior, reading helpful books, taking a class, or getting into therapy. All these are actions put into motion through the positive message you have chosen. Select one of the following affirmations, or make up one for yourself. Just remember that it must be stated in the present tense, eliminating any negative expression such as "I am not a failure." By stating a negative affirmation, the subconscious will hear "failure" and attract more of *that* to you. Also, only use one affirmation so that you do not overwhelm your subconscious with too many messages at one time.

I am highly pleasing to myself.
I am learning to love myself more every day.
The more I love myself, the more others love me.
It is more important for me to please myself than to
    please others.
I am responsible for my sexual self-esteem.
I deserve sexual pleasure.
I accept and acknowledge my individual preferences for
    sexual pleasure.
I feel free to ask my partner to satisfy my individual sexual
    needs.
It is healthy for me to ask for what I want during
    lovemaking.
It is right and perfect for me to have a partner who totally
    pleasures me.
I am a Sex Goddess.

I am a glorious, magnetic, sexual being.
I am one with the MOTHER/GODDESS.

Responding, Rather Than Reacting, to Emotions

You can use your imagination to locate a place in your body where you are feeling strong reactive emotions, then replace those feelings with a calming image. By using this technique, you give yourself time to respond appropriately to a situation. *Reacting* to emotions means behaving impulsively, in emotionally repetitive ways. Reacting defensively in predictable patterns generally culminates in negative results. Initial "gut" feelings to a particular trigger cannot be prevented. However, you can calm your urge to act until you have had time to consider whether what you want to say or do will be in your best interests. Typically, reactive behavior leads to a more destructive outcome than simply reflecting about things, tuning in to your body wisdom, and then responding from a calmer perspective.

When you are aware of a physical feeling in your body, such as a "knot," "butterflies," or an emotion such as sadness or anxiety, you can tune in to your body and identify which part is experiencing the sensation. Give the feeling a shape and a color. As you locate and identify it, you may give it some motion, such as a spinning spiral or a bouncing ball. Create the corresponding shape and opposite color, and allow the new image to cover and calm the original image of your negative emotion. Once you feel the grip of the negative emotion loosening, begin to reflect on what you would like to do or say about the situation. If you feel you can really let the feelings go, make sure you are not simply avoiding conflict. But first, write a letter clarifying your thoughts and feelings, and do not give this letter to anyone. Use it to help clarify your position. When you feel calm and mentally clear, you may choose to talk to someone about it, using the communication skills discussed in the next chapter.

The Mirror Exercise

You will need privacy for this process, especially because it is done in the nude. It may be difficult to be completely nude to begin with, so you may want to put on a silky robe, shift, or wrap. Do not wear an ordinary terry-cloth robe or any other bulky clothing.

Stand in front of a full-length mirror and look carefully at yourself. Set aside the automatic critical thoughts that surface, and concentrate on simply examining what your wonderful face tells you about the life you have lived. Look at yourself with the most compassionate love you can imagine, and find some things you like about the curves and planes, the colors and textures, starting with your head, neck, and hair. Notice the softness of your hair as you touch it, and breathe in its fragrance.

Move gently down your body, noticing your wonderful skin, the most extensive organ of pleasure. See how your breasts curve and swell. Appreciate the beauty of your upper body, the arms that have held others, the hands that have given so much. Lovingly caress the skin over on your upper body, and honor all that you are.

Now move your eyes down to your navel, the place of connection to your mother, and your lifeline as a babe in the womb. Place your hand gently over your belly, that wonderful swell, so uniquely feminine. Notice how your hips curve to make room for your fullness. Move down to your thighs and legs, and notice how strong they are, having supported you through many miles of life. These legs have taken you on your path and have served you well. Finally, turn slightly so you can see your back and buttocks. Lovingly appreciate the strength and support they have given you. Notice when critical thoughts surface, and set them aside. Forgive yourself the inconsistencies of your body, the too thin/too fat judgments we all make.

As you look at your yoni, know that you are a perfect daughter of the Goddess and that your form is a miracle of nature. You are the creative energy of the universe. Take in your whole body, and see its exquisite magnetic sensuality. As a woman in any form, you are the manifestation of the life force. Simply love it.

The Yoni Exercise

Most women are still very uncomfortable looking at themselves candidly in the mirror. It may be especially difficult to examine your yoni with all the cultural inhibitions you have internalized. If you have been sexually abused, be sure to talk to a therapist before engaging in this process. If you decide to proceed, be sure to make an appointment with a therapist afterward.

Begin this process with a satisfying bathing ritual. Perhaps you love to relax in your spa or soak in bath salts that are safe for your vagina. The reason for doing this is preparation and relaxation; it's not because you are unclean in any way.

After you're completely relaxed, anoint yourself with any lotion or oil that is pleasant and non-irritating to your body. Never use any lotion inside your vagina. Enjoy the feel of your skin as you caress yourself. If you choose, light candles in a room where you have a full-length mirror. You could also play tapes of soothing, sensual musical sounds. You should sit on a towel or soft cloth, or you can sit on a stool or chair. You will need to position yourself to be able to see your yoni in the mirror, so make sure your body is in a comfortable, relaxed position that enables you truly to admire your beauty. Make sure you have adequate lighting to see well.

Start softly exploring the outer parts of your yoni with your fingers. This is not intended to be a self-stimulation exercise, but it is a good idea to begin with soft touches. Notice the lovely shape, colors, and textures of this magical gateway to pleasure. Try to see yourself as if for the first time, discovering a wonderful new treasure. When you are ready, open your legs very wide, enough to see inside your yoni. Notice the subtle color differences of the inner and outer labia, which are the flower petals of your yoni. Notice how wonderfully the petals are shaped, and feel the richness of textures. You may notice some moisture, so delight in the magical dew drops of your lubrication. Explore the beauty of your yoni in any way in which you feel comfortable. Just notice if judgmental or negative thoughts emerge when you explore yourself, and deflect these thoughts.

Permit yourself to feel good about your yoni, once

believed by the ancients to be magical. When you feel ready, take some time to hold your yoni with both hands, and lovingly cradle your seat of feminine power. Offer any words that move you, be they prayer, poetry, or a blessing. Your yoni is your sacred life-giver, the cauldron of creation. It is your path to pleasure and your gift to your lover. Honor it.

Whatever you experience with this exercise, please be sure to write it down. This is a powerful source of body wisdom.

Enhancing Your Orgasm

Three things you can do to enhance orgasm are to use fantasy to heighten arousal, to engage in regular self-stimulation, and to exercise your pelvic floor muscles. In addition, there are excellent books in the Suggested Reading section under "Specific Sex Guides."

Using Fantasy

Sexual fantasy is a very important use of the imagination to stimulate and empower your sexuality. Imagining sexual situations does not mean that you have to act on your fantasy, but it is one of the best ways to enhance female orgasm and increase sexual desire. Fantasy actually intensifies sexual arousal because it boosts surges of testosterone. Men have higher levels of testosterone, so the desire to use fantasy for sexual arousal comes naturally. Please note, fantasizing about sex with different partners does not signify disloyalty to your partner, so ladies, there is no harm in using fantasy in order to climax or to arouse yourself! Fantasy is especially useful when your body begins to "numb out," which may occur when you shift into the plateau phase of your sexual response cycle.

You will need to release guilty feelings about your choice of fantasy when it may not seem "normal." Think of your arousing images as additional turn-ons for your mind. Your special fantasies may be precisely the things you were not supposed to do. For example, many women fantasize about sexual activity with another woman, but they feel uncomfortable about it. It is quite normal to find sexual scenarios that are on the far edge of your experience exciting. The dark, interior world of fantasy is worthy of exploration because it is precisely the intersection where curiosity, danger, and excitement meet, which is most sexually stimulating. When you become more aware of your feelings of guilt and shame, you can appropriately eliminate them.

If you have been raised to be a "good girl," you may have split off your sexy side or the "bad girl," from the responsible, caring "good wife." You may need to access what arouses you from the dark side of your desire. Some of the most intense sexual desire inhabits these badlands of our psyches. It is impossible to sanitize sexual desire without it losing its power to excite you.

Often we select pieces of good and bad experiences and weave them into our fantasy images. We use fantasy to celebrate pleasant memories, and treasured sexual experiences from the past. We also use fantasy to rehearse sexual possibilities for the future. We may use seduction scenes in favorite movies to stimulate arousal or to make it "over the edge" to orgasm.

You can read seductive, fictional stories (see the Suggested Reading section in the appendix) to develop strong sensations of desire that can lead to more arousal with your partner. However, many women find explicit men's magazines or the graphic "plumbing" scenes in pornographic movies more upsetting than arousing. Men's fantasy material is often quite different from women's. It is important not to criticize your partner for his fantasies, as you would not want him to criticize yours. It may be that some of your fantasies are fun to share, but some seem to work best in private. By opening up communication about fantasies, you will free your partner from the need for secrecy.

Although fantasy does work well to heighten pleasure and increase desire, it doesn't necessarily improve relationships. If you are hooked on romance novels, you may feel the desire to masturbate to intensely erotic sex scenes. However, if you compare your partner's lack of finesse to these romantic situations, you may be building walls, separating you from your partner. Fantasy is a great arousal booster as long as you do not block him out or depersonalize yourself from the current sexual situation.

Self-Stimulation

Regular masturbation is one of the best ways to increase sexual desire. Self-stimulation can lead to expanding your range of pleasurable behavior and can enhance your orgasm. This is a delicious cycle, because frequent self-pleasuring leads to greater desire for all kinds of sexual activity. Sexual activity stimulates hormone production and boosts hormone levels, especially testosterone and estrogen. This makes you more inclined to be sexual. The hormones, in turn, stimulate the production of pheromones, which make you attractive to the opposite sex. This can lead to greater contact. The more you pursue sexual pleasure, the more sexually responsive you become.

Old beliefs about "scarcity" are hard to dispel. It is as if there was a limited amount of sexual energy available and if you use it up with an orgasm or two, you have less left for your partner. Unfortunately, if you or your partner believe this to be true, it will be. Such is the power of the mind. Through greater understanding, you can reframe your perception to one of sexual "prosperity": *There is an unlimited supply of sexual energy.* In fact, the more you utilize it for pleasuring, connecting, and healing purposes, the more will be generated.

So many of my patients, women as well as men, ask me if masturbating to images is why they have low desire for their mates. The answer is emphatically NO, but with a proviso. If your relationship has become so emotionally distant that you have retreated into auto-erotic sex to the exclusion of your partner, there *is* a problem; but masturbation isn't it. It is the emotional distance and lack of sexual interaction in the relationship that is problematic. Isolating yourself from your partner by spending hours with your computer or by burying your head in a book achieves the same kind of emotional distance. Any activity can create barriers to enhancing your sexual desire for your partner when you choose to shut him out. Fortunately, you can revive the sexual relationship once you have restored the *intimacy.*

— *Self-Pleasuring Exercise:* When you practice self-pleasuring, you must have the time and privacy to relax. Try taking a long bath (no soap, please), and take plenty of time to massage your favorite lotion into your skin. Enjoy the feel of your hands sliding over your body, allowing yourself the gift of feeling sexual pleasure. Take your time with touching. Don't hurry toward direct stimulation of your breasts and yoni, but *tease yourself* with the kind of light, sensual touch you might enjoy from your partner. For example, you may like the feel of gentle stroking on the inside of your thighs and your lower belly. You can gently increase the pressure of stroking, especially in the pelvic area, at about the middle of the crease where the thigh joins the torso. Also, you may enjoy stroking the belly area just above the pubic bone. These are particularly sensitive areas. Women who are easily orgasmic find many areas of the body other than the clitoris or nipples erotically stimulating. Whatever you find pleasurable, keep expanding the possibilities. Don't rush to touch yourself in old, familiar ways that produce the fastest orgasms.

Flexing Your Love Muscle

The pubococcygeal, or PC muscles, are what you use to stop your urine flow. The women-centered Goddess cultures were fully aware of the use of these muscles, as well as of the supposedly "new" discovery of the G-spot (see chapter 11). Strengthening the PC muscles is important for enhancing orgasms. PC exercises are recommended in preparation for natural childbirth, as well as for the relief of stress incontinence. A doctor reported the effect on women's orgasms after he had prescribed PC exercises for women who had problems with stress incontinence (leakage of urine when sneezing, coughing, or laughing). Women told him that they were having orgasms more frequently and with greater intensity. Some women in their 50s and 60s reported having orgasms for the first time in their lives!

Here are some exercises in graduated degrees of difficulty. First, learn to isolate the muscles by stopping and starting your urine flow. Once you recognize how to tighten and relax the PC muscles, start to practice squeezing the muscles, varying the speed by alternating from slow to rapid. Do at least ten sets of ten squeezes throughout each day.

The next step is the *elevator exercise*. Imagine that you are on the ground floor. Start to tighten slowly as you go from the ground floor up to the ninth. Hold the contraction and then slowly let go, one floor at a time. Breathe deeply from the diaphragm by pushing your ribs out when you inhale. You may enjoy adding a sigh or any other sound. After a while, this will become natural to you. The most challenging exercise is to imagine that you are holding a pen with your PC muscles, and write your name, your partner's name, or anything else, alternating tightening and releasing with control.

After you have become used to the sensation of controlled flexing of the PC muscles, you could try it with your partner during sexual stimulation. For example, if your partner is pleasuring your yoni with his fingers, tighten your PC muscles for added sensation. Flexing the PC muscles during intercourse will bring more blood flow to the pelvic floor and may heighten your response. You can also experiment with pushing the PC muscles downwards, as if you were traveling to the basement from an upper floor. If you try this just at the moment before your orgasm, you may intensify the contractions that involuntarily pulse during climax.

The exercise should not be done simply to create a tight vagina for your partner. In fact, if you tighten the muscles without feeling strong sensations of arousal, you may become sore, because your tissues may not be sufficiently swollen for you to enjoy penetration. This should be *for you*. All sexual activities that you experiment with should not be repeated unless you feel the potential for pleasure.

The above exercises are intended to enhance your sexual pleasure and give you opportunities to validate your sexual response. The following chapters will give you skills for putting it all together with a partner.

Chapter Ten

━❦━ ━❦━ ━❦━

Contemporary Relationships: Building Intimacy

Building Your Model for Intimacy

Many women ask, "How do I begin to talk about what I want to change with my partner?" In the "Negotiating for Change" section in this chapter, you will find a potential scenario for your initial conversation. There is much to be learned about changing the dynamics or the "dance" between you and your partner, after you understand and take responsibility for your own behavior. If you do not have a committed relationship at this time, the information in this chapter will help you choose a partner and build skills from the start. You will also find it helpful if you decide to stay single and have part-time relationships. What you learn here will help you obtain more of what you want in *any* relationship.

To begin with, you need a definition of intimacy with clear terms and specific examples. Once you understand this blueprint, you can build your own version in your relationship, using the essential components.

Intimacy: What It Is and What It Is Not

Some couples use the word *intimacy* to mean "sex." They tell me, "We're not intimate anymore," and when I ask them what they mean, they tell me that they've stopped being sexual with each other. Some women say, "When he wants to be intimate, I avoid him." I correct this use of the term immediately, because you can be quite sexual with someone without any intimacy, and you can have an intimate relationship without any sex. It is true that really good sex emerges from intimacy, but sex and intimacy are not synonymous. Men generally say they *feel* intimate with their partners after sex, but the feeling of closeness after sex is not intimacy. What they may mean is that they feel "warm and close," which is not the same.

Intimacy might best be defined as "the desire to know and be known by another." This may seem too simplistic, but as we discuss how it applies at all levels you will find that this definition has profound implications for committed relationships. The desire to know your partner means that you will work on telling each other about your thoughts, feelings, and desires, and you will continue opening yourself up to new information about your partner. Not only will you tell him your deep emotions and thoughts, *without filtering* information, but you will also remain silent, listening to his feelings or views *without judgment*.

Intimacy does *not* exist at the beginning of a relationship. What feels so close and open in a new sexual relationship is really "pseudomutuality," meaning a false sense of sameness in your thoughts and feelings. This is a natural stage in courtship. Couples speak of feeling that they already know one another, or that they think alike. They say, "We finish each other's sentences," or "It feels like we've always known each other." This feeling is based on the *projection* of your ideal lover onto this person. It is what we all do at the beginning stages of love. Eventually, you must learn to listen carefully to what your partner tells you about his experience, and discard your idealized image.

Genuine intimacy fosters a more accurate picture of you and

your partner, without co-dependent assumptions. It is something that you must build and continue reinforcing, repairing damage as it occurs. You should become more connected to your core sense of self, rather than to the person your partner wants you to be. You and your partner should support each other, through negotiating, to act in each one's best interests. In such relationships, you generally feel greater vitality and energy, including the energy for sexual interaction under the right conditions.

If you expect your relationships to consist mostly of struggles with short periods of fulfillment, you are likely to perpetuate those conditions. Relationships are supposed to be based on general feelings of contentment. You should expect to feel overall sexual satisfaction, occasionally interrupted by interpersonal problems. Both of you should expect to work *together* to solve problems, using healthy decision-making skills and conflict-resolution techniques such as those suggested in this chapter. Then you should expect to return to relative contentment, with an enhanced sense of empowerment.

Our culture perpetuates beliefs that do not support these qualities of differentiation. Partners say things such as, "If you really loved me, you would do what I want," or "You should think about our marriage instead of yourself." To serve your best interests, you are not being "selfish," as the popular misconception would have it. Having a deep sense of communion with your beloved is not diminished by respecting each other's boundaries.

Boundaries

Ideally, individuation (connection to the self) and relationship (communion with the other), move in and out of your primary focus. In well-differentiated relationships, you will feel drawn to work on self needs, then relationship needs, in an interweaving pattern. Knowing the difference between your individual needs and those of the relationship is crucial. In order to accomplish this, it may be helpful if you draw a picture of three circles that are not touching. One circle is you (put your initial in it), one circle is your partner (enter his initials), and the third circle is the relationship (mark *R*). The edges of these circles are similar to the border described in the "Secret Garden" exercise.

We acknowledge our sense of self by creating imaginary fences, demarcating the personal property line between "I" and "you" and "us." In healthy relationships, you can choose to invite your partner into your garden at times, and also ask for solitude when appropriate. When your boundaries are clear, you tend to respect your partner's as well. As the poet Robert Frost once said, "Good fences make good neighbors." Appropriate boundaries are neither wide open all the time, nor rigidly walled up. Open borders create enmeshed or co-dependent relationships because the boundaries between you and your partner are blurred. When you are unable to allow your partner into your garden at all, you are emotionally detached, and your boundaries are rigid.

Unfortunately, blurred boundaries represent the popular model of loving relationships, described in romantic songs as, "I can't live without you," and cultural homilies such as "Two become one" and "My better half." To compare this view with the preceding one, draw another set of circles. The first circle should be very large and labeled *R*. Next, draw two overlapping circles of any size inside the large circle marked *R*. Shade the area in common, blotting out overlapping boundaries. This type of relationship leads to dysfunctional patterns of interacting.

Well-differentiated relationships succeed because each partner takes responsibility for personal fulfillment and has more to contribute to the relationship. If your own circle is well nourished, you have the energy to put effort into the third circle. Return to the first set of circles, and draw arrows leading from each individual circle to the relationship circle. Then draw arrows going from the relationship circle to each individual circle to illustrate that the effort you put into the relationship returns positive energy to your individual circles. However, the relationship circle cannot be sustained by the efforts of just one individual. If either of you fails to put energy into the third circle, it will resemble a deflated beach ball. When relationships seem deflated and draining, it is caused by this lack of mutual input.

The Qualities of Intimacy

Four qualities make intimacy possible: respect, honesty, connection, and open communication. Remember the analogy of the blueprint for building intimacy? These qualities are the essential walls needed to support the structure of your house.

— *Respect:* The primary definition of *respect* is "showing honor," which means behaving in ways in which your partner feels honored. Acting with respect demonstrates that you find value in your partner's *individuality.* Each of you has a different image of the term. If you have never asked your partner to describe what behavior would demonstrate your respect for him, I suggest you do so. Write down his answers as well as your own. The results may be surprising. You cannot assume that what makes you feel respected is what your partner wants.

— *Honesty:* The word *honest* is often used to mean "blunt," as in: "I was just being honest." There are some questions you should ask yourself before speaking. Is it true? Is it loving? Does it serve the relationship? This principle is vastly different from the old maxim, "If you can't say something nice, don't say it at all," which is the surest route to emotional distance in a relationship. Each partner owes the other all the information they have about themselves, and must ask their partner for the same information. The communication skills in this chapter are all about delivering information in the best possible way to minimize defensiveness.

Honesty is really about *self-disclosure*. Rather than "being honest" by voicing critical thoughts about your partner, you must work toward telling the truth about yourself. You can speak only about your own experience. The things about yourself that are difficult to express, because you feel vulnerable, are indeed the things that will serve the relationship when they are spoken.

— *Connection:* You experience connection when you are truly present with your partner. Use direct eye contact with no false posturing, disclosing how you feel *in the moment*. There is a here-and-now presence in the eyes, which is very different from that of ordinary, polite conversation. Typically, you feel such a connection when you're communicating vulnerable feelings, which may be those which are somewhat risky to talk about. Sexual encounters are intensified by this connection between two people.

There is a male-female difference in our culture over what comes first: sex or emotional connection. Men tend to find it easier accessing emotions and expressing vulnerability after orgasm. Most women are the opposite. They need to feel emotionally connected before any sexual touching begins. For reclaiming female sexual desire, the best way to establish emotional connection is through communication.

— *Open Communication:* Intimate communication is the key to what happens in the bedroom. It does not simply mean talking. Many couples come to therapy saying, "We communicate just fine; it's the sexual part that doesn't work." When I ask them what they mean by "communicating," they give examples of chatting, gossiping about friends and family members, or talking about their day and the kids. Important as these discussions are, they are not examples of intimate communication.

In any exchange, there are at least two levels of communication: (1) nonverbal cues from facial expressions, tone of voice, or body language; and (2) verbal language, including choice of words. When nonverbal cues do not match the words being said, we call it *incongruent* communication.

The goals for all intimate communication can be summed up in three ways: expressing your feelings congruently, offering information in a nonaccusatory way, and requesting information from your partner. Note that you should ask for information, rather than assume you know your partner's feelings. You can talk about *anything* if you deliver the message in a way that minimizes your partner's defensive reactions. To be *effective,* communication must be congruent with what you are feeling, and it must be nonaccusatory and self-responsible.

"Love Is All We Need"

The belief common to many lovers is that "love is all we need." New love makes us feel that we can solve any problem if only we have our loved one with us. When we finally feel secure that our loved one is a part of our lives, we find that love is not going to solve all the problems of daily life. Even in the best marriages, loving each other does not mean that we always communicate well. Many couples believe that they have lost their love for each other if they constantly disagree, feel emotionally distant, or do not feel sexual desire. In reality, problems in relationships are usually not due to a lack of love, but to a lack of the skills needed to resolve the problems.

Finding ourselves in the midst of a relationship that is not working is one of the most profoundly disturbing stressors in our lives. Many of the couples I see in my office are discouraged. They are profoundly shocked to find that where love was once incredibly uplifting, their lives together have become more distressing than either thought possible. Because they had always believed in the popular romantic myth—that love would be the answer to all their dreams—they start to feel that love has died when they find themselves experiencing tremendous anger and disappointment.

When couples seek help by reading, trying new activities, taking a class, or getting into therapy, there is enough love compelling them to search for a way to renew their relationship. However, *love is not enough.* In the following pages, you'll find some skills to help you build effective communication in your intimate relationships.

Skills for Maintaining and Enhancing Intimacy

There are three areas in which you will need to build skills:

1. Expressing and listening to vulnerable feelings

2. Resolving conflict

3. Negotiating win-win decisions

The cornerstone of all relationship communication is learning to speak from the "I" position, using "I" language. This is the basic building block of all other communication skills.

Using "I" Language

"I" language is more than just a way to express yourself with your partner. It is an attitude of *self-responsibility*. Most of what goes wrong in relationships is based on the failure to share important information. If you are wondering about your partner's experience, *you ask*. If you are wondering what he is thinking, feeling or wanting, *you ask*, using "I" language. You and your partner may feel that you can finish each other's sentences and know what the other wants without even speaking. *Forget trying to do this from now on!* You must not try to mind-read, or assume that you know what your partner really wants, thinks, or feels.

Self-responsibility means acting in your own best interests, while considering the possible effects of your actions on people affected by them. Self-responsibility is telling your partner how you feel about him as soon as you become aware of a reaction. You must not withhold information, or blame your partner for your feelings, nor should you hold him responsible for your behavior. The four principles of self-responsibility are:

1. Say what you mean and mean what you say.

2. Believe what you hear—your partner is the sole expert on his feelings.

3. Assume that you are both on the same team.

4. Accept your partner, rather than judge him.

From now on, when you are speaking to your partner, begin every sentence with "I." Here are some examples: "I feel lonely right now," or "I'd like you to hold me." Do not ask a question. Instead, rephrase your question as a statement such as: "I'd like to know how you feel," rather than "What are you feeling?" Or, "I'd like you to take out the trash,"instead of "Can you take out the trash?" At first you may feel you are too centered on yourself when you start every sentence with "I," but you are being clear about your desires and feelings. You will be better at stating your position, without confusing your partner with hints or questions. From now on, make your feelings or desires known before asking for your partner's.

Using "I" language means that you avoid using sentences starting with: "You should . . .," "Let's . . .," "We should . . .," "I think you . . .," or, "They say. . . ." You can only speak for yourself. You must not expect your partner to read your mind, any more than you can read his. Two other forms of language, with regard to communicating in relationships, are: "you" language, which is the language of blame; and "we" language, which blurs boundaries. With "I" language, you are not speaking for your partner's experience, but merely stating your own. When you ask for your partner's feelings, you accept the answer without interpretation.

The following list of rules for communication offers substitutes for common ways in which people express themselves.

1. Start every sentence with "I," and when you are expressing a feeling, the words "I feel" or "I'm feeling" must be followed by a word that describes the emotion.

Instead of:	**Substitute:**
I feel you need to talk more.	I'd like to hear more about your feelings.
I think you do things to make me . .	I'm unhappy about your behavior . . .
I feel you just want to . . .	I'm feeling hurt because of . . . .

2. When asking for information about your partner's feelings, eliminate the question *why*, and instead use *who, what, when,* or *where* to elicit information. "Why?" requires your partner to justify his behavior.

Instead of:	**Substitute:**
Why are you so quiet?	I'm worried about your silence. I'd like to know if something is bothering you.
Why do you let yourself get upset over one lousy day?	I'm sorry you had a hard day. What can I do to help?

Instead of:	**Substitute:**
Why don't you ever ask for what you want?	I feel really discouraged when I have to figure out what you want, and I'd like your help.
Why are you so picky?	What is it about this that bothers you?
Why are you so tense and upset?	What happened today? When did you start feeling this way?

Eliminate the words *always, never, should,* and *ought.* The words *always* and *never* generalize about the past and predict the future without hope for change. *Should* and *ought* assume that there is a rule you must follow.

Instead of:	**Substitute:**
We should take the time to practice.	I want to take the time to practice.
You never initiate.	I'd like you to initiate.
You always want sex.	I'm feeling emotionally distant, and I'd like to talk.
I ought to get my self-stimulation exercises done.	I want to get started with my self-stimulation exercises.

You must be conscientious about expressing what you know about your feelings and desires. If you truly don't know at a given moment, commit to finding out and letting the other person know when you will talk about it. If you don't give your partner any information about your feelings, he is likely to fill the void with worst-case scenarios.

Using "I" language may be awkward at first, but you can have fun trying to reframe your mistakes. When you take a statement back and rephrase it, you are giving your partner the precious gift of commitment to change. When you hear "you" or "we" language, say, "I'd like to hear that in "I" language, please," or use signs such as pointing to your eye or saying, "Ouch." Remember, you're both learning, and it's not easy to correct habits of language after a lifetime of misuse.

Listening to and Expressing Vulnerable Feelings

Intimate relationships are the only adult relationships in which it is critical to express vulnerable feelings. The most important skill in relationships of all kinds, and especially in intimate ones, is the ability to listen carefully. You must not invalidate each other's feelings by saying, "You shouldn't feel this way," or "That's ridiculous, how could you feel like that?" The best way to learn listening skills is to summarize what your partner is saying. If your partner is someone who can talk continuously for 15 minutes, you will have to learn how to "pace" with him—that is, ask him to pause for a moment until you have summarized what he has said so far. You might say something such as, "Just let me make sure I understand you before you go on." If you are aware that your partner is not listening to you, try asking,

"Would you be willing to tell me what you just heard me say?"

The importance of summarizing your partner's words and asking your partner to do the same for you cannot be emphasized enough. Summarizing what you have heard develops empathy skills. Use your partner's words as much as possible. *Do not interpret* what you think is being said, which is a form of "therapy game"—irritating at best, and enraging at worst. Ask open-ended questions when you would like to encourage your partner to say more about how he is feeling. The following are some examples.

- You sound worried. What happened to make you feel this way?

- I'd like to hear more about what you just said.

- How did you arrive at this thought/feeling/conclusion?

- What was the best/worst/most important part?

- That sounds important. Can you give me an example of it?

Whenever there is a problem with desire discrepancy in a relationship, important information is not being expressed. However, expressing angry feelings in a blaming way inhibits compassionate feelings. Whereas blaming is coercive, vulnerable feelings engage your partner's compassion for you. Expressing the vulnerable feelings beneath the anger helps your partner understand you without him feeling defensive. This does not mean suppressing your anger, but you will need to build a safe environment to be able to express feelings *assertively*.

Creating safety is based on building trust so that you're confident that your partner will not use what you tell him against you, or tell others about your private feelings. Even if your partner does not understand or agree with what you say, he will not punish you with anger, or abandon you once you have told him how you really feel. One of the best ways to create safety is to express and resolve conflict effectively. Some couples are good at communication on a superficial level, but where there is significant conflict, they keep quiet because they lack basic skills to cope with inevitable differences.

Your Way or My Way: Resolving Conflict

Unresolved anger eventually leads to destructive behavior, such as punishing silence and withdrawal of affection. Many forms of "dirty-fighting" are destructive because they are indirect, covert, or emotionally abusive. They tend to perpetuate hurt feelings and retaliation. With some couples, fighting turns into "tit-for-tat" name-calling. Some claim to "always talk things out," but they move too quickly toward Band-Aid solutions. These couples cannot tolerate talking about their differences for long enough to find a true "win-win" solution. Most disturbing are couples who claim to never fight at all. These couples are avoiding the turbulence under the surface, using denial to cover up feelings of emotional distance and resentment. Conflict never openly talked about becomes toxic to sexuality.

There are three components to resolving conflict: eliminating blame, two-way active listening, and taking time out and rescheduling talks. Together, these skills will create safety so that you and your partner can express vulnerable feelings, which enhance intimacy.

— *Eliminating blame*: Both you and your partner need to take responsibility for reframing what to say in "I" language. You must be able to recognize defensive patterns of behavior and be willing to change them. You are blaming when you hear yourself:

- talking in an angry, sarcastic, or resentful tone of voice;
- accusing your partner of imagined motives for their behavior;
- calling your partner pejorative names;
- criticizing or finding fault with your partner;
- assuming that you have been blamed for, or accused of, a given action or specific behavior; and/or
- interpreting what your partner says, or negatively "mind-reading" nonverbal language.

— *Two-way active listening*: This exercise allows you and your partner to talk about conflict in a constructive way. Remember, whenever you want to say something important to your partner, be sure to face each other and make eye contact. When practicing two-way active listening, use a stopwatch to indicate the end of two minutes in order to limit your response so that each of you can remember what the other has said.

One of you can volunteer to start the process by talking about a subject of your choice. Don't pick high-conflict subjects at first. After the first person has completed two minutes or less, the second person summarizes what he or she heard. You will say: "What I heard you say is . . .." or something similar. Be sure you summarize, *in the first person's words,* as accurately as possible. Then, the first person provides accurate feedback after the summary. You could say something such as: "You left out what I said about . . ." Make sure not to add new material when you do the accuracy check; simply restate what you said. The second person now responds to the opening statements, in two minutes or less. The first person summarizes, then checks for accuracy, and then responds again.

You will each go back and forth for about 30 minutes, always summarizing first before responding. Stay within the structure, even though it may seem slow and cumbersome at first. The structure gives you the safety you need to talk about sensitive feelings.

Rules That Create a Safe Environment for Expressing Conflict

1. Use a timer that will ring when 30 to 45 minutes are up. This is a principle called "containment," which means that no matter what subject is broached, you will not continue talking about it after the 30- to 45-minute time limit. Couples creating marathon arguments become drained and ragged and are more likely to regress into blaming language if the discussion continues.

2. Agree at the beginning, before you start talking, on an activity that you will both do together, for about 20 minutes afterwards. For example, plan to take a walk or watch a movie. You don't have to talk at all, but you will need to keep your commitment to doing the activity. This eliminates feelings of abandonment. Maintaining your commitment to stay together says, "I may not like what you said, but I am still your partner."

3. Always schedule regular time for active listening ses-
    sions, at least once a week. Enter them on your calen-
    dars and take turns being responsible for starting with a
    topic of choice. Do not cancel unless it is truly neces-
    sary to do so. Just the fact that you're keeping your
    commitment to meet and practice builds valuable trust.

4. Remember to use "I" language to eliminate blaming.
    Take responsibility for communicating as honestly as
    possible. Ask for information from your partner, and be
    sure to listen with a neutral attitude. The best way to
    make negative feelings shift to more positive ones is to
    allow them to be expressed freely and safely.

Active listening is the foundation for all conflict resolution.
The 30- to 45-minute time limit will eliminate the wear-and-tear
of hopeless feelings that are likely to occur with constant bicker-
ing, or the periodic blowups that result from a total lack of communication. When you have practiced with less intense subjects,
move on to discuss more volatile ones, always staying within the
safety guidelines.

Many areas of high conflict are repetitive, recurring themes.
They will take many sessions to "unpack" and resolve. Desire dis-
crepancies are some of the most volatile and recurrent sources of
conflicts that couples have. You will need to return to this topic
many times over the course of weeks or even months. Each time
you revisit the subject, you will stay within the agreed-upon time
limit, and then stop talking about it until you reschedule a new
appointment.

— *Taking time out and rescheduling talks:* The commitment you make to each other when you are too angry to talk, without blaming, is to ask for a "time-out" by making a "T" sign, or simply saying, "I need a time out to cool down." The next thing to say is, "I'd like to reschedule our talk until . . .," and name a specific day and time. Make sure your partner agrees that the new time is convenient. Either one of you can ask for a time out, and it must be honored by the other. This ensures that you and your partner respect each other's boundaries. By calling for a time-out, you are demonstrating your awareness that your anger does not serve the relationship.

Do not push for resolution after one or two talks. Either your partner will agree to something that is not in his best interests in order to keep the peace, then sabotage the agreement later, or you will both agree to something you don't really want just to reach a compromise. The only sound resolution to conflict is one that is well negotiated and reflects each person's best interests. It is the opposite of *compromise,* a pallid settlement reflecting what is least distasteful.

Negotiating a Win-Win Outcome

Almost all decisions involving both partners must be negotiated so that each individual feels good about the outcome. Win-win solutions are not easy, and some decisions will take many sessions for both of you to find the real "win." Here is a simple formula demonstrating the importance of the commitment to a win/win outcome.

You		Your Partner		Your Relationship
Win	+	Lose	=	Lose
Lose	+	Win	=	Lose
Win	+	Win	=	Win

For example, if you decide to withdraw from any sexual contact with your partner until he has completely altered some aspect of his behavior, it may be a win for you and a loss for your partner. The relationship also loses. If you decide to follow the *concubine solution* in order to accommodate your partner's demands for sex on some preordained schedule, it will be a loss for you and a win for your partner. Again, it is a loss for the relationship. You may stay together with this kind of compromise for some years, but the decline of intimacy due to both partners not getting their needs met, on a deeper level, will eventually lead to breakdown.

Most individuals enter into conflict negotiations with the underlying assumption that the goal is to argue their point until they can prove to their partners that their way is better or more important. Arguing over whose way is better is a win-lose situation from the start. When you and your partner experiment with the attitude that you are both on the same team, each of you will feel more motivated to achieve a true win-win solution.

The Three Win-Win Outcomes

Think of yourselves at a table where each of you has laid out a hand of cards. Your hand represents your true wishes, not filtered by what you think your partner would like to hear. After all

the information (the cards) is out on the table, you begin the negotiation. There are three ways for any outcome to be *win-win*:

1. You both feel good about *doing something separately*
    that fulfills your individual needs. For example, you go
    bowling one night a week with your girlfriends; he has a
    weekly squash game with his buddies. This win-win
    outcome works especially well for recreational activities
    and time spent with your same-sex friends. Such activi-
    ties should lead to both of you having positive feelings
    toward each other when you return. This solution is best
    when *the activity is more important than being together*.
    If your separate activities are gradually pulling you
    away from spending quality time with your partner, you
    will need to renegotiate the decision.

2. You *take turns* choosing the activity you will do to-
    gether. For example, you pick the movie one time, he
    picks the next. Another example: This Christmas you
    go to his parents, next time you go to yours. These
    solutions work well when both partners show their
    commitment to making sure the other partner's turn
    is respected. This "taking turns" outcome works best
    when *being together is more important than the activity.*

3. The third true win-win outcome is negotiating a solution
    that you both like. It is the one you will use most often,
    because decisions impacting the relationship will need
    a shared, alternative solution. For example, you have a
    vacation to plan and one of you wants to go wilderness
    camping, and the other wants to relax by a pool on an

exotic island. Since the purpose of vacations is to have time together to relax and play, thereby renewing your bond, you will need to create a third alternative.

Negotiating the Third Alternative

As you begin to negotiate a third alternative, you both must first decide on the primary goal of the outcome. If you decide that the activity is more important than being together, the first win-win outcome may work well. Sometimes, one of you will feel the primary goal is togetherness, but the other will care more about the activity. For example: He wants to see a new movie, she wants to relax together at home. When this difference is discussed openly, you can use the following exercises to help resolve this impasse.

— *Force-Field Analysis:* Picture a "field" that represents an ongoing problem in your relationship. Draw two parallel horizontal lines, separated by about two inches, to illustrate this. Now draw arrows pointing downwards, above the upper line, and pointing upwards, below the lower line. It will look like this:

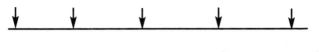

You and your partner can label each downward-pointing arrow to represent the vectors pushing downwards, or those things that are preventing the problem from improving. Next, label the upward-pointing arrows to represent the vectors pushing upwards, or those factors helpful in moving the problem toward a better solution.

One couple worked on the problem of the husband becoming more helpful with child care. One of the down arrows was his tendency to sleep late, then rush to get ready for work, leaving him no time to help get his daughter ready for school. One of the up arrows was his sincere desire to be more involved in his daughter's day-to-day care.

Force-field theory states that you do not have to change the whole set of arrows to improve the situation, or move the field upwards. You only need to strengthen one or two up arrows, and eliminate or weaken one or two of the down arrows. Considering a problem to be negotiated from this perspective will give you and your partner hope that a small, strategic change can create a positive feeling in the relationship. By dividing the problem into vectors, you are able to assess which forces you can most realistically change, on both the positive and negative sides. Identifying factors keeping the problem in its present state allows you to target one or two things. When you change the strength of any of the forces, you will move the whole field, or the problem, into an improved position.

Negotiating for Change

There may be times when you are painfully aware of a behavior or situation that must change. It becomes increasingly hard to deny the problem by making excuses. Perhaps you already know that you cannot tolerate the situation and that you must see some improvement in order to stay in the relationship. You have perceived the need for change and have even developed an idea of what you want. The next step is to talk to your partner. The following is a set of steps designed to negotiate for change:

1. *Set an appointment.* You could say, "I would like to go out to dinner with you on Friday at 7:00. I'd like to spend the time talking to you about something very important to me." Don't get lured into telling your partner what you want to talk about, but reassure him that you think it would be good for the relationship. You will make all the arrangements because you're taking responsibility for the event.

2. *State the problem.* Use the "sandwich technique," which is a statement about what you appreciate in your partner, followed by the words: "My specific concern is . . .," and finished with a hopeful statement about the future. The "bread" represents a genuine positive message that allows your partner to listen without defensiveness, and offers hope for resolving the problem. After you have stated your concern, use the words, "The effect this has on me is . . ." Be sure to use specific examples so that your partner knows exactly what you mean and make sure you are using "I" statements. Do not try to interpret *why* you think he behaves as he does, or impute any motives to him. Finally, use the words "I'm feeling . . ." to give your partner an accurate picture of how you feel.

3. *Obtain partner feedback.* Before you ask you partner to respond, make a specific request to find out what he understood. Say: "Would you be willing to tell me what you just heard me say?" Then listen to his entire attempt to paraphrase before correcting for accuracy. Don't

launch into a discussion about the details or argue with him. Be sure to thank your partner for listening to you and trying to understand your message accurately. The next part of this step is to give your partner the opportunity to respond. Be sure to listen carefully to everything he says, and try to set aside your automatic reactions to emotionally loaded statements. Then summarize what your partner has said, using his words.

4. *Make a direct behavioral request.* When you are negotiating for any kind of positive change, the direct behavioral request is the clearest way to do so. Say: "What I want is . . .," or "What I'd like you to do is . . ." and be as specific as possible. For example: "What I'd like you to do is learn communications skills with me," or "What I want is a date for us to talk each week."

5. *Obtain partner feedback.* Once again, invite your partner to respond to what you have clearly asked for. Do not get drawn into an argument over the "rightness" of the change you request. If verbal manipulation is a problem in your relationship, refer to the next section on "The Broken Record Technique." This will keep you from being distracted from your goal, which is to obtain a contract for change.

6. *Pop the question.* In sales, this part would be called "closing the deal." This is where you say, "Are you willing to try what I ask?" If your partner says, "I'll think about it," that is a good sign, so do not be concerned about pushing for more. You then say, "When can we get back together to talk about it again?" Make sure you

have a specific date set before you finish. If your partner says, "I will try what you suggest," then go on to the next step. It's important to obtain a contract for what is being agreed to. Set a specific date in order to create the contract, and then use the win-win negotiation skills. If your partner says, "I don't understand why you want me to change," go to the following sections on the "Broken Record Technique" and "Exchange Contracting."

7. *Make a contract for change.* When you have general agreement from your partner to work on changing with you, the next step is to create a contract. It requires spelling out the behavior that you are trying to achieve. This should be behavior that both of you can observe so that there's no argument about whether it did or didn't happen. For example, you might agree to set aside 15 minutes each day to sit down together and practice active listening. You may need to schedule additional time to write down the specifics. Force-Field Analysis can be used to identify the targeted areas.

Once you've begun to follow the contract, there will inevitably be mistakes. Try to see mistakes as a learning process, rather than as a betrayal of the relationship. Do not impute motives such as intentional sabotage of the contract or lack of love. When you're experimenting with new behavior, you must take a neutral stance. This means not predicting the outcome, whether it be a negative result or an unrealistically positive one. Schedule regular maintenance sessions to talk about the glitches, and change the steps that haven't worked.

The Broken Record Technique

You may find that as you try to express your needs to your partner, he is unable to listen, but wants to argue about your point of view instead. The "Broken Record" method will keep you firmly in your position, without feeling drawn into a frustrating battle of wits. The "Debater" fighting style is extremely toxic, if it is a repeated pattern, because your partner manipulates you into arguing about some detail of what you have said. You will tend to lose sight of the point you're trying to make. The ensuing argument leaves you drained and angry, releasing the partner from responding specifically to your concerns.

The technique requires you to determine a specific "bottom-line" message that you wish to communicate. It may be a need such as, "It's important for me to feel your full attention in order to become sexually aroused." Your message may be a limit-setting one such as: "I will no longer tolerate your critical comments about my body. They don't make me feel sexy." Whatever your bottom line is, you will be repeating this message many times during the course of your negotiation. This is your "Broken Record Message."

Whatever your partner says in response, simply acknowledge his point of view by saying, "I understand how you might feel this way." This does not mean that you're in agreement with what he says, only that he is entitled to his say. An alternative statement you can use is, "Sometimes this may be true," which is a generality that could be said about many things. Remember to return to your Broken Record Message frequently, and do not defend or justify your position with any other statements. Your feelings are indisputable. Your partner may try to persuade you that you should justify your position, but you must maintain your Broken Record Message in the face of all his efforts to get you to argue with him.

The beauty of this technique is that your partner may not realize for some time that you are repeating yourself. When you continue to acknowledge what he is saying, he may run out of energy, so don't give him anything he can twist out of context. You're simply not playing the debating game. If you achieve your goal of staying with the message you want to convey, rather than being sidetracked into distracting arguments, it is a win-win for you.

Exchange Contracting

One of the simplest and most effective experiments involves your partner agreeing to new behavior as part of an exchange. When a contract is clear, it works like a trade: "I'll do this if you do that." If you first approach your partner with a negotiation for change and he is reluctant, offer to change something important to him in return, and it may motivate him to consider your request. Be very careful to ensure that you are trading behavior requiring an equivalent amount of time and effort on both sides. "I'll be your slave for life if you go to the class with me" is not an equal exchange.

You'll need to create operational steps in order to have a clear idea of the behavior to be exchanged. For example, if your goal is "enhanced intimacy," you may want to use Force-Field Analysis to help you identify specific areas of change. Start with this question: *If all the problems disappeared tomorrow and your relationship felt more intimate, what would be happening that's not happening now?* This is a good way for both of you to envision your relationship as it could be.

If your partner's goal is different, you can each play consultant to the other by helping to define the behavioral steps that will lead to the goal. For example, your partner may set his goal as "more sex." After you've both identified behavioral steps, you can begin negotiation. Have fun with the process. Pretend you're gambling: "I'll see your kiss each day and raise you a full body hug." Or bargain with each other in any way you like. Once you have a contract, check in with each other frequently and make appropriate changes.

Describing Your Sexual Dance

Before you address any change of specific behavior in the bedroom, it is a good idea to describe what usually happens from start to finish. This is your *sexual dance*. You move one way, he moves another way. Your partner's moves may either complement yours or clash with them. Each move has meaning in terms of your willingness to invest in the sexual encounter. Do not use the questions to find fault with your partner or yourself. Just describe what happens. Both you and your partner should answer the following questions. They will lead to some interesting and open discussions about what you both want to change. Each of you should answer the questions separately. After both of you have answered for yourselves, answer the way you think your partner would answer. Then compare notes.

1. Which signals indicate the beginning of a sexual interaction?

2. How do you initiate sexual contact? How does your partner initiate it?

3. How do you know when it's time to begin to touch the breasts and genitals?

4. Which type of touch, on which part of the body *other* than the breasts and genitals, arouses your partner the most?

5. Which touch, movement, or position typically brings your partner to orgasm? What works for you? How do you know when your partner has climaxed?

6. How do you know when sex is over? What typically happens?

After you share your answers, you may need to utilize two-way active listening to communicate difficult or uncomfortable feelings. Where you see repetitive, unchanging, or rigid patterns, you may want to target them for change. Patterns of orgasm that get you or your partner "over the edge" at the final moment are less likely to change than many other sexual patterns, so be sure that you move toward expanded behavior slowly. As you work with specific sexual suggestions, you must also continue practicing communication skills.

Chapter Eleven

~~~~~~~~~~~~~~~~~~~~~~~~~~~~~~~~~~~

Awakening Desire and Enchancing Sexual Pleasure

Sex Exercises: Putting It Together

This chapter provides specific suggestions that promote seductive conditions for erotic encounters. You will need to schedule at least one hour for each exercise. Think of your practice together as an important date, and do not allow other commitments to encroach upon the scheduled time. Some exercises are similar to those in surrogate-partner therapy. They will increase awareness of the physical and emotional experience of surrender to pleasurable feelings. All the exercises should be followed in the suggested sequence in order to enhance or reawaken female sexual desire.

Entraining Your Body Rhythms

Entrainment is a term borrowed from studies of animal behavior and mother-infant bonding. It refers to the tendency for the biological rhythms of two or more bonded individuals—such as baby animals and their mothers—to synchronize with each other. For example, a baby's breathing and heartbeat will entrain with the mother's, creating similar rhythms. Women who live together in the same household or dormitory will tend to have synchronized periods. It is probable that synchronicity occurs among adults living together in an intimate relationship. There is some evidence that just the act of sleeping together may accomplish some biological entrainment.

The following suggestions are significant because they lead to a psychological sense of attunement, as well as promoting biological entrainment. It is important to avoid turning the following exercises into sexual touching.

Spooning

Lie down on your sides, with one of you leaning your back against your partner's stomach, and your partner's arms comfortably around you. Curl up your legs so that you are touching each other from thighs to feet. It may feel somewhat like a double fetal position. Begin to breathe more slowly, and become aware of your partner's breathing rhythm. Notice his rhythm, and when it feels comfortable, breathe together. Don't worry about losing synchronicity; just return to a comfortable rhythm, and refocus your awareness on your partner's breathing. You may find that you move in and out of matching breathing rhythms, or that you fall into synchronized breathing easily.

Skin-to-skin touching promotes the release of oxytocin, the peptide that stimulates your desire to touch more. Breathing together and reducing your heart rate, which happens naturally when you relax, induces a powerful biological bond. As with newborns bonding with their mothers, the scent of your mate in such immediate proximity stimulates the desire to be close.

Performing a Task Together

Planning and making a meal together, working side-by-side in the garden, and even cleaning house together can also promote entrainment. In any given project, moving in cooperative rhythm creates a sense of communion between two people. This is especially true when you've performed tasks together many times so that you flow with each other's rhythm.

Couples who have formed the habit of performing weekly chores separately may be missing out on an opportunity to experience entrainment from such cooperative tasks. Schedule a "project day," at least every once in a while, and be sure you're working with some degree of synchronistic rhythm.

Dancing

Many men complain to me that they "can't dance," which is akin to saying, "I can't sing." They have been conditioned to think that dancing is something that requires a special ability that they don't possess. My usual response is, "You can move, can't you?" For men who have learned to feel rhythm in music or via a drumbeat, the following suggestion will be familiar. As often as possible, put your arms around your partner and move rhythmically as a way to create a very seductive mood. Most women tell me that moving in close proximity to men is one of the sexiest ways to stimulate desire. If you and your partner never dance, here are two ways to start.

— *Mirror dancing:* Begin by standing face-to-face with your partner, and look into each other's eyes. This is a nonverbal process, so save any conversation until it's over. Start to move your arms very slowly, moving with your partner as if you were mirror images of each other. If it is too difficult to maintain eye contact, watch your partner's hands. As you move in wider and more definitive movements, begin to bend at the waist and move your upper torso, keeping pace with your partner as your mirror image. When you become a little more active, start to move your feet and bend your legs, still attempting to flow with the movements of your partner.

You may move into and out of the role of leader. Sometimes your partner's movements will mirror yours, and vice versa. If you feel more free in your movement after a while, hold one hand of your partner's and swing with it. You may even try to twirl yourself or your partner around. At this point, you may feel like moving freely with each other without mirror dancing, or you may feel more comfortable slowing down and returning to the mirror movement. When you've spent at least ten minutes on this exercise, sit together quietly for a few moments and then talk about it.

— *"Dirty Dancing"*: This is fun and may lead to some very sexy feelings. If you recognize your movements when you make love, you already know how to "dirty dance," only this time you will do so standing up. Hold each other around the waist to start, and put on your favorite sexy music—the kind that seems like a seduction, or has a sexual rhythm.

Start to move with your partner, keeping your torsos close together. Move your hips in whatever motion feels sensual, such as "bump-and-grind" movements, or any motion that emanates from your pelvis. Be sure to maintain contact with your partner's body, especially your lower abdomen. Try to make eye contact with each other some of the time. You may feel like moving up and down against your partner's body, either facing forward or facing your partner. Do anything that keeps you in contact with your partner's body and feels very sexy. Since you are dancing in private, it's okay to be as outrageously sensual as you like.

Sensual Exploration: Awakening the Other Senses

This section includes processes used in surrogate-partner therapy that are meant to develop the senses of pleasurable touch, smell, taste, and hearing. The "Trust Walk" exercise is designed to give each of you sensual experiences *excluding sight*. It is also a process used by surrogate partners to break the ice and develop trust with the client.

The Trust Walk

Each of you can take turns on the same day, or plan for each of you to have your own special day for this. The leader should plan some sensual experiences to prepare for your partner. Think of things to explore through touch, smell, hearing, or taste. For example, which wonderfully tasty possibilities can you think of? A juicy peach, yummy chocolate, or delicious grapes are good to taste, but nothing heavy. You want to offer your partner as many sensual delights as possible.

Start by blindfolding your partner so that the visual sense is completely eliminated. You can take the trust walk partly out of doors or completely inside. Lead your partner on a path, making sure you hold him securely so that he doesn't trip or become disoriented. Put your arm around his waist or shoulders so that he can feel your support. Tell your partner when there is a step up or down, a door to pass through, or a turn to make. All along, give your partner things to feel, smell, and taste. Remember, this is called a trust walk, so no tricks or jokes. Along the way, keep asking your partner how he's doing, and if there is a need for you to stand closer or hold him more securely. Your job, as leader, is to be the most compassionate, trustworthy, nurturing partner you can be.

Face Caress

For this process, you will take turns being both the toucher and the receiver. As the toucher, you will sit on the floor with you back supported by a pillow against a wall. Your partner's head can be between your legs on a pillow, nestled close enough for your arms to rest comfortably while caressing his face. You should take a moment to relax, breathing slowly and deeply. Your partner should also relax and be willing to accept all the attention. There should be no talking.

The toucher should keep eyes open in order to prevent any accidental discomfort. Be very careful because the face is sensitive. As the toucher, begin by holding your partner's head in the position of the healing helmet. End in this position as well. Place your two thumbs side by side on his forehead so that the rest of your hand can cup the top of his head. Place your fingers around the temples. Hold that position gently, for a few moments, breathing with your partner. Try and shift your energy to your heart. As you do so, imagine warmth emanating from the center of your heart into your hands, radiating loving feelings to your partner.

Begin to move your fingertips softly and gently over

your partner's forehead. Feel the bone structure of his brow. Lightly touch his eyelid with a gentle motion that does not disturb the skin. Feel the softness of the eyes and lashes. Stroke the cheeks in a circular motion. Notice how fascinating it is to touch even the beard stubble or mustache on a man. You might like to stroke his hair and gently massage the scalp. Continue to send loving energy, radiating through your hands, guiding your caress. Imagine your partner, your precious friend and lover, as a gift to you of companionship and pleasure.

After ten minutes or so, experiment with touching your partner in ways that you would like to be touched. Imagine what would feel good to you, and share that with your partner nonverbally through your caress. When you're ready, end the caress with the healing helmet position—hands cupped around the head with thumbs side-by-side over the forehead. Rest there for a moment before switching positions. Now, the receiver becomes the toucher and follows the same pattern. End the session with spooning, side-to-side, one partner's back to the other's front, legs curled up together. Breathe together for a few minutes, and talk about your experiences if you like.

A variation on the face caress involves washing each other's hair in a bath. Take turns, with the active partner sitting with his or her back against the back of the tub, and the receiver sitting in front with his or her back against the partner's chest. Use very mild, nonallergenic shampoo, and just enjoy massaging your partner's head, neck, and shoulders, as well as playing with his soapy hair and loving your partner in this wonderful way.

Full-Body Sensual Touch

This exercise is a variation of one of Masters and Johnson's sex therapy techniques. If you have specific fears about touch, it would be wise to seek a therapist who can assist you in processing your feelings and supporting your progress. There are many gradual steps you can take with this exercise, and it should be repeated many times. It's a good idea to only touch each other's backs the first time if you have strong negative feelings about any sexual touching. The back is a safe place to start because it's associated with nurturing rather than sexual touch.

The purpose of gradual touch is to allow the receiver to relax into pleasurable sensations from the partner's touch, without any demand for sexual performance. The toucher's focus is to develop the awareness of touch, purely for its own sake. The process is called "non-demand touch," because there is no specific sexual touching in this exercise. If you become aroused during the process, just enjoy the feelings. You can plan time for sex later, but there must be clear separation between the touch experience and any sexual encounter.

Take turns starting as toucher, but each of you should have a turn in every session. Use a private room or an area with no distractions. Make sure the temperature is appropriate for nudity. If either one of you is uncomfortable being totally nude, you can wear underwear or a bathing suit. Think about where you want the receiver to lie down, because you both need to be comfortable as active toucher. If one of you has a back problem, it would be an excellent idea to get a massage table. Otherwise, the receiver can lie on a bed or on the floor. You may light candles or a fire, play soft music, dim the lights, or do anything else pleasurable to the senses.

You will be touching the receiver from head to foot, front to back, eliminating the breasts and genitals, for the first few times. Focus on the sensations of your hands. Try to explore the various textures, and find some interesting temperature differences. Take time to touch the whole body, and do not hurry through this process. You are not doing this as a massage, but to enhance your own touching sensitivity. Your partner is to tell you if anything tickles, hurts, or is uncomfortable in any way. Otherwise, the receiver can just relax into oblivion. Allow each of you at least 20 minutes to have a turn.

Be alert to distracting thoughts that may arise, as clues to what may be hindering your focus on the sensations, both as receiver and toucher. As toucher, when you begin to get distracted by thoughts, learn to refocus on the awareness of sensation through your hands. The enhanced awareness will continue to teach you more about your sense of touch each time.

When you have both taken turns as toucher, lie down together in the spoon position for a while, and synchronize your breathing. You may feel like talking about your experiences, but be very careful not to give a critical review of your partner's technique. You are deepening intimacy at both a verbal and a nonverbal level, so allow the process to grow and prosper with positive feelings.

Awakening Female Sexual Energy

At any stage of life, a woman can become cut off from her sexual feelings, much to her dismay as well as her partner's. Most women tell me they genuinely want to feel desire for their partners, but they just don't know how. Every desperate effort of the partner to "do it right" seems to increase repulsion, similar to magnets with the same poles placed end to end. The purpose of these techniques is to bring to the surface the fire that has been buried by layers of emotional distress. Female sexual desire must be awakened slowly.

First, you must learn about female *readiness*, which is the mental, emotional, and physical sense of being ready for sexual touch. The following exercises focus on pleasure for the woman. No attempt has been made to "make it even" for the male because it is intended for the specific purpose of awakening feminine sexual energy. Further reading for specific sexual suggestions can be found in the appendix.

(What follows is instruction for men.)

It might be a good idea for you both to read the following pages together, perhaps while soaking in a bath or relaxing in some other way. As you practice the specific sexual touching, be careful not to circumvent the communication skills, assuming that all you need to learn is sexual technique. If you have skipped the previous chapter and have gone directly to the sex exercises, you may also have a pattern of moving too rapidly into direct sexual touching in your relationship. Even if you and your partner have great sexual compatibility, you may want to try these suggestions for fun and enhancement. Just about any woman will love to be touched in these ways.

Erotic Massage

You will be receiving feedback from your partner in both verbal and nonverbal ways. One form of nonverbal feedback is hand-guiding. This requires your partner to place her hand on top of yours, moving it to where she wants to be touched. She will also indicate the exact type of touch she desires by applying pressure on your hand or raising your hand slightly for lighter touch.

The other form of nonverbal feedback is body cues. You will be focusing your awareness on your partner's responses as you touch, but you should not act on your interpretation of her body cues until you have received verbal confirmation. A woman's body shows signs of erotic pleasure by rippling of the skin, goose bumps, erect nipples, reddening of skin color, or genital lubrication. She may also arch her pelvis, lean her breasts forward, moan, spread her legs, and raise them at the knees. However, refrain from moving too rapidly. Do not proceed to any specific genital touch until you have completed the full-body erotic massage. Just enjoy watching her receive pleasure, without having to do anything else.

Your partner should lie comfortably on her back on one side of the bed, on a pad on the floor, or on a massage table. Make sure you can kneel or stand comfortably during the process, because if you show any signs of stress or fatigue, she will lose her sense of permission to enjoy herself. If you cannot fully participate, you must reschedule for a time when you are able to give her your full attention.

Choose a body massage oil that is safe for contact with her genitals. You will not be applying it inside her yoni, but oil not recommended for sensitive areas should be avoided. Begin with your hands resting gently, one on her head, and one on her belly. Try to radiate loving, warm energy through your hands. Breathe deeply and imagine energy, generated from your groin, moving all the way up and down your spine as you inhale and exhale. Make sure you feel a sense of connection to your partner, and center your awareness on pure giving. Begin with long, "connecting" strokes over the whole length and width of her body. Try to use a rhythmic flow, alternating strokes over her arms, legs, thighs, and breasts. Do not go over the nipples or pubic area yet; just pleasure her with relaxing message strokes.

Begin to move the energy toward her chest and pelvic area, with the direction of your strokes. For example, stroke all the way up her thighs, ending just at the crease where the leg meets the torso. Stroke the arms upwards, cross over the shoulder, and down to the breasts. Take your time, and do not rush this pleasurable stroking. You are raising the fire of Kundalini energy. (Ladies, focus completely on your body sensations, and breathe from deep inside your belly. Imagine the energy coming from your womb and moving up and down the spine. Visualize a vibrant red/orange with this energy.)

Now, tease the rising energy by stroking lightly with your fingertips on sensitive areas of her body, close to her breasts and genitals, but not directly on them. (You may find it hard to identify with this light, teasing approach because you may prefer much stronger, direct stimulation.) Let your fingertips tease and dance all over her body, paying attention to her hand-guiding cues for special places where she likes to be touched or for where she wants more or less pressure. Even if she guides your hand to her yoni, do not touch it yet. It is always better to continue to tease and play for a while. Try running your fingers up and down her inner thigh, ending just before her yoni, or gently tease the soft sides of her torso and under her arm, unless she indicates that this is uncomfortable. Circle around her breasts one way and then the other. Enjoy the effect you are having on her, which you can detect by the way her nipples harden and her body moves.

Gently brush over her nipples, and playfully tease them with your fingertips. Never rub hard or pinch them. At high states of arousal, this may be stimulating, but the kind of process you are working with here is awakening, not pushing for orgasmic release. Always refrain from exclusive focus on the nipples, and return to circling her breasts as a way to tease her energy higher. Occasionally, return to the long, connecting strokes over her entire body. Move your touch down to her belly, and use both hands, alternately stroking her belly in a circular motion. Make sure you receive feedback about how much pressure to use. Enjoy her erotic movements and sounds.

Very slowly, move your strokes downwards toward the pubic bone, continuing the circular movement, alternating with both hands. Gently tug at the pubic hair. Be sure not to pull small amounts of hair, but tug a handful gently, asking for feedback. Now, place the heel of your hand over the entire yoni, facing toward her open legs. Let your palm rest gently over her yoni lips and mons veneris (the area covered with pubic hair). Again, focus your awareness on the warmth emanating from your hand. Imagine that the energy is radiating from your genitals directly to her yoni, moving up and down from her spine to yours and back again. If your partner enjoys it, try caressing her all over with your tongue, hair, or silky material.

The next step in this awakening process is the female genital caress and stimulating finger-play. It may be helpful to do the erotic massage for several sessions before she is ready for this caress. Let her decide what she is ready for, and when. However, once you begin female genital caress, do not hurry to intensify touch. Always stay slightly behind her readiness to make sure she is truly relaxed, allowing her to surrender to the pleasurable feelings. She may try to hurry things along if she is afraid you'll get bored. Always reassure her that she should relax and take all the pleasure for herself.

Female Genital Caress

Begin by placing your hands on your female partner's head and belly, as in the erotic massage. Make some long strokes over her whole body in order to establish a relaxed state and a sense of connection, using nonallergenic body oil. Then face your partner's yoni, either kneeling if she is on a bed, or standing if she is on a massage table.

Place your hand over her yoni, with the heel and palm of your hand over her outer lips and your fingers spread over her mons area. Make sure that the oil is warm (not hot) before you slowly drip a small amount onto your fingers, and let it gently flow through them onto her yoni. Slowly, begin to move the heel of your hand upwards, applying slight pressure on her outer yoni lips. Then drag your spread fingers gently downwards over the whole, outer area. Continue stroking like this for a few moments unless she indicates that she doesn't enjoy it. Remember not to put any fingers inside her until she is much more aroused. You might try gently dragging your middle finger over her clitoris and between her outer lips, but just for a tease. Return to stroking her inner thighs periodically, as in the erotic massage. When massaging her yoni, apply just enough pressure to move the skin back and forth over the tissue underneath. Never rub hard. When she is reaching orgasm later on, she may indicate she wants more pressure, but not at this point. Return often to light, gentle touches that barely brush the inner thighs and pubic hair, unless she finds this teasing uncomfortable.

Use both thumbs to part her outer lips gently (make sure your fingernails are cut and smooth), and slide your thumbs along the crease between the inner and outer yoni lips. Make sure there is plenty of oil or lubrication. Add more oil periodically. Friction does not feel good to women unless they are highly aroused, and some do not want it even then. You can place her outer lips between the thumbs and forefingers of both hands, and gently squeeze and pull outwards, away from her body.

Before touching the clitoris, gently push and pull on the inner lips and the hood of the clitoris to provide plenty of pleasing stimulation before any direct touch. Some women cannot tolerate the head of the clitoris being touched at all because it is too sensitive, so always ask first. If she wants you to proceed, caress around the clitoris with two fingers in a circular motion. Then alternate with upward strokes, from the bottom of the lips toward the clitoris. When you are using one hand, try to keep the other resting on her abdomen, or tracing a circular massage motion on her belly. Women often do this during masturbation. Play with gentle fingers around her inner lips and clitoris. Do not concentrate on the clitoris as if you were trying to rub the head of your penis. Most women use subtle movements to touch themselves until they are ready to climax. Make sure you get verbal feedback about any discomfort.

Inner Yoni Massage

The next step is the inner yoni massage, including stimulation of the G-spot, the sensitive area on the roof of the vaginal walls. You should repeat several sessions of the female genital caress before proceeding to pleasure your partner with your fingers inside of her. Always do some erotic massage and sensual stroking before moving onto stimulation of the inner yoni. Use plenty of lubrication specifically made for genital use. When placing your fingers inside a woman, never make the mistake of assuming that you have to simulate the in-and-out friction of penile thrusting. This misconception has been unfortunately fostered by the term "finger-fucking" from street language. Most of the stroking you will use is either circular, side-to-side, or up-and-down jiggling with your fingers bent in a 45-degree angle. Use your whole wrist with these motions, not just your fingers.

When your partner is ready for direct stimulation of the walls of her inner yoni, proceed very slowly, even if your partner wriggles and attempts to thrust toward your hand. If she does this, gently place the heel and palm of your hand over her outer lips for a moment, and help her breathe deeply to relax. The best way to allow her fire to build is to give her plenty of time to feel the sensations, without prematurely going for a release. Always start with a finger gently inserted up to the first knuckle, or use your thumb, since it is shorter and thicker than your other fingers. Slowly rock your finger from side to side, using the image of a clock face over her yoni. Begin by rocking your finger at 12:00, and move to each hour position on the outer third of her yoni walls, around the "clock." Your partner can give you feedback as to which area feels best. Try jiggling your crooked middle finger around the clock, with the knuckle stimulating the outer sides of the opening. Notice the beautiful changes in color of your partner's yoni as she engorges and lubricates.

She may be ready for you to stimulate the upper roof of her yoni, which is the G-spot. Continue massaging her vaginal walls gently, and lovingly use your middle finger in a "beckoning" gesture to stroke the roof, where it feels slightly grainy or rough. This is the same tissue as the male's prostate gland and can be very sensitive to stimulation, especially when she is very aroused. Some women find stimulation of this area an acquired taste, so do not try to rub this spot immediately. As always, stay attuned to her feedback and move cautiously. You may feel this area swell with your gentle stimulation. If she likes it, use two fingers of your other hand to stimulate the lower walls of her yoni, or alternate stroking the G-spot by circling your two fingers around her vagina.

At this point, if she is ready for orgasm, by all means reach for the sky! Be sure to allow her hand-guiding and verbal feedback to indicate her wishes. She may desire stimulation of her clitoris, either by you or her own hand. When she has had one orgasm or several, hold your fingers still inside her, or place your hand on her outer lips, and gently rock your palm until she starts to build again. Then use whatever stimulation she favors. She may want to bring herself to orgasm, since she knows just the right touch. Continue the cycle of slowing down or stopping stimulation, and then returning to jiggling, rocking, or circling as long as she desires. Some women enjoy intercourse after several such orgasms.

Ladies' Night

If your partner wants to experiment with some form of play that involves penetration, you can try this exercise. Schedule a "ladies' night," where you are passive (at last!), on your back. Your lady may now play with your body in any way she desires, without hurting you. She may choose to rub you all over with her hair; or lick, nip, or kiss you wherever she likes, including your penis.

(What follows is instruction for women.)

One idea that may be fun is for you to straddle your male partner's body and rub your yoni wherever you want. Experiment with inserting just the tip of his penis inside your yoni, or rub against his shaft and tease him with your yoni lips until he cries for mercy and reaches orgasm. Any penetration is controlled completely by your movements. He is not to thrust or move his pelvis. This may be difficult to maintain indefinitely, but you can help him calm his urge for orgasm by gently cupping his genitals and staying still until he relaxes. When you decide you would like to have him fully inside you, you can mount his penis and move to your own rhythm as you enjoy riding him, wherever you want to go!

This exercise is especially effective if you have been averse to intercourse for any reason, because it gives you total control. If you have worked up to this process by practicing all the touch experiences beforehand, you will be able to decide when you are ready for intercourse, and you may choose to repeat this Ladies' Night exercise often. You can learn to follow your rhythms for your own pleasure, with obvious benefits to your partner.

Chapter Twelve

Spiritual Sexuality

The Feminine Way

By now, I hope you understand that your life and your sexuality are integral parts of your whole being. Your sexuality is not purely physical, but a function of body-mind-spirit interaction. You can see that low sexual desire is not a mechanical problem, but stems from a lack of self-love and self-acceptance, inhibiting surrender to your natural sexual energy. Abundant sexual desire is not something you have lost. *It never left you, and it is within your power to reawaken!*

We need an understanding of female sexuality reflecting women's unique experiences of themselves as sexual beings. The feminine way is nothing less than erotic pleasure, intimate communion with a partner, and joining one's energy with the Life Force. When the notion of sex is strictly limited to a masculine template into which women are supposed to fit, *there is no counterpoint of active, female energy.* If the feminine way is to be represented in contemporary, sexual knowledge *in equal measure,* female desire must be clearly represented as an active urge, as powerful as the male's, but very different. Ancient knowledge holds that the female polarity is the powerful, *magnetic pull* of sexual surrender. In its highest expression, it is *spiritual sex.*

Spiritual Sex

In a recent article, therapist and sex researcher Gina Ogden states, "From my professional perspective the disconnection of sex and spirit is the single, greatest contributor to low sexual desire, especially for women."[1] This observation correlates with my experience working with couples over many years. She continues by noting that when couples come to treatment with desire problems, women express the feeling that something is missing, which results in their feeling sexually incomplete. The "something" that is missing is the spiritual connection.

No matter how advanced our biological research becomes, conception and birth remain two of life's great miracles. They are the embodiment of Divine Life through the transmutation of energy into matter. This is a unique power of the feminine way. Women intuitively know the link between spirituality and sexuality through direct experience of embodying the Life Force in the creation of a child. Thus, the linking of sex and spirit is essential to female sexuality. The essence of spiritual sex is enhanced awareness, ecstatic inspiration, and merging with the Life Force.

The Great Marriage

From the ritual of The Great Marriage, we see the mystery of male-female sexual union as it was perceived by the Goddess cultures. The ritual enacted several times a year at festivals brought renewal to Earth and balance to male-female energy in the universe. The participants were seen as representatives of the Goddess and her divine consort, the priestess and the king enacting the sacred will of Divine Desire in a powerful spiritual-sexual act.

The Great Marriage Made Real

In order to create an image of how the Great Marriage might have been enacted in an actual sexual experience, let us return to the story of Inanna a few years after her sexual initiation. Inanna had been raised on the island of Crete in a sex-positive, woman-centered society, honoring sexual expression of many kinds as a gift of the Great Mother.

Inanna's relationship with Tor, her gymnastics partner, had lasted long enough for her to be able to explore her sexuality and discover what pleased her. She had learned how to communicate her needs to her partner and also how to be attentive to information about his desires. Having a strong sense of self, she was careful to choose the right conditions for her. She knew that some sexual situations dissipated her energy, and she listened to her Guardian about what was in her own best interests with regard to sex. Inanna and Tor were excellent friends, and they had been lovers for over a year. As their personal paths separated, their sexual attachment diminished. They continued to be friends after he chose to pursue training as a craftsman. He eventually married and started a family with another woman.

Inanna had worked as an apprentice healer with her grandmother, but at the age of 25, she decided to enter the temple to train as a Priestess of the Goddess. In ancient times, becoming a priestess did not preclude having sexual encounters. However, since she had chosen to belong to the Goddess, she would have no obligations to any man.

Inanna served in the temple, developing her spiritual discipline, as well as learning the practical arts connected with healing herbs and physical treatments for all types of ailments. She was able to practice her skills with many of the city dwellers who came to the temple for tonics, ointments, healing massage, and various other kinds of physical and psychological treatment. She watched the wise Crone priestesses in their compassionate handling of situations in which they knew that hope and positive emotions were all that were needed. She saw them offer tonic herbs and words that would promote a sense of well-being. They seemed to know instinctively what to suggest, by way of spiritual practices and quest journeys, that the petitioner could undertake to promote personal healing. Inanna learned how to use special potions that enhance the "second sight" of divination, and she became adept in the art of dream incubation—that is, she was able to enter dreams at will, with total recall. She also found out how to apply the knowledge gained to the problems of waking life.

Inanna's mother had been High Priestess for more than five years. In this capacity, she was often consulted for advice on everything from marital discord to divinatory guidance in decisions affecting the whole community. She was adept in the art of dream incubation at a very advanced level, and was respected for the wise counsel that came from her visions. She perfectly embodied the characteristics of the Mother Goddess, accepting responsibility for her children. In addition to her service to the community, it was the High Priestess's responsibility to oversee training of the priestesses and to recognize each one's special talents and capabilities.

There came a day when Inanna's mother approached her with a request. She made it clear to her daughter that her service to the Great Mother was needed, but she had to carry out the mission of her own free will. She asked Inanna to serve as representative of the Goddess at the Sacred Marriage ceremony in May. During her training, Inanna had learned the deeper, spiritual significance of this rite, and she knew what was being asked of her. She was to join with a specially chosen priest in a private and powerful ceremony that would ensure continued guidance and abundance for their beloved city. Her heart was beating very fast as she accepted. She was both scared and excited to have been chosen for this honor.

The following month proved to be an intense time of psychological preparation for this very important ceremony. She ate sparingly of special food and plants, promoting optimal energy and health for the body. She spent her early morning hours in meditation, often at beautiful, natural locations, where she felt especially close to the Great Mother. She asked for wisdom and strength to transmute the powerful energy of the Life Force so that it might infuse the land and her people with abundant healing life. After some intensive physical training, she was taught the ancient secrets of transmuting sexual energy through the body, by means of special breathing techniques, sounds, and visual images. She was schooled in the art of joining with the spiral dance of Life Force energy in dream states. She learned to enter those states and to return to normal awareness at will. In all her training, she was made aware of the Divine Love of the Mother, as well as the Mother's desire for her children to honor her gift of life with sacred, sexual union.

The day of the Sacred Marriage ceremony dawned cold and misty, with the promise of spring warmth. Inanna awakened from a deep slumber. All night she had dreamed of communion with the Great Mother, dancing on a river of light that playfully swirled around and inside her. As she became fully awake, Inanna was thinking about her partner in the forthcoming ceremony, knowing that he too had spent the month in preparation to receive and generate Life Force energy through his union with her. She felt strangely elated and even curious about him. As she meditated, using the breathing techniques that had become second nature to her by now, Inanna felt that she was in a calm, yet alert state, prepared for what was to come. This felt like the most important day of her life.

Inanna trusted that the love of the Goddess would move through her. She would surrender to Divine Purpose even if it meant that her life was to change permanently. If the Goddess willed, she might bear a child of this union, and it would be a joy for all her people. If it meant that she would be risking her life to give birth, Inanna would accept the sacrifice. She felt ready to face the challenge of childbirth. She knew that giving birth was an auspicious gateway into the Stage of the Mother, which she was ready to enter if such was Divine Will.

Inanna's carefully chosen handmaidens entered her chamber to bring her the special herbal tea. They proceeded to help her perform the ablutions that would prepare her to be a perfect vessel for the Life Force. The women felt especially honored to have been chosen to attend her. After the ritual cleansing, her handmaidens anointed her with fragrant oils and rubbed her body with special preparations that made her skin glow. They oiled and dressed her hair with great care so that she looked both regal and sensuous. She was brought the extraordinary diaphanous robe that was to be her only raiment. It was made of the softest, most luxuriant fabric she had ever felt.

The handmaidens placed a crown of flowers upon Inanna's head, and as she contemplated her reflection in a highly polished bowl, she knew that she was Goddess in her most magnetic and vibrant, sexual self. When all was ready, the High Priestess came for her and intoned the words of prayer for the success of the union, expressing the hope of her people. Inanna was ready.

The handmaidens preceded Inanna down a long passageway leading to the labyrinth. This was the spiral path down into the earth, ending in a beautiful chamber representing the womb of the Great Mother. The magnificent voices of the priests and priestesses joined in a wonderful harmony of male and female. They blended together in the song of The Great Harmony of All That Is. As their voices swelled at the entrance to the Chamber of the Mother's Womb, Inanna's body pulsed with the rhythm of their primordial sounds. The celebrants bowed and backed away as she entered. The chamber was perfumed with the most exotic scents she had ever smelled. Her body moved as if in a trance, yet she felt vibrantly alive.

Inanna's partner was waiting for her in the chamber, standing under the apex of the domed ceiling draped with silk. His hair was crowned with flowers matching her own. She thought for a moment that they looked like the faerie folk, hair tressed in flowers and clothed only in flowing, diaphanous robes. There was a radiant aura about him, glowing in the shimmering light of a hundred votive candles. He turned as she walked in, and he caught his breath, clearly in awe of her beauty. She smiled at him bravely, hardly trusting her voice to speak. The energy around them was intense with the prayers of the whole community flowing toward their union.

Inanna stepped before him and held out her hands in an intimate gesture of greeting. He was a stranger, yet his face was familiar, like someone known to her for lifetimes. She knew him, and from the look that registered in his eyes, she could tell that he knew her, too. Inanna was aware of a drawing sensation in the center of her womb. It was the most intense sexual desire she had ever felt. She knew what they were destined to enact here, yet there seemed to be a suspension of time that stilled her movements. Inanna's athletic body wanted to dance, yet there was time. There was all the time they would ever need. He motioned her to sit on a cushion opposite his. Then, he served her rich, aromatic tea and honey cakes, yet she was scarcely hungry. The offering was but a ritual acknowledgment of ceremonial greeting.

She studied his hands as he served her, wondering how those long, slender fingers would feel on her breasts and between the lips of her yoni. She knew he was deliberately moving slowly and sensuously toward the moment of contact. Except for her taking his hands in hers, they had not touched at all. Yet, her skin felt the electric current of his arms passing near her. Once again, they caressed each other with their eyes. It was as if they were each studying the other in order to unlock the secrets of their souls behind the eyes. Inanna's mouth opened, her moist lips swelling with desire. She ached for the contact of his touch. He hesitated, smiling in recognition of the signs of her eager sexuality, yet he controlled his own desire with the practiced, slow breathing of an adept. Her breathing also slowed as she struggled to remember all the practices she had been taught. She began the power breathing, moving energy from the base of her spine upwards, and slowly exhaling with long, slow sighs. He nodded his appreciation of her discipline, and she thought she saw a flash of fierce, sharp heat pass through him. Then she, too, smiled in her delight for his passion.

What happened next surprised them both. A sound began to build around them, a harmony of chords neither one had ever heard before. It moved through them, vibrating their energy centers, attuning them to a rhythm that felt very ancient and yet very present. Inanna could no longer contain her need to move, and she rose to join in a dance with the swirling currents of air. He watched her intently as she moved with the grace of a gazelle in motion, her joy overtaking any shyness she had felt. He was entranced by the overwhelming sensuality of her movements.

Inanna danced around the chamber, returning to where he was sitting in his meditative stillness, and she began to seduce him with her movements. Her eyes locked onto his, and they gazed deeply at each other. The waiting was over. They were drawn into the current of spiraling energy. He caught her robe as she pressed her hips into his hands, and she gasped as she felt it slipping away. She shivered with the teasing, sensual feel of the soft fabric flowing over her skin. He continued to lock his eyes onto hers as he slowly moved his hands over her body for the first time. She felt herself melting into the liquid heat emanating from the center of her womb. He watched in delight as he saw her reaction to his touch, deliberately teasing her with its lightness. His caress was so sensual that she thought she might faint from the intense pleasure shooting through her body. She began again with her disciplined breathing, this time using the charged breathing to build her fire. It was fortunate that she had continued to practice it until it came naturally, because she was now aware that all her training had been destined for this moment.

Inanna stepped over his shoulder and pressed her yoni to his lips, silently begging him to taste her there, to use his tongue to stroke her fire higher. As his tongue stroked her gently, she pressed into him. When he finally suckled her pleasure center, she exploded with orgasm, arching her back fiercely. He held her buttocks securely and exhaled his warm breath on her yoni, her sounds of pleasure continuing in a long, slow exhalation of A-a-a-a-a-h! His fingers slipped inside her, pulsing her yoni walls gently to keep her waves of orgasm coming. Her hips were rolling in unstoppable motion. After several waves passed, she gracefully lowered her body forward to a crouch. At that moment, her yoni found what it wanted most.

Inanna drew his erect penis into her to ease her aching longing for him to be inside her. He filled her, supporting her hips to keep himself from thrusting fully upwards into her. Now she was making primordial sounds with her fire breathing. He moaned in his own need, yet still he held her from moving forcefully down on him. Once again, he locked eyes with her. She saw his eyes beaming with the adoration she needed, in order to feel a sense of communion with his soul. He began to pulsate his groin muscles and move her down slowly so that she could feel his gentle moment-by-moment penetration. That slow joining was the last conscious act of individual will he could remember. Inanna's strong yoni muscles finally pulled him upwards in a long, suspended moment of surrender to the forces of desire that joined them together. His eyes pooled as tears of emotion welled up from deep within the center of his being. His sobs echoed the intense waves of timeless, limitless release from his physical boundaries. There was no longer location in space, nor division between them. There was just sound and light and energy. There was yet time, endless time, to move with the spiral dance of pulsing Life Force, making and unmaking them in boundless bliss.

🦅🦅 🦅🦅 🦅🦅 🦅🦅 🦅🦅 🦅🦅

Epilogue

Relationships in the New Millennium

For the Men

Our culture is already in the process of change, partly due to the reemergence of feminine values. Relationships and family structures are in a state of extreme flux, as the traditional patriarchal view of marriage loses its hold on a large segment of the population. It may be that the evolving familial and organizational structures are confusing or upsetting to some of you. You may ask, "What's in it for me if I make the changes suggested in this book?" You may think you are "kicking yourselves in the shins" by letting go of the perks still operating for you in the traditional system.

As a man, you can choose not to live under the shadow of 5,000 years of sexual limitation. If what you want is a sexier partner, there is no advantage in limiting her sexual expression. The basis for your fears about your partner's free sexual expression is potential betrayal and abandonment. Actually, she may increase her interest in you as a result of the changes. There are significant benefits for those of you wanting to balance the equation of male and female energy in your own relationships. There is a growing number of couples exploring expanded sexuality and more satisfying sexual relationships.

Since men and women in conflict cause serious damage to their individual psyches, their families, and their sexuality, it

makes sense to find a more effective way for affectional and sexual needs to be met. The drain of energy from win-lose arguments
could be ended, and this energy could be freed to focus on creative projects. Negotiation, rather than relentless battles, would be
the norm. When you build trust and intimacy with your partner,
you no longer waste valuable time watching out for betrayal.

The change required of you involves negotiating with your
partner to meet her desires. In many ways, you have nothing to
lose but your misplaced perceptions of how things *ought* to be.
All it takes is the application of communication skills that allow
for both your needs, interweaving sensual and sexual activities
from each other's desires. There would be room for the exploration of new behavior in a fun-filled, mutually satisfying adven-
ture. When sex is well negotiated and the sexual equation is balanced, your relationship will take whatever creative form you
both choose, based on mutual trust and understanding.

The playful child in you can discover new delights as long as
there is a sense of permission and safety. Boredom from repetitive
sexual patterns, rigidly followed, will be replaced by the exploration of uncharted territory. It will include opening to a wider
range of sexual choices. There will be plenty of discussion, feedback, and decisions to discard the "duds," keeping an experi-
mental attitude. Each couple can create their own rules, incor-
porating growth into their system. Many experiences can har-
ness the qualities of sexuality that are both healing and consciousness expanding.

It may seem preposterous to view sexual relationships in such
lofty terms. Yet, it no longer makes sense to deny the spiritual
dimension of our sexuality, as if we had "lower" physical urges
and "higher" spiritual functions, disconnected from the body.
Since sexual energy is the source of our connection to the Life
Force, the benefits of physical, emotional, and mental health are

obvious. There is truly an endless supply of loving sexual energy. Consequently, there are more unlimited playful moments
and times of pleasure and contentment than most of us can ever
imagine.

Cultural Changes

We desperately need a new blueprint for human relationships
to replace the current patriarchal arrangement that has prevailed
during the last 5,000 years. Even the relatively new emphasis on
"romantic love" as a prerequisite for marriage does not provide
lasting conditions for female sexual desire. The simplistic notions
of romantic love, encouraging the choice of life partners based on
fleeting, lust-driven impulses, serve humanity no better than
rigidly limiting female sexual expression. The chaos of constantly making and unmaking familial ties from divorce, impulsive
sexual betrayals, and parental abandonment is hardly the ideal
structure for human growth.

It is obvious that we humans are a work in progress. The variety of ways in which we have organized the critical functions of
society demonstrates that there are no limitations on structuring
human relationships. Sexual activity, pair-bonding, child-rearing,
and life-partnership need not be bound together in just one structural form, that of patriarchal marriage.

When facing new times, we must open the dialogue for finding a more flexible model of union between males and females. It
must take into the account the radical social, psychological, and
spiritual changes of the new millennium. The information high-
way of computer networking already gives people data for new
lifestyle options. Many now perceive themselves differently,
based on new images of a wider variety of human sexual choices.

Let us hope we can create new and more satisfactory ways to nurture human life and adult sexual love.

We will need to discard the whole panoply of unrealistic expectations and unfounded assumptions upon which patriarchal marriage and family units continue to exist as our culture's conceptual ideal. In doing so, we can hope to save the psyches of countless individuals who continue to struggle with trying to fit into this model, even when it is not meeting their needs. Many nontraditional families suffer the economic, social, and psychological consequences of not conforming to the outmoded, structural form.

Those who decry the high divorce statistics of current times are incorrectly targeting the loss of "moral fiber." However, we will ultimately have to heed the female half of humanity's need to act in its own best interests if the rate of divorce is to be reduced significantly. This will require a tremendous shift in our thinking. Acknowledging the feminine way requires a paradigm shift of such enormous implications that institutions as we know them will be permanently changed in the outcome. It could lead us to a more egalitarian model of social structure, as outlined by Riane Eisler's Partnership Model.[1]

Freedom to Choose

There is much to be done to establish cultural support for women freely choosing when, where, and with whom they desire to be sexual. Support for the feminine perspective must originate with women helping women to heal their wounded psyches. We can choose to live by our feminine truth: All women gain power by supporting each other's growth. The "beauty myths" that pit women against women, especially Crones against Maidens

(Snow White, Cinderella, Sleeping Beauty) need to be exposed as false images. We must replace these distorted tales of women in competition with each other. We can choose to establish new images of women's ways in the psyches of our children, reflecting collaboration and mutual empathy.

As mothers, we can choose to instill the Goddess image as a source of self-esteem for our daughters. A strong, internalized concept of Divine Femininity will help insulate them from the influences of sex-negative messages in our culture. With our help, the new breed of Maidens will be able to hold true to their Guardians, against the strongest efforts to undermine them that they will surely encounter. With our support, Maidens will be able to assess conditions for appropriate and safe sexual exploration, rather than behave in sexually self-destructive ways.

As adult women, we can choose to feel good about our Divine Feminine nature. We can internalize the rightness of our unique way, based on feminine values. Our bodies are our best teachers, and we can choose to master the lessons of the blood mysteries. We can honor all the stages of women's lives—Maiden, Mother, and Crone—and celebrate the events initiating us into each stage: First Blood, Childbirth, and Menopause. In particular, we can learn to honor our yonis as the seat of our power of magnetic attraction. They are the magical source of sexual pleasure and the gateway to new life. Finally, we can choose to honor our women's way of knowing, derived from our body wisdom. Our intuition is the gift of the Divine Feminine. As it was in ancient times, and can once again be acknowledged, our prophetic vision is a source of Divine Guidance.

Our visions for ourselves are our surest paths to channeling the creative power of the Life Force toward whatever goals for change we wish to create. I sincerely hope you will build a vision for yourself, and then live it. Your vision will allow you to realize your sexual power. However, you must give yourself permission to do so, and let go of the fears limiting your sexual expression. In *A Return to Love,* Marianne Williamson explains our dilemma:

> Our deepest fear is not that we are inadequate. Our deepest fear is that we are powerful beyond measure. It is our light, not our darkness, that most frightens us. We ask ourselves, who am I to be brilliant, gorgeous, talented and fabulous? Actually, who are [we] <u>not</u> to be? . . . As we let our own light shine, we unconsciously give other people permission to do the same.[2]

It is a powerful, inspirational message. When you examine your own fears of freely expressed sexuality, you can use the insight to give yourself permission to shine.

In the future, women as well as men will be able to express themselves as the free and loving sexual beings they were meant to be. As a woman, you can choose to rewrite the script for male-female lovemaking so that you feel empowered, surrendering to your natural desire in the feminine way. Female sexuality is essential to the creative force of life, and you can choose to express it in you own way.

Sexual energy is the light of the universe shining through you. It is your creative force. Use it well.

A Prayer for the New Millennium

In the new millennium, we may finally recognize that Earth *is* the Mother, and we cannot dominate nature without peril to our lives. As we emerge from the long, dark night of sexual oppression, it is my sincere prayer that we will witness the renewal of ancient wisdom and undergo a major transformation in our time. As we overturn limits on feminine power, we can make the shift into perceiving sexuality as sacred for both men and women. Together, men and women can choose to make violence against other humans unconscionable, and incorporate the values of the Earth-honoring cultures.

May we balance male and female energy in a positive way, living as life-affirming, sex-positive, pleasure-centered caretakers of the Earth.

May we relinquish the fear of sexual energy and allow the Life Force to express itself radiantly within us.

May we acknowledge the divine feminine and masculine as equal and necessary polarities that are meant to dance together with the erotic, pulsing Divine Source.

May we respect all varieties of human sexual expression that harm no one and increase the Life Force energy.

May we finally know ourselves as the loving and creative beings we are in our true nature.

May the Earth, our Mother, continue to offer her gifts of abundance to humankind. May we cooperate as one family in accordance with universal laws.

May we finally manifest the "peace of a thousand years" and live a thousand times a thousand years in harmony with the Divine Life Force.

APPENDIX

Endnotes

Introduction: The Great Marriage
1. Morgan, Elaine. *The Descent of Woman*. New York: Stein and Day, 1972, p. 73.
2. Eisler, Riane. *Sacred Pleasure*. San Francisco: HarperSanFrancisco, 1995.

Chapter One: Why Women Seek Sex Therapy
1. Laake, Deborah. *Secret Ceremonies*. New York: Island Books, 1994.
2. Borysenko, Joan. *A Woman's Book of Life*. New York: G. P. Putnam's Sons, 1996.
3. Schrof, Joannie M. and Betsy Wagner. "Sex in America." *U.S. News & World Report*, Oct. 17, 1994, pp. 74-81.
4. Touchman, Barbara. *A Distant Mirror*. New York: Ballantine Books, 1978.
5. "Army Report on Sexual Harassment," *Contemporary Sexuality*, Vol. 31, No.11, p. 4.

Chapter Two: Ancient Wisdom and Female Sexuality
1. Stone, Merlin. *When God Was a Woman*. San Diego: Harcourt Brace, 1976.
2. Eisler, Riane. *The Chalice and the Blade*. New York: Harper Collins, 1988.
3. Silko, Leslie Marmon. "Yellow Woman and A Beauty of Spirit," *Los Angeles Times Magazine*, Dec. 19, 1993, pp. 52-54, 64-66.
4. Starhawk. *The Spiral Dance*. Tenth anniversary edition. San Francisco: HarperSanFrancisco, 1989.
5. Gadon, Elinor. *The Once and Future Goddess*. San Francisco: HarperSanFrancisco, 1989.
6. Camphausen, Rufus. *The Yoni: Ancient Symbol of Female Creative Power*. Rochester, VT: Inner Realities, 1996.
7. Lubell, Winifred Milius. *The Metamorphosis of Baubo*. Nashville: Vanderbuilt University Press, 1994.
8. Bradley, Marion Zimmer. *The Mists of Avalon*. New York: Knopf, 1983.
9. Camphausen. Op. cit., pp. 36-48.
10. Andrews, Lynn V. *Shakkai*. New York: Harper Collins, 1992.
11. Gadon. Op. cit., p. 123.
12. Eisler, Riane. *Sacred Pleasure*. San Francisco: HarperSanFrancisco, 1995.
13. Patai, Raphael. *The Hebrew Goddess*. New York: Avon, 1978.

Chapter Three: The Three Faces of the Goddess
1. Grant, Joan. *Winged Pharao*. New York: Berkeley, 1977.
2. Andrews, Lynn V. *Flight of the Seventh Moon*. New York: Harper & Row, 1984.

Chapter Four: Reclaiming Your Goddess Sexuality
1. Starhawk. *The Spiral Dance*. Tenth anniversary edition. San Francisco: HarperSanFrancisco, 1989, p. 5.

Chapter Five: Awakening: The Path of the Maiden
1. Crenshaw, Teresa. *The Alchemy of Love and Lust*. New York: G. P. Putnam's Sons, 1996.

2.	Cassell, Carol. *Swept Away*. New York: Bantam Books, 1985.
3.	Pipher, Mary. *Reviving Ophelia*. New York: Ballantine Books, 1994.
4.	Fein, Ellen and Sherrie Schneider. *The Rules*. New York: Warner Books, 1995
5.	Williamson, Marianne. *A Woman's Worth*. New York: Random House, 1993.
6.	Silko, Leslie Marmon. "Yellow Woman and a Beauty of Spirit," *Los Angeles Times Magazine*, Dec. 19, 1993, pp. 52-54, 64-66.

Chapter Six: Initiation: The Circle of the Mother
1.	Williamson, Marianne. *A Woman's Worth*. New York: Random House, 1993.
2.	Borysenko, Joan. *A Woman's Book of Life*. New York: G.P. Putnam 's Sons, 1996.
3.	Ibid., p. 122.
4.	Hay, Louise. *Empowering Women*. Carlsbad, CA: Hay House, 1997, p. 157.
5.	Crenshaw, Teresa. *The Alchemy of Love and Lust*. New York: G. P. Putnam's Sons, 1996, pp. 172-175.
6.	Goleman, Daniel. *Emotional Intelligence*. New York: Bantam Books, 1995.
7.	Ogden, Gina. *Women Who Love Sex*. New York: Pocket Books, 1994.
8.	Ibid. p. 27.

Chapter Seven: Coronation: The Wisdom of the Crone
1.	Andrews, Lynn V. *Woman at the Edge of Two Worlds*. New York: Harper Collins, 1993.
2.	Crenshaw, Teresa. *The Alchemy of Love and Lust*. New York: G. P. Putnam's Sons, 1996.
3.	Greer, Germaine. *The Change*. New York: Fawcett Columbine, 1991.
4.	Ibid., pp. 118-119.
5.	Crenshaw. Op. cit., chapter 6.
6.	Borysenko, Joan. *A Woman's Book of Life*. New York: G. P. Putnam's Sons, 1996.
7.	Gordon, Barbara. *Jennifer Fever: Older Men/Younger Women*. New York.: Random House, 1989.
8.	Sheehy, Gail. *The Silent Passage*. New York: Random House, 1992, p.145.

Chapter Eight: Making Sense of Your Personal Story
1.	If you would like more information about parental influences, read: Forward, Susan. *Toxic Parents*. New York: Bantam Books, 1990.

Chapter Nine: Healing and Enhancing Your Sexuality
1.	Jones, Laurie Beth. *The Path*. New York: Hyperion, 1996.
2.	Andrews, Lynn V. *Woman at the Edge of Two Worlds*. New York: HarperCollins, 1993.

Chapter Twelve: Spiritual Sexuality
1.	Ogden, Gina. "Spiritual Sex." *New Woman*, July, 1998, p. 105.

Epilogue: Relationships in the New Millennium
1.	Eisler, Riane and David Loye. *The Partnership Way: New Tools for Living and Learning* (available through Center for Partnership Studies, P.O. Box 51936, Pacific Grove, CA 93950).
2.	Marianne Williamson. *A Return to Love*. New York: HarperPerennial, 1996, p. 190.

Suggested Reading

Goddess Cultures

Eisler, Riane. *The Chalice and the Blade.* New York: Harper Collins, 1988.

_____. *Sacred Pleasure.* San Francisco: HarperSanFrancisco, 1995

Gadon, Elinor W. *The Once and Future Goddess.* San Francisco: HarperSanFrancisco, 1989.

Patai, Raphael. *The Hebrew Goddess.* New York: Avon. 1978.

Stone, Merlin. *When God Was a Woman.* New York: Dial Press, 1976.

Priestesses/Sacred Virgins

Hall, Nor. *The Moon and the Virgin.* New York: Harper & Row, 1980.

Qualls-Corbett, Nancy. *The Sacred Prostitute.* Toronto, Canada: Inner City Books, 1988.

Shepsut, Asia. *Journey of the Priestesses.* London: The Aquarian Press, 1993.

Stubbs, Kenneth Ray, ed. *Women of the Light.* Larkspur, CA: Secret Garden, 1994.

Maiden-Stage Issues

Brown, Lyn Mikel and Carol Gilligan. *Meeting at the Crossroads.* New York: Ballantine Books, 1992.

Friday, Nancy. *The Power of Beauty.* New York: Harper Collins, 1996.

Pipher, Mary. *Reviving Ophelia.* New York: Ballantine Books, 1994.

Mother-Stage Issues

Hansen, Maren. *Mother Mysteries.* Boston: Shambhala Publications, 1997.

Wallerstein, Judith S. and Sandra Blakeslee. *The Good Marriage.* New York: Warner Books, 1995.

Crone-Stage Issues

Barbach, Lonnie. *The Pause.* New York: Penguin Group, 1994.

Greer, Germaine. *The Change.* New York: Fawcett Columbine, 1991.

Kenton, Leslie. *Passage to Power: Natural Menopause Revolution.* Carlsbad, CA: Hay House, 1998.

Women: All Stages

Borysenko, Joan. *A Woman's Book of Life.* New York: G. P. Putnam's Sons, 1996.

Hay, Louise, *Empowering Women.* Carlsbad, CA: Hay House, 1997.

Ogden, Gina. *Women Who Love Sex.* New York: Pocket Books, 1994.

Resnick, Stella. *The Pleasure Zone.* Berkeley, CA: Conari Press, 1997.

Help for Troubled Relationships

Evans, Patricia. *The Verbally Abusive Relationship.* Holbrook, MA: Adams Media Corp., 1996.

Norwood, Robin. *Women Who Love Too Much.* New York: Pocket Books, 1986.

Specific Sex Guides
Anand, Margo. *The Art of Sexual Ecstasy*. Los Angeles: Jeremy P. Tarcher. Inc., 1989.
Birch, Robert. *Oral Caress: The Loving Guide to Exciting a Woman*. Columbus, Ohio: PEC Publications, 1996.
Gabriel, Bonnie. *The Fine Art of Erotic Talk*. New York: Bantam Books, 1996.
Joannides, Paul. *The Guide to Getting It On*. Hollywood, CA: Goofy Foot Press, 1996.
Stubbs, Kenneth Ray. *Sacred Orgasms*. Larkspur, CA: Secret Garden, 1992.
Wink, Cathy and Anne Semans. *The New Good Vibrations Guide to Sex*. 2nd ed. San Francisco: Cleis Press, 1994.

Erotic Fiction
Barbach, Lonnie, ed. *The Erotic Edge*. New York: Plume Books, 1996.
Fortune, Dion. *The Sea Priestess*. York Beach, ME: Weiser, 1985.
Jaivin, Linda. *Eat Me*. New York: Bantam Books, 1997.
Kensington Ladies Erotica Society. *Ladies Home Erotica*. Berkeley, CA: Ten Speed Press, 1986.
Nin, Anais, *Delta of Venus*. New York: Bantam Books, 1977.

Adult Video Guide
Winks, Cathy. *The Good Vibrations Guide to Adult Videos*. San Francisco: Down There Press, 1998.

There are many excellent educational books and videos that are women-friendly and offer a variety of ideas and options. Send for a catalog of The Sexuality Library, which describes the special features of the books they carry and even has an ingenious rating system to identify the outstanding features of each video. Call (800) 289-8423, or write to: The Sexuality Library, Open Enterprises Cooperative, Inc., 938 Howard St., Suite 101, San Francisco, CA 94103.

In New York, you can contact: Eve's Garden, at (800) 848-3837.

Mind-Body Healing
Borysenko, Joan. *Minding the Body, Mending the Mind*. New York: Bantam Books, 1988.
Chopra, Deepak. *Quantum Healing*. New York: Bantam Books, 1989.
Cousins, Norman. *Anatomy of an Illness*. New York: W. W. Norton Co., 1979.
Hay, Louise. *You Can Heal Your Life*. Carlsbad, CA: Hay House, 1984.
Siegel, Bernie. *Love, Medicine & Miracles*. New York: Harper Collins, 1990.
Weil, Andrew. *Spontaneous Healing*. New York: Fawcett Columbine, 1995.

Historical Sex Education Publications
Drake, Emma T. Angell, M.D., *What a Woman of Forty-Five Ought to Know*. London: The Vir Publishing Co. 1902.
Nystrom, Anton. *The Natural Laws of Sexual Life*. St. Louis, MO.: C. V. Mosby Company, 1923. Copyright by author 1908.
Wood-Allen, Mary, M.D. *What a Young Girl Ought to Know*. London: The Vir Publishing Co., 1897.

Internet Resources

http://runningdeer.com/cwwe/wwwboard.htm • Crone-Wise Woman-Elder Home Page

http://members.aol.com/YnisAvalon/Sisterhood-of-Avalon.htm • The Sisterhood of Avalon home page.

http://www.primenet.com/~queen/woman.html • Wild Women of the Web Page

http://scriptorium.lib.duke.edu/women/cdover.html • Duke Women's Archives: Collection • Overview

http://www.amug.org/~dtmms • Chuluaqui-Quodoushka Fire Medicine information. Harley SwiftDeer Reagan, Medicine Chief of Deer Tribe Metis Medicine Society.

http://www.yoni.com/booklist.shtml • The Yoni Booklist

http://www.eliki.com/realsm/kat/goddess.html • Goddesses of the World

http://www.teleport.com/nonprofit/sister~spirit/#top • SisterSpirit Sharing Spirituality

http://www.cyberglobe.net/magicalblend/catalog/books/goddess.html The Magical Blend • On-Line Catalog: Goddess books.

http://www.tantra.com for information about tantra

Self-Help Resources

The following list of resources can be used for more information about recovery options for addictions, health concerns, death and bereavement, and other issues. The addresses and telephone numbers listed are for the national headquarters; look in your local yellow pages under "Community Services" for resources closer to your area.

In addition to the following groups, other self-help organizations may be available in your area to assist your healing and recovery for a particular life crisis not listed here. Consult your telephone directory, call a counseling center or help line near you, or contact:

Attorney Referral Network
(800) 624-8846

National Self-Help Clearinghouse
25 West 43rd St., Room 620
New York, NY 10036
(800) 952-2075

***

AIDS

AIDS Hotline
(800) 342-2437

Children with AIDS (CWA)
Project of America
(800) 866-AIDS (24-hour hotline)

The Names Project – AIDS Quilt
(800) 872-6263

National AIDS Network
(800) 342-2437

Project Inform
19655 Market St., Ste. 220
San Francisco, CA 94103
(415) 558-8669

PWA Coalition
50 W. 17th St.
New York, NY 10011

Spanish AIDS Hotline
(800) 344-7432

TDD (Hearing Impaired) AIDS Hotline
(800) 243-7889

***

ALCOHOL ABUSE

Al-Anon Family Headquarters
200 Park Ave. South
New York, NY 10003
(757) 563-1600

Alcoholics Anonymous (AA)
General Service Office
475 Riverside Dr.
New York, NY 10115
(212) 870-3400

Children of Alcoholics Foundation
33 West 60th St., 5th Floor
New York, NY 10023
(212) 757-2100 ext. 6370
(212) 757-2208 (fax)
(800) 359-COAF

Meridian Council, Inc.
Administrative Offices
4 Elmcrest Terrace
Norwalk, CT 06850

Mothers Against Drunk Driving (MADD)
(254) 690-6233

National Association of Children of Alcoholics (NACOA)
11426 Rockville Pike, Ste. 100
Rockville, MD 20852
(301) 468-0985
(888) 554-2627

National Clearinghouse for Alcohol and Drug Information (NCADI)
P.O. Box 234
Rockville, MD 20852
(301) 468-2600

National Council on Alcoholism and Drug Dependency (NCADD)
12 West 21st St.
New York, NY 10010
(212) 206-6770

National Council on Alcohol & Drugs
(800) 475-HOPE

Women for Sobriety
(800) 333-1606

***

ANOREXIA/BULIMIA

**American Anorexia/Bulimia
Association, Inc.**
293 Central Park West, Ste. 1R
New York, NY 10024
(212) 575-6200

Eating Disorder Organization
6655 S. Yale Ave.
Tulsa, OK 74136
(918) 481-4044

***

CANCER

National Cancer Institute
(800) 4-CANCER

***

CHILDREN'S ISSUES

Child Molestation

Adults Molested As Children United (AMACU)
232 East Gish Rd.
San Jose, CA 95112
(800) 422-4453

National Committee for Prevention of Child Abuse
332 South Michigan Ave., Ste. 1600
Chicago, IL 60604
(312) 663-3520

Children's and Teens' Crisis Intervention

Boy's Town Crisis Hotline
(800) 448-3000

Children of the Night
(800) 551-1300

Covenant House Hotline
(800) 999-9999

Kid Save
(800) 543-7283

National Runaway and Suicide Hotline
(800) 448-3000

Youth Nineline
(Referrals for parents/teens about drugs, homelessness, runaways)
(800) 999-9999

***

Missing Children

Missing Children-Help Center
410 Ware Blvd., Ste. 400
Tampa, FL 33619
(800) USA-KIDS

National Center for Missing and Exploited Children
1835 K St. NW
Washington, DC 20006
(800) 843-5678

***

Children with Serious Illnesses (fulfilling wishes)

Brass Ring Society
National Headquarters
551 East Semoran Blvd., Suite E-5
Fern Park, FL 32730
(407) 339-6188
(800) 666-WISH

Make-a-Wish Foundation
(800) 332-9474

***

CO-DEPENDENCY

Co-Dependents Anonymous
(602) 277-7991

***

DEATH/GRIEVING/SUICIDE

Grief Recovery Helpline
(800) 445-4808

Grief Recovery Institute
8306 Wilshire Blvd., Ste. 21A
Beverly Hills, CA 90211
(213) 650-1234

National Hospice Organization (NHO)
1901 Moore St. #901
Arlington, VA 22209
(703) 243-5900

National Sudden Infant Death Syndrome
Two Metro Plaza, Ste. 205
Landover, MD 20785
(800) 221-SIDS

Seasons: Suicide Bereavement
P.O. Box 187
Park City, UT 84060
(801) 649-8327

Share
(Recovering from violent death of friend or family member)
100 E 8th St., Suite B41
Cincinnati, OH 45202
(513) 721-5683

Survivors of Suicide
Call your local Mental Health Association for the branch nearest you.

Widowed Persons Service
(202) 434-2260
(800) 424-3410 ext. 2260

***

DEBTS

Credit Referral
(Information on local credit counseling services)
(800) 388-CCCS

Debtors Anonymous
General Service Office
P.O. Box 400
Grand Central Station
New York, NY 10163-0400
(212) 642-8220

***

DIABETES

American Diabetes Association
(800) 232-3472

***

DRUG ABUSE

Cocaine Anonymous
(800) 347-8998

National Cocaine-Abuse Hotline
(800) 262-2463
(800) COCAINE

National Institute of Drug Abuse (NIDA)
Parklawn Building
5600 Fishers Lane, Room 10A-39
Rockville, MD 20852
(301) 443-6245 (for information)
(800) 662-4357 (for help)

World Service Office (CA)
3740 Overland Ave., Ste. C
Los Angeles, CA 90034-6337
(310) 559-5833
(800) 347-8998 (to leave message)

***

EATING DISORDERS

Eating Disorder Organization
6655 S. Yale Ave.
Tulsa, OK 74136
(918) 481-4044

Overeaters Anonymous
National Office
P.O. Box 44020
Rio Rancho, NM 87174-4020
(505) 891-2664

***

GAMBLING

Gamblers Anonymous
National Council on Compulsive Gambling
444 West 59th St., Room 1521
New York, NY 10019
(212) 903-4400

***

HEALTH ISSUES

Alzheimer's Disease Information
(800) 621-0379

American Chronic Pain Association
P.O. Box 850
Rocklin, CA 95677
(916) 632-0922

American Foundation of Traditional Chinese Medicine
505 Beach St.
San Francisco, CA 94133
(415) 776-0502

American Holistic Health Association
P.O. Box 17400
Anaheim, CA 92817
(714) 779-6152

Chopra Center for Well Being
Deepak Chopra, M.D.
7630 Fay Ave.
La Jolla, CA 92037
(619) 551-7788

The Fetzer Institute
9292 West KL Ave.
Kalamazoo, MI 49009
(616) 375-2000

Hippocrates Health Institute
1443 Palmdale Court
West Palm Beach, FL 33411
(561) 471-8876

Hospicelink
(800) 331-1620

Institute for Noetic Sciences
P.O. Box 909, Dept. M
Sausalito, CA 94966-0909
(800) 383-1394

The Mind-Body Medical Institute
185 Pilgrim Rd.
Boston, MA 02215
(617) 632-9525

National Health Information Center
P.O. Box 1133
Washington, DC 20013-1133
(800) 336-4797

Optimum Health Care Institute
6970 Central Ave.
Lemon Grove, CA 91945
(619) 464-3346

Preventive Medicine Research Institute
Dean Ornish, M.D.
900 Bridgeway, Ste. 2
Sausalito, CA 94965
(415) 332-2525

World Research Foundation
20501 Ventura Blvd., Ste. 100
Woodland Hills, CA 91364
(818) 999-5483

***

HOUSING RESOURCES

Acorn
(Nonprofit network of low- and moderate-income housing)
739 8th St., S.E.
Washington, DC 20003
(202) 547-9292

***

IMPOTENCE

Impotence Institute of America
P.O. Box 410
Bowie, MD 20718-0410
(800) 669-1603
www.impotenceworld.org

***

INCEST

Incest Survivors Resource Network
International, Inc.
P.O. Box 7375
Las Cruces, NM 88006-7375
(505) 521-4260 (Hours: Monday –
Saturday, 2 – 4 P.M. and
11 P.M. – Midnight / Eastern time)

***

PET BEREAVEMENT

Bide-A-Wee Foundation
410 E. 38th St.
New York, NY 10016
(212) 532-6395

The Animal Medical Center
510 E. 62nd St.
New York, NY 10021
(212) 838-8100

Holistic Animal Consulting Center
29 Lyman Ave.
Staten Island, NY 10305
(718) 720-5548

***

RAPE/SEXUAL ISSUES

Austin Rape Crisis Center
1824 East Oltorf
Austin, TX 78741
(512) 440-7273

National Council on Sexual Addictions and Compulsivity
1090 S. Northchase Parkway, Suite 200
South Marietta, GA 30067
(770) 989-9754

Sexually Transmitted Disease Referral
(800) 227-8922

***

SMOKING ABUSE

Nicotine Anonymous
2118 Greenwich St.
San Francisco, CA 94123
(415) 750-0328

***

SPOUSAL ABUSE

National Coalition Against Domestic Violence
P.O. Box 34103
Washington, DC 20043-4103
(202) 544-7358

National Domestic Violence Hotline
(800) 799-SAFE

***

STRESS REDUCTION

The Biofeedback & Psychophysiology Clinic
The Menninger Clinic
P.O. Box 829
Topeka, KS 66601-0829
(913) 350-5000

New York Open Center
(In-depth workshops to invigorate the spirit)
83 Spring St.
New York, NY 10012
(212) 219-2527

Omega Institute
(A healing, spiritual retreat community)
260 Lake Dr.
Rhinebeck, NY 12572-3212
(914) 266-4444 (info)
(800) 944-1001 (to enroll)

Rise Institute
P.O. Box 2733
Petaluma, CA 94973
(707) 765-2758

The Stress Reduction Clinic
Center for Mindfulness
University of Massachusetts Medical Center
55 Lake Ave. North
Worcester, MA 01655
(508) 856-1616
(508) 856-2656

*** ***

About the Author

Linda E. Savage, Ph.D., is a licensed psychologist and marriage and family therapist in California, and a member of the Institute of Marital and Sexual Therapy. She has a private practice specializing in couples therapy, effective communication skills, and women's issues. Dr. Savage is also a sex therapist and has supervised surrogate partner therapy as well as couples treatment for sexual issues since 1984. Research in the field of sexual healing and relationship intimacy has been her passion for more than 25 years.

Dr. Savage has taught psychology at National University and has presented seminars and lectures on a wide variety of sexual issues. Her expertise in this area has made her educational presentations popular on television, as well as with groups. She is a graduate of Mount Holyoke College and the University of Massachusetts, and a Diplomate of the American Board of Sexology.

Dr. Savage lives in Vista, California, with her husband and daughter.

The author would love to hear from you about the impact this book has made on your life. Please feel free to contact her at the following address or websites:

Linda E. Savage, Ph.D.
914 So. Santa Fe Ave., #197
Vista, CA 92084
e-mail: **goddesstherapy@home.com**

www.sexualtherapy.com
The Institute for Marital and Sexual Therapy

www.sexologist.org
The American Board of Sexology

We hope you enjoyed this Hay House book.
If you would like to receive a free catalog featuring additional
Hay House books and products, or if you would like informa-
tion about the Hay Foundation, please contact:

Hay House, Inc.
P.O. Box 5100
Carlsbad, CA 92018-5100

(760) 431-7695 or **(800) 654-5126**
(760) 431-6948 (fax) or **(800) 650-5115 (fax)**

Please visit the Hay House Website at:
www.hayhouse.com